ILLUSTRATED COURSE GUIDES
Microsoft® Word 2010

Basic

ILLUSTRATED COURSE GUIDES
Microsoft® Word 2010

Basic

Jennifer Duffy

Australia • Brazil • Japan • Korea • Mexico • Singapore • Spain • United Kingdom • United States

COURSE TECHNOLOGY
CENGAGE Learning™

Illustrated Course Guide: Microsoft® Word 2010—Basic
Jennifer Duffy

Vice President, Publisher: Nicole Jones Pinard

Executive Editor: Marjorie Hunt

Associate Acquisitions Editor: Brandi Shailer

Senior Product Manager: Christina Kling Garrett

Associate Product Manager: Michelle Camisa

Editorial Assistant: Kim Klasner

Director of Marketing: Cheryl Costantini

Senior Marketing Manager: Ryan DeGrote

Marketing Coordinator: Kristen Panciocco

Contributing Authors: Carol Cram, Elizabeth Eisner Reding

Developmental Editors: Pamela Conrad, Jeanne Herring

Content Project Manager: Heather Hopkins

Copy Editor: Mark Goodin

Proofreader: Harold Johnson

Indexer: BIM Indexing and Proofreading Services

QA Manuscript Reviewers: Nicole Ashton, John Frietas, Serge Palladino, Susan Pedicini, Jeff Schwartz, Danielle Shaw, Marianne Snow

Print Buyer: Fola Orekoya

Cover Designer: GEX Publishing Services

Cover Artist: Mark Hunt

Composition: GEX Publishing Services

For product information and technology assistance, contact us at
Cengage Learning Customer & Sales Support, 1-800-354-9706
For permission to use material from this text or product, submit all requests online at **www.cengage.com/permissions**
Further permissions questions can be emailed to
permissionrequest@cengage.com

Trademarks:

Some of the product names and company names used in this book have been used for identification purposes only and may be trademarks or registered trademarks of their respective manufacturers and sellers.

Microsoft and the Office logo are either registered trademarks or trademarks of Microsoft Corporation in the United States and/or other countries. Course Technology, Cengage Learning is an independent entity from Microsoft Corporation, and not affiliated with Microsoft in any manner.

Library of Congress Control Number: 2010935559

ISBN-13: 978-0-538-74833-9
ISBN-10: 0-538-74833-8

Course Technology
20 Channel Center Street
Boston, MA 02210
USA

Cengage Learning is a leading provider of customized learning solutions with office locations around the globe, including Singapore, the United Kingdom, Australia, Mexico, Brazil, and Japan. Locate your local office at:
international.cengage.com/region

Cengage Learning products are represented in Canada by Nelson Education, Ltd.

To learn more about Course Technology, visit **www.cengage.com/coursetechnology**

To learn more about Cengage Learning, visit **www.cengage.com**

Purchase any of our products at your local college store or at our preferred online store **www.cengagebrain.com**

Printed in the United States of America
1 2 3 4 5 6 7 8 9 18 17 16 15 14 13 12 11 10

Brief Contents

Contents

Preface

Welcome to *Illustrated Course Guide: Microsoft® Word 2010 Basic*. If this is your first experience with the Illustrated Course Guides, you'll see that this book has a unique design: each skill is presented on two facing pages, with steps on the left and screens on the right. The layout makes it easy to learn a skill without having to read a lot of text and flip pages to see an illustration.

This book is an ideal learning tool for a wide range of learners—the "rookies" will find the clean design easy to follow and focused with only essential information presented, and the "hotshots" will appreciate being able to move quickly through the lessons to find the information they need without reading a lot of text. The design also makes this a great reference after the course is over! See the illustration on the right to learn more about the pedagogical and design elements of a typical lesson.

What's New In This Edition

- **Fully Updated.** Highlights the new features of Microsoft Word 2010 and includes updated examples and exercises throughout. Unit D includes increased coverage of research tools, including adding citations, endnotes, and bibliographies. A new appendix covers cloud computing concepts and using Microsoft Office Web Apps.

- **Maps to SAM 2010.** This book is designed to work with SAM (Skills Assessment Manager) 2010. **SAM Assessment** contains performance-based, hands-on SAM exams for each unit of this book, and **SAM Training** provides hands-on training for skills covered in the book. Some exercises are available in **SAM Projects**, which is auto-grading software that provides both learners and instructors with immediate, detailed feedback (SAM sold separately.) See page xii for more information on SAM.

Each two-page spread focuses on a single skill.

Introduction briefly explains why the lesson skill is important.

A case scenario motivates the the steps and puts learning in context.

Tips and troubleshooting advice, right where you need it—next to the step itself.

Clues to Use boxes provide useful information related to the lesson skill.

UNIT A
Word 2010

Saving a Document

To store a document permanently so you can open it and edit it at another time, you must save it as a **file**. When you **save** a document you give it a name, called a **filename**, and indicate the location where you want to store the file. Files created in Word 2010 are automatically assigned the .docx file extension to distinguish them from files created in other software programs. You can save a document using the Save button on the Quick Access toolbar or the Save command on the File tab. Once you have saved a document for the first time, you should save it again every few minutes and always before printing so that the saved file is updated to reflect your latest changes. You save your memo using a descriptive filename and the default file extension.

STEPS

TROUBLE
If you don't see the extension .docx as part of the filename, the setting in Windows to display file extensions is not active.

1. **Click the Save button on the Quick Access toolbar**
   The first time you save a document, the Save As dialog box opens, as shown in Figure A-5. The default filename, Memorandum, appears in the File name text box. The default filename is based on the first few words of the document. The default file extension, .docx, appears in the Save as type list box. Table A-3 describes the functions of some of the buttons in the Save As dialog box.

2. **Type WD A-Morocco Tour Memo in the File name text box**
   The new filename replaces the default filename. Giving your documents brief descriptive filenames makes it easier to locate and organize them later. You do not need to type .docx when you type a new filename.

3. **Navigate to the drive and folder where you store your Data Files**
   You can navigate to a different drive or folder in several ways. For example, you can click a drive or folder in the Address bar or the navigation pane to go directly to that location. Click the double arrow in the Address bar to display a list of drives and folders. You can also double-click a drive or folder in the folder window to change the active location. When you are finished navigating to the drive or folder where you store your Data Files, that location appears in the Address bar. Your Save As dialog box should resemble Figure A-6.

QUICK TIP
To save a document so it can be opened in an older version of Word, click the Save as type list arrow, then click Word 97-2003 Document (*.doc).

4. **Click Save**
   The document is saved to the drive and folder you specified in the Save As dialog box, and the title bar displays the new filename, WD A-Morocco Tour Memo.docx.

5. **Place the insertion point before conference in the first sentence, type large, then press [Spacebar]**
   You can continue to work on a document after you have saved it with a new filename.

6. **Click**
   Your change to the memo is saved. After you save a document for the first time, you must continue to save the changes you make to the document. You also can press [Ctrl][S] to save a document.

Windows Live and Microsoft Office Web Apps

All Office programs include the capability to incorporate feedback—called online collaboration—across the Internet or a company network. Using **cloud computing** (work done in a virtual environment), you can take advantage of Web programs called Microsoft Office Web Apps, which are simplified versions of the programs found in the Microsoft Office 2010 suite. Because these programs are online, they take up no computer disk space and are accessed using Windows Live SkyDrive, a free service from Microsoft. Using Windows Live SkyDrive, you and your colleagues can create and store documents in a "cloud" and make the documents available to whomever you grant access. To use Windows Live SkyDrive, you need a free Windows Live ID, which you obtain at the Windows Live Web site. You can find more information in the "Working with Windows Live and Office Web Apps" appendix.

Word 8 Creating Documents with Word 2010

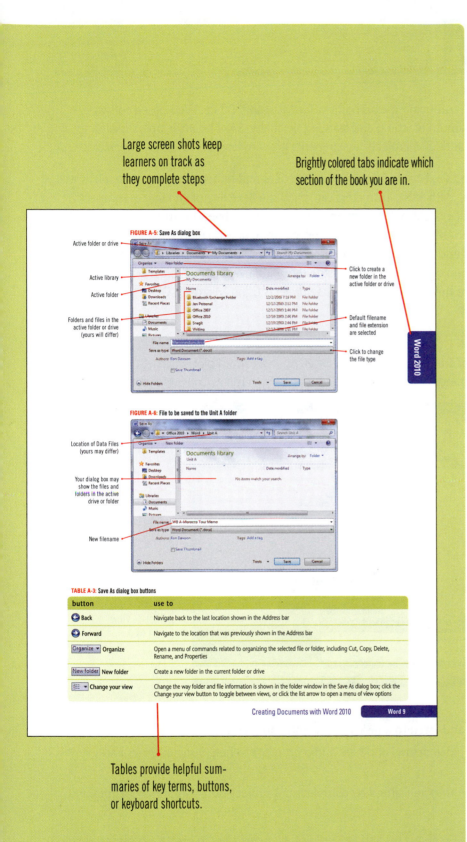

Large screen shots keep learners on track as they complete steps

Brightly colored tabs indicate which section of the book you are in.

FIGURE A-5: Save As dialog box

Active folder or drive

Active library

Active folder

Folders and files in the active folder or drive (yours will differ)

Click to create a new folder in the active folder or drive

Default filename and file extension are selected

Click to change the file type

Word 2010

FIGURE A-6: File to be saved to the Unit A folder

Location of Data Files (yours may differ)

Your dialog box may show the files and folders in the active drive or folder

New filename

TABLE A-3: Save As dialog box buttons

button	use to
Back	Navigate back to the last location shown in the Address bar
Forward	Navigate to the location that was previously shown in the Address bar
Organize	Open a menu of commands related to organizing the selected file or folder, including Cut, Copy, Delete, Rename, and Properties
New folder	Create a new folder in the current folder or drive
Change your view	Change the way folder and file information is shown in the folder window in the Save As dialog box; click the Change your view button to toggle between views, or click the list arrow to open a menu of view options

Creating Documents with Word 2010   Word 9

Tables provide helpful summaries of key terms, buttons, or keyboard shortcuts.

Assignments

The lessons use Quest Specialty Travel, a fictional adventure travel company, as the case study. The assignments on the light yellow pages at the end of each unit increase in difficulty. Assignments include:

- **Concepts Review** consist of multiple choice, matching, and screen identification questions.

- **Skills Reviews** are hands-on, step-by-step exercises that review the skills covered in each lesson in the unit.

- **Independent Challenges** are case projects requiring critical thinking and application of the unit skills. The Independent Challenges increase in difficulty, with the first one in each unit being the easiest. Independent Challenges 2 and 3 become increasingly open-ended, requiring more independent problem solving.

- **SAM Projects** is live-in-the-application autograding software that provides immediate and detailed feedback reports to learners and instructors. Some exercises in this book are available in SAM Projects. (Purchase of a SAM Projects pincode is required.)

- **Real Life Independent Challenges** are practical exercises in which learners create documents to help them with their every day lives.

- **Advanced Challenge Exercises** set within the Independent Challenges provide optional steps for more advanced learners.

- **Visual Workshops** are practical, self-graded capstone projects that require independent problem solving.

About SAM

SAM is the premier proficiency-based assessment and training environment for Microsoft Office. Web-based software along with an inviting user interface provide maximum teaching and learning flexibility. SAM builds learners' skills and confidence with a variety of real-life simulations, and SAM Projects' assignments prepare learners for today's workplace.

The SAM system includes Assessment, Training, and Projects, featuring page references and remediation for this book as well as Course Technology's Microsoft Office textbooks. With SAM, instructors can enjoy the flexibility of creating assignments based on content from their favorite Microsoft Office books or based on specific course objectives. Instructors appreciate the scheduling and reporting options that have made SAM the market-leading online testing and training software for over a decade. Over 2,000 performance-based questions and matching Training simulations, as well as tens of thousands of objective-based questions from many Course Technology texts, provide instructors with a variety of choices across multiple applications. SAM Projects is auto-grading software that lets learners complete projects using Microsoft Office and then receive detailed feedback on their finished projects.

SAM Assessment

- Content for these hands-on, performance-based tasks includes Word, Excel, Access, PowerPoint, Internet Explorer, Outlook, and Windows. Includes tens of thousands of objective-based questions from many Course Technology texts.

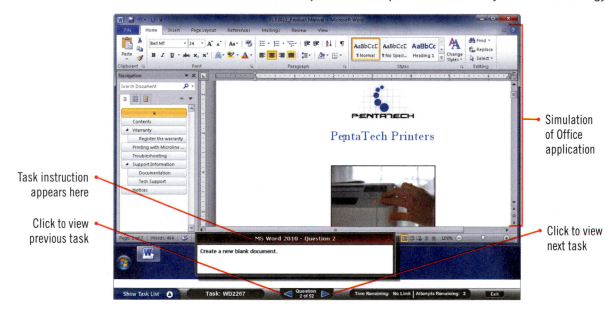

SAM Training

- Observe mode allows the learners to watch and listen to a task as it is being completed.
- Practice mode allows the learner to follow guided arrows and hear audio prompts to help visual learners know how to complete a task.
- Apply mode allows the learner to prove what they've learned by completing a project using on-screen instructions.

SAM Projects

- Live-in-the-application assignments in Word, Excel, Access and PowerPoint allow learners to create a project using the Microsoft Office software and then receive immediate, detailed feedback on their completed project.
- Learners receive detailed feedback on their project within minutes.
- Unique anti-cheating detection feature is encrypted into the data files to ensure learners complete their own assignments.

Instructor Resources

The Instructor Resources CD is Course Technology's way of putting the resources and information needed to teach and learn effectively into your hands. With an integrated array of teaching and learning tools that offer you and your learners a broad range of technology-based instructional options, we believe this CD represents the highest quality and most cutting edge resources available to instructors today. The resources available with this book are:

- **Instructor's Manual**—Available as an electronic file, the Instructor's Manual includes detailed lecture topics with teaching tips for each unit.

- **Sample Syllabus**—Prepare and customize your course easily using this sample course outline.

- **PowerPoint Presentations**—Each unit has a corresponding PowerPoint presentation that you can use in lecture, distribute to your learners, or customize to suit your course.

- **Figure Files**—The figures in the text are provided on the Instructor Resources CD to help you illustrate key topics or concepts. You can create traditional overhead transparencies by printing the figure files. Or you can create electronic slide shows by using the figures in a presentation program such as PowerPoint.

- **Solutions to Exercises**—Solutions to Exercises contains every file learners are asked to create or modify in the lessons and end-of-unit material. Also provided in this section, there is a document outlining the solutions for the end-of-unit Concepts Review, Skills Review, and Independent Challenges. An Annotated Solution File and Grading Rubric accompany each file and can be used together for quick and easy grading.

- **Data Files for Learners**—To complete most of the units in this book, learners will need Data Files. You can post the Data Files on a file server for learners to copy. The Data Files are available on the Instructor Resources CD-ROM, the Review Pack, and can also be downloaded from cengagebrain.com. For more information on how to download the Data Files, see the inside back cover.

Instruct learners to use the Data Files List included on the Review Pack and the Instructor Resources CD. This list gives instructions on copying and organizing files.

- **ExamView**—ExamView is a powerful testing software package that allows you to create and administer printed, computer (LAN-based), and Internet exams. ExamView includes hundreds of questions that correspond to the topics covered in this text, enabling learners to generate detailed study guides that include page references for further review. The computer-based and Internet testing components allow learners to take exams at their computers, and also saves you time by grading each exam automatically.

Content for Online Learning.

Course Technology has partnered with the leading distance learning solution providers and class-management platforms today. To access this material, visit www.cengage.com/webtutor and search for your title. Instructor resources include the following: additional case projects, sample syllabi, PowerPoint presentations, and more. For additional information, please contact your sales representative. For learners to access this material, they must have purchased a WebTutor PIN-code specific to this title and your campus platform. The resources for learners might include (based on instructor preferences): topic reviews, review questions, practice tests, and more.

Acknowledgements

Instructor Advisory Board

We thank our Instructor Advisory Board who gave us their opinions and guided our decisions as we updated our texts for Microsoft Office 2010. They are as follows:

Terri Helfand, Chaffey Community College

Barbara Comfort, J. Sargeant Reynolds Community College

Brenda Nielsen, Mesa Community College

Sharon Cotman, Thomas Nelson Community College

Marian Meyer, Central New Mexico Community College

Audrey Styer, Morton College

Richard Alexander, Heald College

Xiaodong Qiao, Heald College

Student Advisory Board

We also thank our Student Advisory Board members, who shared their experiences using the book and offered suggestions to make it better: **Latasha Jefferson**, Thomas Nelson Community College, **Gary Williams**, Thomas Nelson Community College, **Stephanie Miller**, J. Sargeant Reynolds Community College, **Sarah Styer**, Morton Community College, **Missy Marino**, Chaffey College

Author Acknowledgements

Jennifer Duffy Many talented people at Course Technology worked tirelessly to shape this book—thank you all. I am especially grateful to Pam Conrad, editor extraordinaire, whose dedication, wisdom, and precision are evident on every page.

Read This Before You Begin

Frequently Asked Questions

What are Data Files?

A Data File is a partially completed Word document or another type of file that you use to complete the steps in the units and exercises to create the final document that you submit to your instructor. Each unit opener page lists the Data Files that you need for that unit.

Where are the Data Files?

Your instructor will provide the Data Files to you or direct you to a location on a network drive from which you can download them. For information on how to download the Data Files from cengagebrain.com, see the inside back cover.

What software was used to write and test this book?

This book was written and tested using a typical installation of Microsoft Office 2010 Professional Plus on a computer with a typical installation of Microsoft Windows 7 Ultimate.

The browser used for any Web-dependent steps is Internet Explorer 8.

Do I need to be connected to the Internet to complete the steps and exercises in this book?

Some of the exercises in this book require that your computer be connected to the Internet. If you are not connected to the Internet, see your instructor for information on how to complete the exercises.

What do I do if my screen is different from the figures shown in this book?

This book was written and tested on computers with monitors set at a resolution of 1024 $\times$ 768. If your screen shows more or less information than the figures in the book, your monitor is probably set at a higher or lower resolution. If you don't see something on your screen, you might have to scroll down or up to see the object identified in the figures.

The Ribbon—the blue area at the top of the screen—in Microsoft Office 2010 adapts to different resolutions. If your monitor is set at a lower resolution than 1024 $\times$ 768, you might not see all of the buttons shown in the figures. The groups of buttons will always appear, but the entire group might be condensed into a single button that you need to click to access the buttons described in the instructions.

COURSECASTS **Learning on the Go. Always Available...Always Relevant.**

Our fast-paced world is driven by technology. You know because you are an active participant—always on the go, always keeping up with technological trends, and always learning new ways to embrace technology to power your life. Let CourseCasts, hosted by Ken Baldauf of Florida State University, be your guide into weekly updates in this ever-changing space. These timely, relevant podcasts are produced weekly and are available for download at http://coursecasts.course.com or directly from iTunes (search by CourseCasts). CourseCasts are a perfect solution to getting learners (and even instructors) to learn on the go!

Getting Started with Microsoft Office 2010

Microsoft Office 2010 is a group of software programs designed to help you create documents, collaborate with coworkers, and track and analyze information. Each program is designed so you can work quickly and efficiently to create professional-looking results. You use different Office programs to accomplish specific tasks, such as writing a letter or producing a sales presentation, yet all the programs have a similar look and feel. Once you become familiar with one program, you'll find it easy to transfer your knowledge to the others.  This unit introduces you to the most frequently used programs in Office, as well as common features they all share.

OBJECTIVES

Understand the Office 2010 suite

Start and exit an Office program

View the Office 2010 user interface

Create and save a file

Open a file and save it with a new name

View and print your work

Get Help and close a file

Understanding the Office 2010 Suite

Microsoft Office 2010 features an intuitive, context-sensitive user interface, so you can get up to speed faster and use advanced features with greater ease. The programs in Office are bundled together in a group called a **suite** (although you can also purchase them separately). The Office suite is available in several configurations, but all include Word, Excel, and PowerPoint. Other configurations include Access, Outlook, Publisher, and other programs.  Each program in Office is best suited for completing specific types of tasks, though there is some overlap in capabilities.

DETAILS

The Office programs covered in this book include:

- **Microsoft Word 2010**

  When you need to create any kind of text-based document, such as a memo, newsletter, or multipage report, Word is the program to use. You can easily make your documents look great by inserting eye-catching graphics and using formatting tools such as themes, which are available in most Office programs. **Themes** are predesigned combinations of color and formatting attributes you can apply to a document. The Word document shown in Figure A-1 was formatted with the Solstice theme.

- **Microsoft Excel 2010**

  Excel is the perfect solution when you need to work with numeric values and make calculations. It puts the power of formulas, functions, charts, and other analytical tools into the hands of every user, so you can analyze sales projections, calculate loan payments, and present your findings in style. The Excel worksheet shown in Figure A-1 tracks personal expenses. Because Excel automatically recalculates results whenever a value changes, the information is always up to date. A chart illustrates how the monthly expenses are broken down.

- **Microsoft PowerPoint 2010**

  Using PowerPoint, it's easy to create powerful presentations complete with graphics, transitions, and even a soundtrack. Using professionally designed themes and clip art, you can quickly and easily create dynamic slide shows such as the one shown in Figure A-1.

- **Microsoft Access 2010**

  Access helps you keep track of large amounts of quantitative data, such as product inventories or employee records. The form shown in Figure A-1 was created for a grocery store inventory database. Employees use the form to enter data about each item. Using Access enables employees to quickly find specific information such as price and quantity without hunting through store shelves and stockrooms.

Microsoft Office has benefits beyond the power of each program, including:

- **Common user interface: Improving business processes**

  Because the Office suite programs have a similar **interface**, or look and feel, your experience using one program's tools makes it easy to learn those in the other programs. In addition, Office documents are **compatible** with one another, meaning that you can easily incorporate, or **integrate**, an Excel chart into a PowerPoint slide, or an Access table into a Word document.

- **Collaboration: Simplifying how people work together**

  Office recognizes the way people do business today, and supports the emphasis on communication and knowledge sharing within companies and across the globe. All Office programs include the capability to incorporate feedback—called **online collaboration**—across the Internet or a company network.

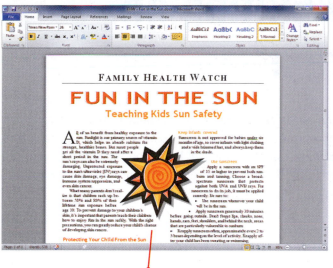

Newsletter created in Word

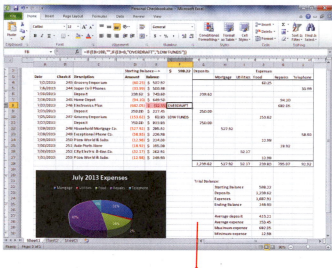

Checkbook register created in Excel

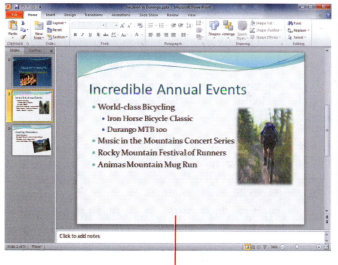

Tourism presentation created in PowerPoint

Store inventory form created in Access

Deciding which program to use

Every Office program includes tools that go far beyond what you might expect. For example, although Excel is primarily designed for making calculations, you can use it to create a database. So when you're planning a project, how do you decide which Office program to use? The general rule of thumb is to use the program best suited for your intended task, and make use of supporting tools in the program if you need them. Word is best for creating text-based documents, Excel is best for making mathematical calculations, PowerPoint is best for preparing presentations, and Access is best for managing quantitative data. Although the capabilities of Office are so vast that you *could* create an inventory in Excel or a budget in Word, you'll find greater flexibility and efficiency by using the program designed for the task. And remember, you can always create a file in one program, and then insert it in a document in another program when you need to, such as including sales projections (Excel) in a memo (Word).

Starting and Exiting an Office Program

The first step in using an Office program is to open, or **launch**, it on your computer. The easiest ways to launch a program are to click the Start button on the Windows taskbar or to double-click an icon on your desktop. You can have multiple programs open on your computer simultaneously, and you can move between open programs by clicking the desired program or document button on the taskbar or by using the [Alt][Tab] keyboard shortcut combination. When working, you'll often want to open multiple programs in Office and switch among them as you work. Begin by launching a few Office programs now.

STEPS

QUICK TIP
You can also launch a program by double-clicking a desktop icon or clicking the program name on the Start menu.

1. **Click the Start button on the taskbar**

   The Start menu opens. If the taskbar is hidden, you can display it by pointing to the bottom of the screen. Depending on your taskbar property settings, the taskbar may be displayed at all times, or only when you point to that area of the screen. For more information, or to change your taskbar properties, consult your instructor or technical support person.

2. **Click All Programs, scroll down if necessary in the All Programs menu, click Microsoft Office as shown in Figure A-2, then click Microsoft Word 2010**

   Word 2010 starts, and the program window opens on your screen.

QUICK TIP
It is not necessary to close one program before opening another.

3. **Click on the taskbar, click All Programs, click Microsoft Office, then click Microsoft Excel 2010**

   Excel 2010 starts, and the program window opens, as shown in Figure A-3. Word is no longer visible, but it remains open. The taskbar displays a button for each open program and document. Because this Excel document is **active**, or in front and available, the Excel button on the taskbar appears slightly lighter.

QUICK TIP
As you work in Windows, your computer adapts to your activities. You may notice that after clicking the Start button, the name of the program you want to open appears in the Start menu above All Programs; if so, you can click it to start the program.

4. **Point to the Word program button on the taskbar, then click**

   The Word program window is now in front. When the Aero feature is turned on in Windows 7, pointing to a program button on the taskbar displays a thumbnail version of each open window in that program above the program button. Clicking a program button on the taskbar activates that program and the most recently active document. Clicking a thumbnail of a document activates that document.

5. **Click on the taskbar, click All Programs, click Microsoft Office, then click Microsoft PowerPoint 2010**

   PowerPoint 2010 starts and becomes the active program.

6. **Click the Excel program button on the taskbar**

   Excel is now the active program.

TROUBLE
If you don't have Access installed on your computer, proceed to the next lesson.

7. **Click on the taskbar, click All Programs, click Microsoft Office, then click Microsoft Access 2010**

   Access 2010 starts and becomes the active program. Now all four Office programs are open at the same time.

8. **Click Exit on the navigation bar in the Access program window, as shown in Figure A-4**

   Access closes, leaving Excel active and Word and PowerPoint open.

Using shortcut keys to move between Office programs

As an alternative to the Windows taskbar, you can use a keyboard shortcut to move among open Office programs. The [Alt][Tab] keyboard combination lets you either switch quickly to the next open program or file or choose one from a gallery. To switch immediately to the next open program or file, press [Alt][Tab]. To choose from all open programs and files, press and hold [Alt], then press and release [Tab] without releasing [Alt]. A gallery opens on screen, displaying the filename and a thumbnail image of each open program and file, as well as of the desktop. Each time you press [Tab] while holding [Alt], the selection cycles to the next open file or location. Release [Alt] when the program, file, or location you want to activate is selected.

FIGURE A-2: Start menu

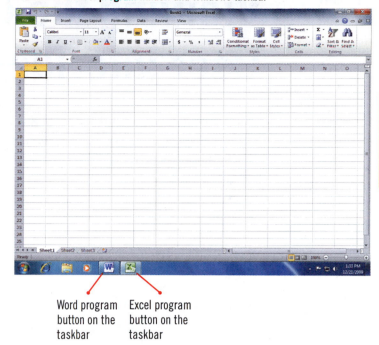

All programs menu (yours will look different)

Start button

Taskbar

FIGURE A-3: Excel program window and Windows taskbar

Word program button on the taskbar

Excel program button on the taskbar

FIGURE A-4: Access program window

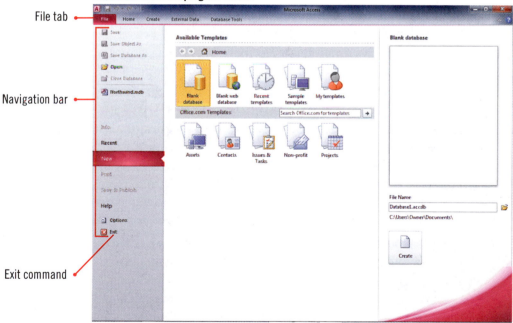

File tab

Navigation bar

Exit command

Windows Live and Microsoft Office Web Apps

All Office programs include the capability to incorporate feedback—called online collaboration—across the Internet or a company network. Using **cloud computing** (work done in a virtual environment), you can take advantage of Web programs called Microsoft Office Web Apps, which are simplified versions of the programs found in the Microsoft Office 2010 suite. Because these programs are online, they take up no computer disk space and are accessed using

Windows Live SkyDrive, a free service from Microsoft. Using Windows Live SkyDrive, you and your colleagues can create and store documents in a "cloud" and make the documents available to whomever you grant access. To use Windows Live SkyDrive, you need a free Windows Live ID, which you obtain at the Windows Live Web site. You can find more information in the "Working with Windows Live and Office Web Apps" appendix.

Viewing the Office 2010 User Interface

One of the benefits of using Office is that the programs have much in common, making them easy to learn and making it simple to move from one to another. Individual Office programs have always shared many features, but the innovations in the Office 2010 user interface mean even greater similarity among them all. That means you can also use your knowledge of one program to get up to speed in another. A **user interface** is a collective term for all the ways you interact with a software program. The user interface in Office 2010 provides intuitive ways to choose commands, work with files, and navigate in the program window.  Familiarize yourself with some of the common interface elements in Office by examining the PowerPoint program window.

STEPS

QUICK TIP

In addition to the standard tabs on the Ribbon, **contextual tabs** open when needed to complete a specific task; they appear in an accent color and close when no longer needed. To minimize the display of the buttons and commands on tabs, click the Minimize the Ribbon button 🔼 on the right end of the Ribbon.

1. **Click the PowerPoint program button** 📙 **on the taskbar**

   PowerPoint becomes the active program. Refer to Figure A-5 to identify common elements of the Office user interface. The **document window** occupies most of the screen. In PowerPoint, a blank slide appears in the document window, so you can build your slide show. At the top of every Office program window is a **title bar** that displays the document name and program name. Below the title bar is the **Ribbon**, which displays commands you're likely to need for the current task. Commands are organized onto **tabs**. The tab names appear at the top of the Ribbon, and the active tab appears in front. The Ribbon in every Office program includes tabs specific to the program, but all Office programs include a File tab and Home tab on the left end of the Ribbon.

2. **Click the File tab**

   The File tab opens, displaying **Backstage view**. The navigation bar on the left side of Backstage view contains commands to perform actions common to most Office programs, such as opening a file, saving a file, and closing the current program. Just above the File tab is the **Quick Access toolbar**, which also includes buttons for common Office commands.

3. **Click the File tab again to close Backstage view and return to the document window, then click the Design tab on the Ribbon**

   To display a different tab, you click the tab on the Ribbon. Each tab contains related commands arranged into **groups** to make features easy to find. On the Design tab, the Themes group displays available design themes in a **gallery**, or visual collection of choices you can browse. Many groups contain a **dialog box launcher**, an icon you can click to open a dialog box or task pane from which to choose related commands.

QUICK TIP

Live Preview is available in many galleries and menus throughout Office.

4. **Move the mouse pointer** 🖱 **over the Angles theme in the Themes group as shown in Figure A-6, but do not click the mouse button**

   The Angles theme is temporarily applied to the slide in the document window. However, because you did not click the theme, you did not permanently change the slide. With the **Live Preview** feature, you can point to a choice, see the results right in the document, and then decide if you want to make the change.

QUICK TIP

If you accidentally click a theme, click the Undo button 🔄 on the Quick Access toolbar.

5. **Move** 🖱 **away from the Ribbon and towards the slide**

   If you had clicked the Angles theme, it would be applied to this slide. Instead, the slide remains unchanged.

QUICK TIP

You can also use the Zoom button in the Zoom group on the View tab to enlarge or reduce a document's appearance.

6. **Point to the Zoom slider** 🔽 **on the status bar, then drag** 🔽 **to the right until the Zoom level reads 166%**

   The slide display is enlarged. Zoom tools are located on the status bar. You can drag the slider or click the Zoom In or Zoom Out buttons to zoom in or out on an area of interest. **Zooming in**, or choosing a higher percentage, makes a document appear bigger on screen, but less of it fits on the screen at once; **zooming out**, or choosing a lower percentage, lets you see more of the document but at a reduced size.

7. **Drag** 🔽 **on the status bar to the left until the Zoom level reads 73%**

FIGURE A-5: PowerPoint program window

Quick Access toolbar

Ribbon

Clipboard dialog box launcher

Title bar

Tabs

Document window

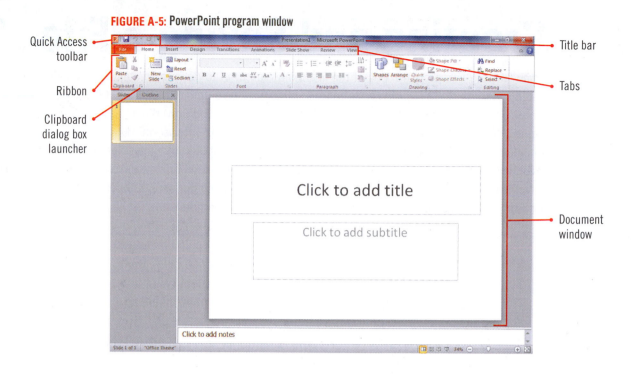

FIGURE A-6: Viewing a theme with Live Preview

Angles theme

Mouse pointer

Live Preview of Angles theme applied to document

Zoom slider

Zoom In button

Zoom level

Zoom Out button

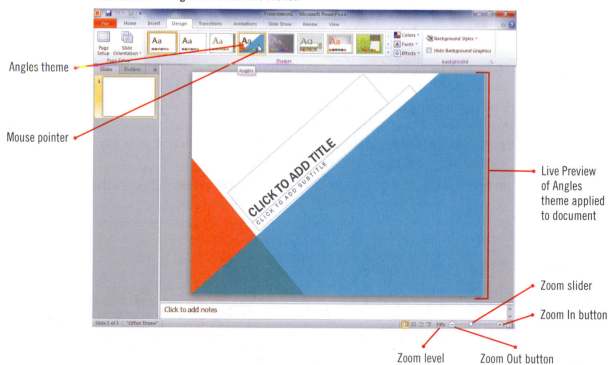

Using Backstage view

Backstage view in each Microsoft Office program offers "one stop shopping" for many commonly performed tasks, such as opening and saving a file, printing and previewing a document, defining document properties, sharing information, and exiting a program.

Backstage view opens when you click the File tab in any Office program, and while features such as the Ribbon, Mini toolbar, and Live Preview all help you work *in* your documents, the File tab and Backstage view help you work *with* your documents.

Creating and Saving a File

When working in a program, one of the first things you need to do is to create and save a file. A **file** is a stored collection of data. Saving a file enables you to work on a project now, then put it away and work on it again later. In some Office programs, including Word, Excel, and PowerPoint, a new file is automatically created when you start the program, so all you have to do is enter some data and save it. In Access, you must expressly create a file before you enter any data. You should give your files meaningful names and save them in an appropriate location so that they're easy to find. Use Word to familiarize yourself with the process of creating and saving a document. First you'll type some notes about a possible location for a corporate meeting, then you'll save the information for later use.

STEPS

1. **Click the Word program button** 🔲 **on the taskbar**

2. **Type Locations for Corporate Meeting, then press [Enter] twice**
   The text appears in the document window, and the **insertion point** blinks on a new blank line. The insertion point indicates where the next typed text will appear.

3. **Type Las Vegas, NV, press [Enter], type Orlando, FL, press [Enter], type Boston, MA, press [Enter] twice, then type your name**
   Compare your document to Figure A-7.

> **QUICK TIP**
> A filename can be up to 255 characters, including a file extension, and can include upper- or lowercase characters and spaces, but not ?, ", /, \, <, >, *, |, or :.

4. **Click the Save button** 🔲 **on the Quick Access toolbar**
   Because this is the first time you are saving this document, the Save As dialog box opens, as shown in Figure A-8. The Save As dialog box includes options for assigning a filename and storage location. Once you save a file for the first time, clicking 🔲 saves any changes to the file *without* opening the Save As dialog box, because no additional information is needed. The Address bar in the Save As dialog box displays the default location for saving the file, but you can change it to any location. The File name field contains a suggested name for the document based on text in the file, but you can enter a different name.

5. **Type OF A-Potential Corporate Meeting Locations**
   The text you type replaces the highlighted text. (The "OF A-" in the filename indicates that the file is created in Office Unit A. You will see similar designations throughout this book when files are named. For example, a file named in Excel Unit B would begin with "EX B-" .)

> **QUICK TIP**
> Saving a file to the Desktop creates a desktop icon that you can double-click to both launch a program and open a document.

6. **In the Save As dialog box, use the Address bar or Navigation Pane to navigate to the drive and folder where you store your Data Files**
   Many students store files on a flash drive, but you can also store files on your computer, a network drive, or any storage device indicated by your instructor or technical support person.

> **QUICK TIP**
> To create a new blank file when a file is open, click the File tab, click New on the navigation bar, then click Create near the bottom of the document preview pane.

7. **Click Save**
   The Save As dialog box closes, the new file is saved to the location you specified, then the name of the document appears in the title bar, as shown in Figure A-9. (You may or may not see the file extension ".docx" after the filename.) See Table A-1 for a description of the different types of files you create in Office, and the file extensions associated with each.

TABLE A-1: Common filenames and default file extensions

file created in	is called a	and has the default extension
Word	document	.docx
Excel	workbook	.xlsx
PowerPoint	presentation	.pptx
Access	database	.accdb

FIGURE A-7: Document created in Word

Save button

Your name should appear here

Insertion point

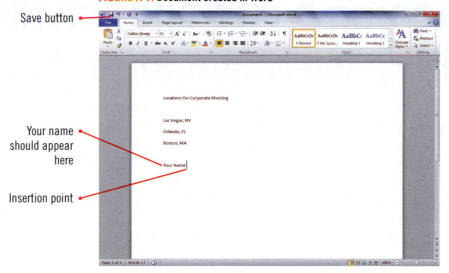

FIGURE A-8: Save As dialog box

Address bar

Navigation Pane; your links and folders may differ

File name field; your computer may not display file extensions

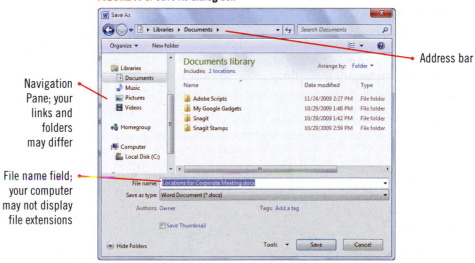

FIGURE A-9: Saved and named Word document

Filename appears in title bar

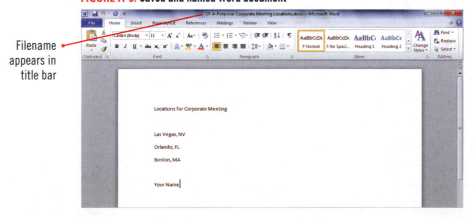

Using the Office Clipboard

You can use the Office Clipboard to cut and copy items from one Office program and paste them into others. The Office Clipboard can store a maximum of 24 items. To access it, open the Office Clipboard task pane by clicking the dialog box launcher 🔲 in the Clipboard group on the Home tab. Each time you copy a selection, it is saved in the Office Clipboard. Each entry in the Office Clipboard includes an icon that tells you the program it was created in. To paste an entry, click in the document where you want it to appear, then click the item in the Office Clipboard. To delete an item from the Office Clipboard, right-click the item, then click Delete.

Opening a File and Saving It with a New Name

In many cases as you work in Office, you start with a blank document, but often you need to use an existing file. It might be a file you or a coworker created earlier as a work in progress, or it could be a complete document that you want to use as the basis for another. For example, you might want to create a budget for this year using the budget you created last year; you could type in all the categories and information from scratch, or you could open last year's budget, save it with a new name, and just make changes to update it for the current year. By opening the existing file and saving it with the Save As command, you create a duplicate that you can modify to your heart's content, while the original file remains intact. Use Excel to open an existing workbook file, and save it with a new name so the original remains unchanged.

STEPS

QUICK TIP

Click Recent on the navigation bar to display a list of recent workbooks; click a file in the list to open it.

1. **Click the Excel program button on the taskbar, click the File tab, then click Open on the navigation bar**

   The Open dialog box opens, where you can navigate to any drive or folder accessible to your computer to locate a file.

2. **In the Open dialog box, navigate to the drive and folder where you store your Data Files**

   The files available in the current folder are listed, as shown in Figure A-10. This folder contains one file.

TROUBLE

Click Enable Editing on the Protected View bar near the top of your document window if prompted.

3. **Click OFFICE A-1.xlsx, then click Open**

   The dialog box closes, and the file opens in Excel. An Excel file is an electronic spreadsheet, so it looks different from a Word document or a PowerPoint slide.

4. **Click the File tab, then click Save As on the navigation bar**

   The Save As dialog box opens, and the current filename is highlighted in the File name text box. Using the Save As command enables you to create a copy of the current, existing file with a new name. This action preserves the original file and creates a new file that you can modify.

QUICK TIP

The Save As command works identically in all Office programs, except Access; in Access, this command lets you save a copy of the current database object, such as a table or form, with a new name, but not a copy of the entire database.

5. **Navigate to the drive and folder where you store your Data Files if necessary, type OF A-Budget for Corporate Meeting in the File name text box, as shown in Figure A-11, then click Save**

   A copy of the existing workbook is created with the new name. The original file, Office A-1.xlsx, closes automatically.

6. **Click cell A19, type your name, then press [Enter], as shown in Figure A-12**

   In Excel, you enter data in cells, which are formed by the intersection of a row and a column. Cell A19 is at the intersection of column A and row 19. When you press [Enter], the cell pointer moves to cell A20.

7. **Click the Save button on the Quick Access toolbar**

   Your name appears in the workbook, and your changes to the file are saved.

Working in Compatibility Mode

Not everyone upgrades to the newest version of Office. As a general rule, new software versions are **backward compatible**, meaning that documents saved by an older version can be read by newer software. To open documents created in older Office versions, Office 2010 includes a feature called Compatibility Mode. When you use Office 2010 to open a file created in an earlier version of Office, "Compatibility Mode" appears in the title bar, letting you know the file was created in an earlier but usable version of the program. If you are working with someone who may not be using the newest version of the software, you can avoid possible incompatibility problems by saving your file in another, earlier format. To do this in an Office program, click the File tab, click Save As on the navigation bar, click the Save as type list arrow in the Save As dialog box, then click an option on the list. For example, if you're working in Excel, click Excel 97-2003 Workbook format in the Save as type list to save an Excel file so that it can be opened in Excel 97 or Excel 2003.

FIGURE A-10: Open dialog box

Available files in this folder

Open button

Open list arrow

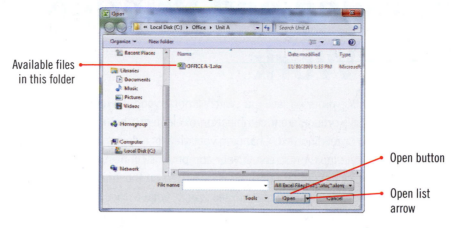

FIGURE A-11: Save As dialog box

New filename

Save as type list arrow

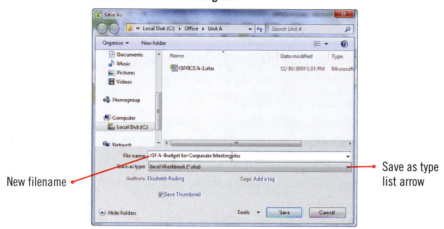

FIGURE A-12: Your name added to the workbook

Address for cell A19 formed by column A and row 19

Cell A19; type your name here

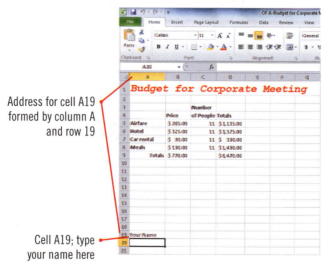

Exploring File Open options

You might have noticed that the Open button on the Open dialog box includes an arrow. In a dialog box, if a button includes an arrow you can click the button to invoke the command, or you can click the arrow to choose from a list of related commands. The Open list arrow includes several related commands, including Open Read-Only and Open as Copy. Clicking Open Read-Only opens a file that you can only save with a new name; you cannot save changes to the original file. Clicking Open as Copy creates a copy of the file already saved and named with the word "Copy" in the title. Like the Save As command, these commands provide additional ways to use copies of existing files while ensuring that original files do not get changed by mistake.

Viewing and Printing Your Work

Each Microsoft Office program lets you switch among various **views** of the document window to show more or fewer details or a different combination of elements that make it easier to complete certain tasks, such as formatting or reading text. Changing your view of a document does not affect the file in any way, it affects only the way it looks on screen. If your computer is connected to a printer or a print server, you can easily print any Office document using the Print button on the Print tab in Backstage view. Printing can be as simple as **previewing** the document to see exactly what a document will look like when it is printed and then clicking the Print button. Or, you can customize the print job by printing only selected pages or making other choices. Experiment with changing your view of a Word document, and then preview and print your work.

STEPS

1. **Click the Word program button** 📄 **on the taskbar**

   Word becomes the active program, and the document fills the screen.

2. **Click the View tab on the Ribbon**

   In most Office programs, the View tab on the Ribbon includes groups and commands for changing your view of the current document. You can also change views using the View buttons on the status bar.

3. **Click the Web Layout button in the Document Views group on the View tab**

   The view changes to Web Layout view, as shown in Figure A-13. This view shows how the document will look if you save it as a Web page.

4. **Click the Print Layout button on the View tab**

   You return to Print Layout view, the default view in Word.

5. **Click the File tab, then click Print on the navigation bar**

   The Print tab opens in Backstage view. The preview pane on the right side of the window automatically displays a preview of how your document will look when printed, showing the entire page on screen at once. Compare your screen to Figure A-14. Options in the Settings section enable you to change settings such as margins, orientation, and paper size before printing. To change a setting, click it, and then click the new setting you want. For instance, to change from Letter paper size to Legal, click Letter in the Settings section, then click Legal on the menu that opens. The document preview is updated as you change the settings. You also can use the Settings section to change which pages to print and even the number of pages you print on each sheet of printed paper. If you have multiple printers from which to choose, you can change from one installed printer to another by clicking the current printer in the Printer section, then clicking the name of the installed printer you want to use. The Print section contains the Print button and also enables you to select the number of copies of the document to print.

6. **Click the Print button in the Print section**

   A copy of the document prints, and Backstage view closes.

QUICK TIP

You can add the Quick Print button 🖨 to the Quick Access toolbar by clicking the Customize Quick Access Toolbar button, then clicking Quick Print. The Quick Print button prints one copy of your document using the default settings.

Customizing the Quick Access toolbar

You can customize the Quick Access toolbar to display your favorite commands. To do so, click the Customize Quick Access Toolbar button ▼ in the title bar, then click the command you want to add. If you don't see the command in the list, click More Commands to open the Quick Access Toolbar tab of the current program's Options dialog box. In the Options dialog box, use the Choose commands from list to choose a category, click the desired command in the list on the left, click Add to add it to the Quick Access toolbar, then click OK. To remove a button from the toolbar, click the name in the list on the right in the Options dialog box, then click Remove. To add a command to the Quick Access toolbar on the fly, simply right-click the button on the Ribbon, then click Add to Quick Access Toolbar on the shortcut menu. To move the Quick Access toolbar below the Ribbon, click the Customize Quick Access Toolbar button, and then click Show Below the Ribbon.

FIGURE A-13: Web Layout view

Web Layout button

View buttons on status bar

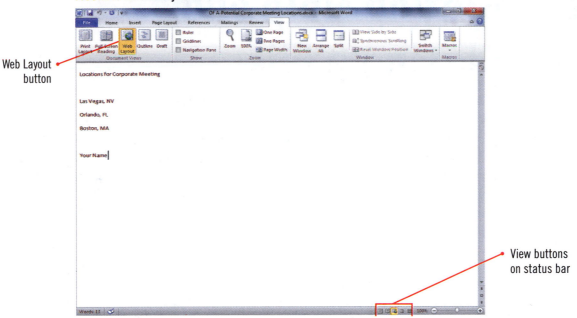

FIGURE A-14: Print tab in Backstage view

Print button

Click to select a different installed printer

Settings section

Preview of document

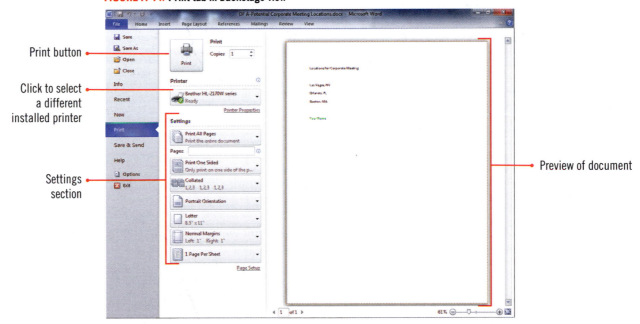

Creating a screen capture

A **screen capture** is a digital image of your screen, as if you took a picture of it with a camera. For instance, you might want to take a screen capture if an error message occurs and you want Technical Support to see exactly what's on the screen. You can create a screen capture using features found in Windows 7 or Office 2010. Windows 7 comes with the Snipping Tool, a separate program designed to capture whole screens or portions of screens. To open the Snipping Tool, click it on the Start menu or click All Programs, click Accessories, then click Snipping Tool. After opening the Snipping Tool, drag the pointer on the screen to select the area of the screen you want to capture. When you release the mouse button, the screen capture opens in the Snipping Tool window, and

you can save, copy, or send it in an e-mail. In Word, Excel, and PowerPoint 2010, you can capture screens or portions of screens and insert them in the current document using the Screenshot button on the Insert tab. And finally, you can create a screen capture by pressing [PrtScn]. (Keyboards differ, but you may find the [PrtScn] button in or near your keyboard's function keys.) Pressing this key places a digital image of your screen in the Windows temporary storage area known as the **Clipboard**. Open the document where you want the screen capture to appear, click the Home tab on the Ribbon (if necessary), then click the Paste button on the Home tab. The screen capture is pasted into the document.

Office 2010

Getting Help and Closing a File

You can get comprehensive help at any time by pressing [F1] in an Office program. You can also get help in the form of a ScreenTip by pointing to almost any icon in the program window. When you're finished working in an Office document, you have a few choices regarding ending your work session. You can close a file or exit a program by using the File tab or by clicking a button on the title bar. Closing a file leaves a program running, while exiting a program closes all the open files in that program as well as the program itself. In all cases, Office reminds you if you try to close a file or exit a program and your document contains unsaved changes. Explore the Help system in Microsoft Office, and then close your documents and exit any open programs.

STEPS

1. **Point to the Zoom button on the View tab of the Ribbon**

   A ScreenTip appears that describes how the Zoom button works and explains where to find other zoom controls.

2. **Press [F1]**

   The Word Help window opens, as shown in Figure A-15, displaying the home page for help in Word on the right and the Table of Contents pane on the left. In both panes of the Help window, each entry is a hyperlink you can click to open a list of related topics. The Help window also includes a toolbar of useful Help commands and a Search field. The connection status at the bottom of the Help window indicates that the connection to Office.com is active. Office.com supplements the help content available on your computer with a wide variety of up-to-date topics, templates, and training. If you are not connected to the Internet, the Help window displays only the help content available on your computer.

3. **Click the Creating documents link in the Table of Contents pane**

   The icon next to Creating documents changes, and a list of subtopics expands beneath the topic.

4. **Click the Create a document link in the subtopics list in the Table of Contents pane**

   The topic opens in the right pane of the Help window, as shown in Figure A-16.

5. **Click Delete a document under "What do you want to do?" in the right pane**

   The link leads to information about deleting a document.

6. **Click the Accessibility link in the Table of Contents pane, click the Accessibility features in Word link, read the information in the right pane, then click the Help window Close button**

7. **Click the File tab, then click Close on the navigation bar; if a dialog box opens asking whether you want to save your changes, click Save**

   The Potential Corporate Meeting Locations document closes, leaving the Word program open.

8. **Click the File tab, then click Exit on the navigation bar**

   Word closes, and the Excel program window is active.

9. **Click the File tab, click Exit on the navigation bar to exit Excel, click the PowerPoint program button on the taskbar if necessary, click the File tab, then click Exit on the navigation bar to exit PowerPoint**

   Excel and PowerPoint both close.

Help toolbar

Search field

The colors of
your links may
differ if the
links have
been visited
previously

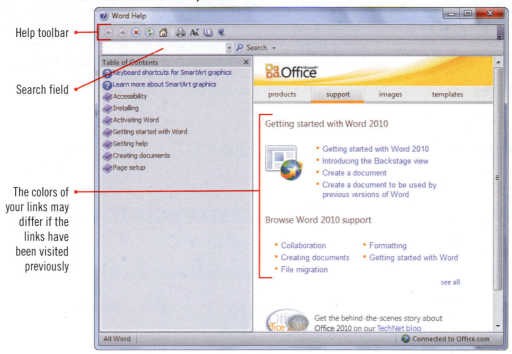

FIGURE A-16: Create a document Help topic

Print button

Icon indicates
expanded topic

Create a
document link

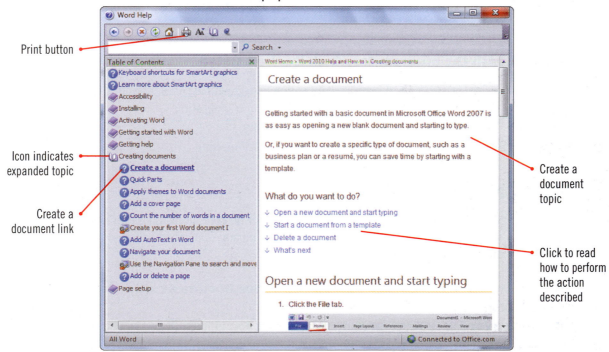

Create a
document
topic

Click to read
how to perform
the action
described

Recovering a document

Each Office program has a built-in recovery feature that allows you to open and save files that were open at the time of an interruption such as a power failure. When you restart the program(s) after an interruption, the Document Recovery task pane opens on the left side of your screen displaying both original and recovered versions of the files that were open. If you're not sure which file to open

(original or recovered), it's usually better to open the recovered file because it will contain the latest information. You can, however, open and review all versions of the file that were recovered and save the best one. Each file listed in the Document Recovery task pane displays a list arrow with options that allow you to open the file, save it as is, delete it, or show repairs made to it during recovery.

Practice

For current SAM information, including versions and content details, visit SAM Central (http://www.cengage.com/samcentral). If you have a SAM user profile, you may have access to hands-on instruction, practice, and assessment of the skills covered in this unit. Since various versions of SAM are supported throughout the life of this text, check with your instructor for the correct instructions and URL/Web site for accessing assignments.

Concepts Review

Label the elements of the program window shown in Figure A-17.

FIGURE A-17

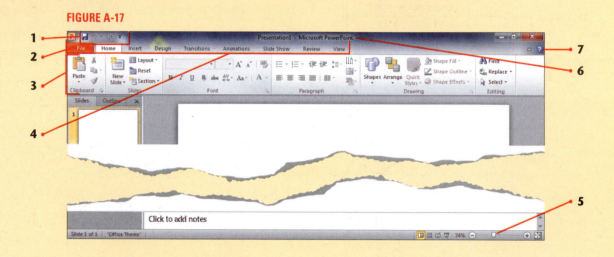

Match each project with the program for which it is best suited.

8. Microsoft Access   a. Corporate convention budget with expense projections
9. Microsoft Excel   b. Business cover letter for a job application
10. Microsoft Word   c. Department store inventory
11. Microsoft PowerPoint   d. Presentation for city council meeting

Independent Challenge 1

You just accepted an administrative position with a local independently owned produce vendor that has recently invested in computers and is now considering purchasing Microsoft Office for the company. You are asked to propose ways Office might help the business. You produce your document in Word.

a. Start Word, then save the document as **OF A-Microsoft Office Document** in the drive and folder where you store your Data Files.
b. Type **Microsoft Word**, press [Enter] twice, type **Microsoft Excel**, press [Enter] twice, type **Microsoft PowerPoint**, press [Enter] twice, type **Microsoft Access**, press [Enter] twice, then type your name.
c. Click the line beneath each program name, type at least two tasks suited to that program (each separated by a comma), then press [Enter].

Advanced Challenge Exercise

- Press the [PrtScn] button to create a screen capture.
- Click after your name, press [Enter] to move to a blank line below your name, then click the Paste button in the Clipboard group on the Home tab.

d. Save the document, then submit your work to your instructor as directed.
e. Exit Word.

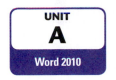

Creating Documents with Word 2010

Files You Will Need:

WD A-1.docx

Microsoft Word 2010 is a word processing program that makes it easy to create a variety of professional-looking documents, from simple letters and memos to newsletters, research papers, blog posts, business cards, résumés, financial reports, and other documents that include multiple pages of text and sophisticated formatting. In this unit, you will explore the editing and formatting features available in Word and create two documents. You have been hired to work in the Marketing Department at Quest Specialty Travel (QST), a tour company that specializes in cultural tourism and adventure travel. Shortly after reporting to your new office, Ron Dawson, the vice president of marketing, asks you to use Word to create a memo to the marketing staff and a fax to one of the tour developers.

OBJECTIVES

Understand word processing software

Explore the Word program window

Start a document

Save a document

Select text

Format text using the Mini toolbar

Create a document using a template

View and navigate a document

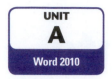

Understanding Word Processing Software

A **word processing program** is a software program that includes tools for entering, editing, and formatting text and graphics. Microsoft Word is a powerful word processing program that allows you to create and enhance a wide range of documents quickly and easily. Figure A-1 shows the first page of a report created using Word and illustrates some of the Word features you can use to enhance your documents. The electronic files you create using Word are called **documents**. One of the benefits of using Word is that document files can be stored on a hard disk, CD, flash drive, or other storage device, making them easy to transport, exchange, and revise. Before beginning your memo to the marketing staff, you explore the editing and formatting features available in Word.

DETAILS

You can use Word to accomplish the following tasks:

- **Type and edit text**

  The Word editing tools make it simple to insert and delete text in a document. You can add text to the middle of an existing paragraph, replace text with other text, undo an editing change, and correct typing, spelling, and grammatical errors with ease.

- **Copy and move text from one location to another**

  Using the more advanced editing features of Word, you can copy or move text from one location and insert it in a different location in a document. You also can copy and move text between documents. This means you don't have to retype text that is already entered in a document.

- **Format text and paragraphs with fonts, colors, and other elements**

  The sophisticated formatting tools in Word allow you to make the text in your documents come alive. You can change the size, style, and color of text, add lines and shading to paragraphs, and enhance lists with bullets and numbers. Creatively formatting text helps to highlight important ideas in your documents.

- **Format and design pages**

  The page-formatting features in Word give you power to design attractive newsletters, create powerful résumés, and produce documents such as research papers, business cards, CD labels, and books. You can change the paper size and orientation of your documents, organize text in columns, and control the layout of text and graphics on each page of a document. For quick results, Word includes preformatted cover pages, pull quotes, and headers and footers, as well as galleries of coordinated text, table, and graphic styles that you can rely on to give documents a polished look. If you are writing a research paper, Word makes it easy to manage reference sources and create footnotes, endnotes, and bibliographies.

- **Enhance documents with tables, charts, diagrams, and graphics**

  Using the powerful graphics tools in Word, you can spice up your documents with pictures, photographs, lines, shapes, and diagrams. You also can illustrate your documents with tables and charts to help convey your message in a visually interesting way.

- **Use Mail Merge to create form letters and mailing labels**

  The Word Mail Merge feature allows you to send personalized form letters to many different people. You can also use Mail Merge to create mailing labels, directories, e-mail messages, and other types of documents.

- **Share documents securely**

  The security features in Word make it quick and easy to remove comments, tracked changes, and unwanted personal information from your files before you share them with others. You can also add a password or a digital signature to a document and convert a file to a format suitable for publishing on the Web.

Add headers to every page

Insert graphics

Format the size and appearance of text

Create columns of text

Create tables

Add lines

Add bullets to lists

Create charts

Align text in paragraphs evenly

Add page numbers in footers

Word 2010

Quest Specialty Travel Marketing Report   May 2013

Client Profile

A typical QST client is a 42-year-old professional with an annual household income of $84,000. He or she works in the city, owns a home in an urban or suburban area, and has no children living at home.

- 73% graduated from college.
- 32% have a graduate level degree.
- 60% earn more than $60,000 per year.
- 8% earn more than $200,000 per year.
- 45% are employed as professionals.
- 29% are retired.

QST Client Survey Results

In an effort to develop an economic profile of Quest Specialty Travel clients, the marketing department hired the market research firm Takeshita Consultants, Inc. to create and administer a survey of the QST client base. A secondary goal of the survey was to identify the areas in which QST can improve its tour offerings in each region. Over 8,600 people completed the survey, which was distributed by e-mail and mailed to everyone who has purchased a QST tour in the past five years. Surveys were also completed by people who visited the QST Web site but have not purchased a QST tour. Forty-two percent of the survey recipients responded to the survey.

Survey Methods

The survey was distributed to purchasing clients via mail and e-mail during January and February 2013. The survey was also available on the QST Web site, and was completed by over 1,800 non-clients. The table below shows the distribution of respondents by delivery mode and by sex.

Travel Preferences

Respondents report they enjoy independent domestic travel, but they prefer an organized tour when traveling abroad. Most cited guide expertise as the primary reason for selecting a QST tour.

Preferred Destination

Pie chart legend:
- Africa
- Asia
- Australia/NZ
- Europe
- Latin America
- North America

Values: 6%, 15%, 21%, 18%, 8%, 32%

Client Satisfaction

On the whole, QST clients gave the quality of QST tours a favorable review. Clients rated the expertise and professionalism of the guides as excellent, the range of tours as very good, and the accommodations and food served as excellent. Equally favorable ratings were given to the sales staff and the attractiveness of QST printed materials. Clients did express interest in a wider selection of tours in South East Asia, particularly Laos, Cambodia, and Vietnam, as well as more European offerings. The response time for tour information ordered from the Web site could also be improved.

Survey Delivery Mode	Male	Female
E-mail to clients	6,657	7,801
Mail to clients	1,567	1,238
Web site clients	563	442
Web site non-clients	898	987
Other	365	122
Total	10,050	10,590
	Grand Total	20,640

▶ 1

Planning a document

Before you create a new document, it's a good idea to spend time planning it. Identify the message you want to convey, the audience for your document, and the elements, such as tables or charts, you want to include. You should also think about the tone and look of your document—are you writing a business letter, which should be written in a pleasant, but serious tone and have a formal appearance, or are you creating a flyer that must be colorful, eye-catching, and fun to read? The purpose and audience for your document determine the appropriate design. Planning the layout and design of a document involves deciding how to organize the text, selecting the fonts to use, identifying the graphics to include, and selecting the formatting elements that will enhance the message and appeal of the document. For longer documents, such as newsletters, it can be useful to sketch the layout and design of each page before you begin.

Exploring the Word Program Window

When you start Word, a blank document appears in the document window in Print Layout view. 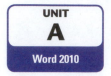 You examine the elements of the Word program window.

1. **Start Word**

   The **Word program window** opens, as shown in Figure A-2. The blinking vertical line in the document window is the **insertion point**. It indicates where text appears as you type.

2. **Move the mouse pointer around the Word program window**

   The mouse pointer changes shape depending on where it is in the Word program window. You use pointers to move the insertion point or to select text to edit. Table A-1 describes common pointers in Word.

   QUICK TIP
   The buttons visible on your Ribbon may differ.

3. **Place the mouse pointer over a button on the Ribbon**

   When you place the mouse pointer over a button or some other elements of the Word program window, a ScreenTip appears. A **ScreenTip** is a label that identifies the name of the button or feature, briefly describes its function, conveys any keyboard shortcut for the command, and includes a link to associated help topics, if any.

Using Figure A-2 as a guide, find the elements described below in your program window:

- The **title bar** displays the name of the document and the name of the program. Until you give a new document a different name, its temporary name is Document1. The title bar also contains resizing buttons and the program Close button. These buttons are common to all Windows programs.

- The **Quick Access toolbar** contains buttons for saving a document and for undoing, redoing, and repeating a change. You can modify the Quick Access toolbar to include the commands you use frequently.

- The **File tab** provides access to **Backstage view**, where you manage files and the information about them. Backstage view includes commands related to working with documents, such as opening, printing, and saving a document. The File tab also provides access to resources for help using Word and to the Word Options dialog box, which is used to customize the way you use Word.

  QUICK TIP
  To display a different tab, you simply click its name on the Ribbon.

- The **Ribbon** contains the Word tabs. Each **tab** on the Ribbon includes buttons for commands related to editing and formatting, documents. The commands are organized in **groups**. For example, the Home tab includes the Clipboard, Font, Paragraph, Styles, and Editing groups. The Ribbon also includes the **Microsoft Word Help button**, which you use to access the Word Help system.

- The **document window** displays the current document. You enter text and format your document in the document window.

  TROUBLE
  Click the View Ruler button [⬚] at the top of the vertical scroll bar to display the rulers if they are not already displayed.

- The rulers appear in the document window in Print Layout view. The **horizontal ruler** displays left and right document margins as well as the tab settings and paragraph indents, if any, for the paragraph in which the insertion point is located. The **vertical ruler** displays the top and bottom document margins.

- The **vertical scroll bar** and the **horizontal scroll bar** are used to display different parts of the document in the document window. The scroll bars include **scroll boxes** and **scroll arrows**, which you can use to scroll through a document.

- The **status bar** displays the page number of the current page, the total number of pages and words in the document, and the status of spelling and grammar checking. It also includes the view buttons, the Zoom level button, and the Zoom slider. You can customize the status bar to display other information.

- The **view buttons** on the status bar allow you to display the document in Print Layout, Full Screen Reading, Web Layout, Outline, or Draft view.

- The **Zoom level** button and the **Zoom slider** provide quick ways to enlarge and decrease the size of the document in the document window, making it easy to zoom in on a detail of a document or to view the layout of the document as a whole.

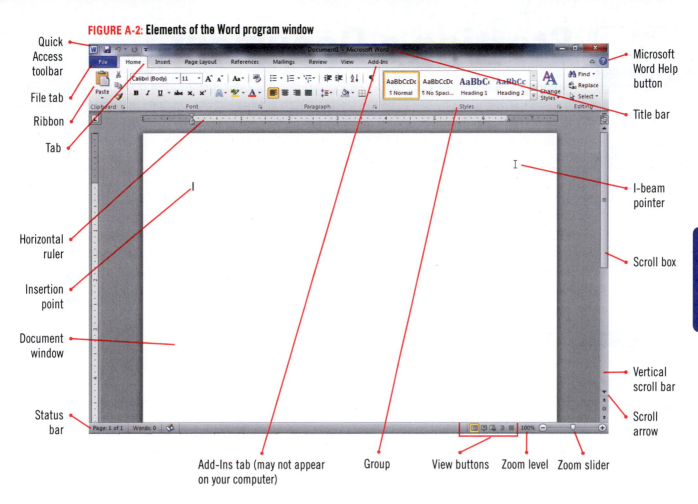

FIGURE A-2: Elements of the Word program window

Quick Access toolbar · File tab · Ribbon · Tab · Horizontal ruler · Insertion point · Document window · Status bar

Microsoft Word Help button · Title bar · I-beam pointer · Scroll box · Vertical scroll bar · Scroll arrow

Add-Ins tab (may not appear on your computer) · Group · View buttons · Zoom level · Zoom slider

TABLE A-1: Common mouse pointers in Word

name	pointer	use to
I-beam pointer	I	Move the insertion point in a document or to select text
Click and Type pointers, including left-align and center-align	I≡ or I≡	Move the insertion point to a blank area of a document in Print Layout or Web Layout view; double-clicking with a Click and Type pointer automatically applies the paragraph formatting (alignment and indentation) required to position text or a graphic at that location in the document
Selection pointer	⟍	Click a button or other element of the Word program window; appears when you point to elements of the Word program window
Right-pointing arrow pointer	⟍	Select a line or lines of text; appears when you point to the left edge of a line of text in the document window
Hand pointer	☝	Open a hyperlink; appears when you point to a hyperlink in a task pane or when you press [Ctrl] and point to a hyperlink in a document
Hide white space pointer	⇥⇤	Hide the white space in the top and bottom margins of a document in Print Layout view
Show white space pointer	⇥⇤	Show the white space in the top and bottom margins of a document in Print Layout view

Starting a Document

You begin a new document by simply typing text in a blank document in the document window. Word includes a **word-wrap** feature so that as you type Word automatically moves the insertion point to the next line of the document when you reach the right margin. You only press [Enter] when you want to start a new paragraph or insert a blank line.  You type a quick memo to the marketing staff.

STEPS

1. Type Memorandum, then press [Enter] twice

Each time you press [Enter] the insertion point moves to the start of the next line.

2. Type TO:, then press [Tab] twice

Pressing [Tab] moves the insertion point several spaces to the right. You can use the [Tab] key to align the text in a memo header or to indent the first line of a paragraph.

3. Type QST Managers, then press [Enter]

The insertion point moves to the start of the next line.

4. Type: FROM: [Tab] [Tab] Ron Dawson [Enter]
            DATE: [Tab] [Tab] July 7, 2013 [Enter]
            RE: [Tab] [Tab] Marketing Meeting [Enter] [Enter]

Red or green wavy lines may appear under the words you typed, indicating a possible spelling or grammar error. Spelling and grammar checking is one of the many automatic features you will encounter as you type. Table A-2 describes several of these automatic features. You can correct any typing errors you make later.

5. Type The next marketing staff meeting will be held on the 11th of July at 1 p.m. in the conference room on the ground floor., then press [Spacebar]

As you type, notice that the insertion point moves automatically to the next line of the document. You also might notice that Word automatically changed "11th" to "11th" in the memo. This feature is called **AutoCorrect**. AutoCorrect automatically makes typographical adjustments and detects and adjusts typing errors, certain misspelled words (such as "taht" for "that"), and incorrect capitalization as you type.

6. Type Heading the agenda will be the launch of our new High Atlas Trek, a rigorous ten-day walking tour of the sunny valleys, remote Berber villages, and steep slopes of Morocco's High Atlas, scheduled for September 2015.

When you type the first few characters of "September," the Word AutoComplete feature displays the complete word in a ScreenTip. **AutoComplete** suggests text to insert quickly into your documents. You can ignore AutoComplete for now. Your memo should resemble Figure A-3.

7. Press [Enter], then type Kai Haketa is in Marrakech hammering out the details. A preliminary draft of the tour brochure is attached. Bring your creative ideas for launching this exciting new tour to the meeting.

When you press [Enter] and type the new paragraph, notice that Word adds more space between the paragraphs than it does between the lines in each paragraph. This is part of the default style for paragraphs in Word, called the **Normal style**.

8. Position the I pointer after for (but before the space) in the last line of the first paragraph, then click

Clicking moves the insertion point after "for."

9. Press [Backspace] three times, then type to depart in

Pressing [Backspace] removes the character before the insertion point.

10. Move the insertion point before staff in the first sentence, then press [Delete] six times to remove the word "staff" and the space after it

Pressing [Delete] removes the character after the insertion point. Figure A-4 shows the revised memo.

FIGURE A-3: Memo text in the document window

Memo title

Blank lines between paragraphs

Memo header

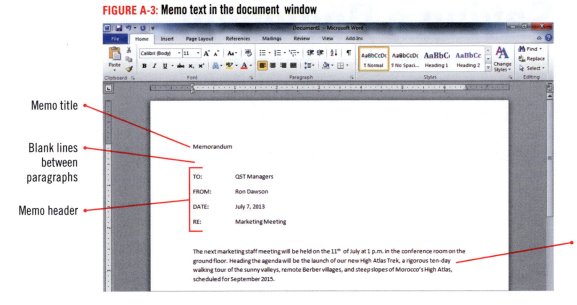

Text wraps to the next line (yours may wrap differently)

FIGURE A-4: Edited memo text

Text inserted in the memo

Normal style leaves more space between paragraphs than between lines

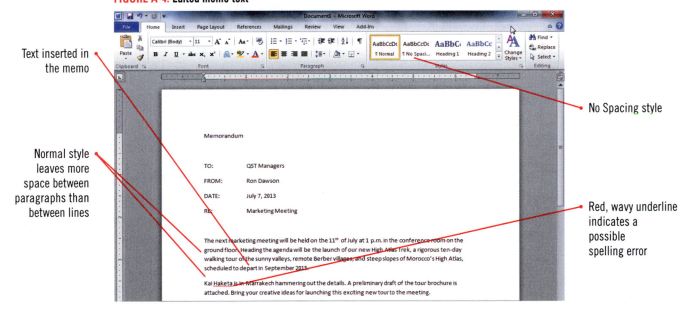

No Spacing style

Red, wavy underline indicates a possible spelling error

TABLE A-2: Automatic features that appear as you type in Word

feature	what appears	to use
AutoComplete	A ScreenTip suggesting text to insert appears as you type	Press [Enter] to insert the text suggested by the ScreenTip; continue typing to reject the suggestion
AutoCorrect	A small blue box appears when you place the pointer over text corrected by AutoCorrect; an AutoCorrect Options button ⬚ appears when you point to the blue box	Word automatically corrects typos, minor spelling errors, and capitalization, and adds typographical symbols (such as © and ™) as you type; to reverse an AutoCorrect adjustment, click the AutoCorrect Options list arrow, then click the option that will undo the action
Spelling and Grammar	A red wavy line under a word indicates a possible misspelling; a green wavy line under text indicates a possible grammar error	Right-click red- or green-underlined text to display a shortcut menu of correction options; click a correction option to accept it and remove the wavy underline

Saving a Document

To store a document permanently so you can open it and edit it at another time, you must save it as a **file**. When you **save** a document you give it a name, called a **filename**, and indicate the location where you want to store the file. Files created in Word 2010 are automatically assigned the .docx file extension to distinguish them from files created in other software programs. You can save a document using the Save button on the Quick Access toolbar or the Save command on the File tab. Once you have saved a document for the first time, you should save it again every few minutes and always before printing so that the saved file is updated to reflect your latest changes. 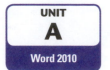 You save your memo using a descriptive filename and the default file extension.

STEPS

1. **Click the Save button 🖫 on the Quick Access toolbar**

   The first time you save a document, the Save As dialog box opens, as shown in Figure A-5. The default filename, Memorandum, appears in the File name text box. The default filename is based on the first few words of the document. The default file extension, .docx, appears in the Save as type list box. Table A-3 describes the functions of some of the buttons in the Save As dialog box.

2. **Type WD A-Morocco Tour Memo in the File name text box**

   The new filename replaces the default filename. Giving your documents brief descriptive filenames makes it easier to locate and organize them later. You do not need to type .docx when you type a new filename.

3. **Navigate to the drive and folder where you store your Data Files**

   You can navigate to a different drive or folder in several ways. For example, you can click a drive or folder in the Address bar or the navigation pane to go directly to that location. Click the double arrow in the Address bar to display a list of drives and folders. You can also double-click a drive or folder in the folder window to change the active location. When you are finished navigating to the drive or folder where you store your Data Files, that location appears in the Address bar. Your Save As dialog box should resemble Figure A-6.

4. **Click Save**

   The document is saved to the drive and folder you specified in the Save As dialog box, and the title bar displays the new filename, WD A-Morocco Tour Memo.docx.

5. **Place the insertion point before conference in the first sentence, type large, then press [Spacebar]**

   You can continue to work on a document after you have saved it with a new filename.

6. **Click 🖫**

   Your change to the memo is saved. After you save a document for the first time, you must continue to save the changes you make to the document. You also can press [Ctrl][S] to save a document.

Windows Live and Microsoft Office Web Apps

All Office programs include the capability to incorporate feedback—called online collaboration—across the Internet or a company network. Using **cloud computing** (work done in a virtual environment), you can take advantage of Web programs called Microsoft Office Web Apps, which are simplified versions of the programs found in the Microsoft Office 2010 suite. Because these programs are online, they take up no computer disk space and are accessed using Windows Live SkyDrive, a free service from Microsoft. Using Windows Live SkyDrive, you and your colleagues can create and store documents in a "cloud" and make the documents available to whomever you grant access. To use Windows Live SkyDrive, you need a free Windows Live ID, which you obtain at the Windows Live Web site. You can find more information in the "Working with Windows Live and Office Web Apps" appendix.

FIGURE A-5: Save As dialog box

Active folder or drive

Active library

Active folder

Folders and files in the active folder or drive (yours will differ)

Click to create a new folder in the active folder or drive

Default filename and file extension are selected

Click to change the file type

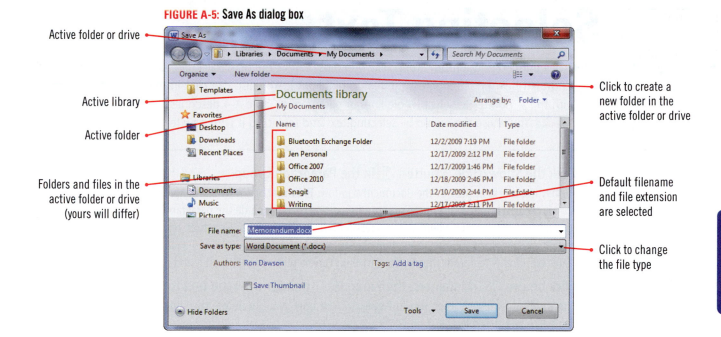

FIGURE A-6: File to be saved to the Unit A folder

Location of Data Files (yours may differ)

Your dialog box may show the files and folders in the active drive or folder

New filename

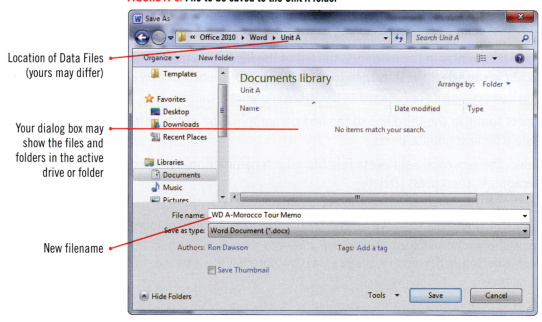

TABLE A-3: Save As dialog box buttons

button	use to
⬅ Back	Navigate back to the last location shown in the Address bar
➡ Forward	Navigate to the location that was previously shown in the Address bar
Organize ▾ Organize	Open a menu of commands related to organizing the selected file or folder, including Cut, Copy, Delete, Rename, and Properties
New folder New folder	Create a new folder in the current folder or drive
▤ ▾ Change your view	Change the way folder and file information is shown in the folder window in the Save As dialog box; click the Change your view button to toggle between views, or click the list arrow to open a menu of view options

Selecting Text

Before deleting, editing, or formatting text, you must **select** the text. Selecting text involves clicking and dragging the I-beam pointer across the text to highlight it. You also can click in the margin to the left of text with the ⌐ pointer to select whole lines or paragraphs. Table A-4 describes the many ways to select text. 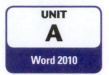 You revise the memo by selecting text and replacing it with new text.

1. **Click the Show/Hide ¶ button ¶ in the Paragraph group**

   Formatting marks appear in the document window. **Formatting marks** are special characters that appear on your screen but do not print. Common formatting marks include the paragraph symbol (¶), which shows the end of a paragraph—wherever you press [Enter]; the dot symbol (·), which represents a space—wherever you press [Spacebar]; and the arrow symbol (→), which shows the location of a tab stop—wherever you press [Tab]. Working with formatting marks turned on can help you to select, edit, and format text with precision.

   QUICK TIP
   You deselect text by clicking anywhere in the document window.

2. **Click before QST Managers, then drag the I pointer over the text to select it**

   The words are selected, as shown in Figure A-7. For now, you can ignore the faint toolbar that appears over text when you first select it.

3. **Type Marketing Staff**

   The text you type replaces the selected text.

4. **Double-click Ron, type your first name, double-click Dawson, then type your last name**

   Double-clicking a word selects the entire word.

   TROUBLE
   If you delete text by mistake, immediately click the Undo button ↺ on the Quick Access toolbar to restore the deleted text to the document.

5. **Place the pointer in the margin to the left of the RE: line so that the pointer changes to ⌐, click to select the line, then type RE: [Tab] [Tab] Launch of new Morocco trekking tour**

   Clicking to the left of a line of text with the ⌐ pointer selects the entire line.

6. **Select sunny in the third line of the first paragraph, type green, select steep slopes, then type stunning granite peaks**

7. **Select the sentence Kai Haketa is in Marrakech hammering out the details. in the second paragraph, then press [Delete]**

   Selecting text and pressing [Delete] removes the text from the document.

   QUICK TIP
   Always save before and after editing text.

8. **Click ¶, then click the Save button 💾 on the Quick Access toolbar**

   Formatting marks are turned off, and your changes to the memo are saved. The Show/Hide ¶ button is a **toggle button**, which means you can use it to turn formatting marks on and off. The edited memo is shown in Figure A-8.

FIGURE A-7: Text selected in the memo

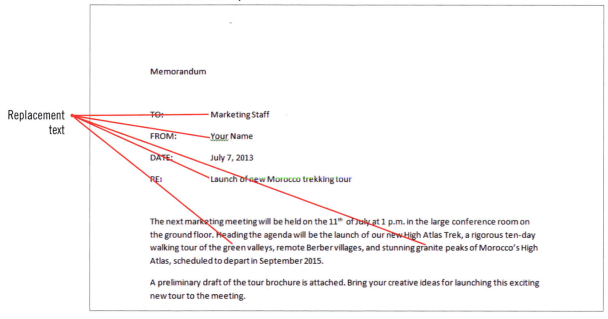

Selected text

Left document margin

FIGURE A-8: Edited memo with replacement text

Replacement text

TABLE A-4: Methods for selecting text

to select	use the pointer to
Any amount of text	Drag over the text
A word	Double-click the word
A line of text	Click with the ↗ pointer to the left of the line
A sentence	Press and hold [Ctrl], then click the sentence
A paragraph	Triple-click the paragraph or double-click with the ↗ pointer to the left of the paragraph
A large block of text	Click at the beginning of the selection, press and hold [Shift], then click at the end of the selection
Multiple nonconsecutive selections	Select the first selection, then press and hold [Ctrl] as you select each additional selection
An entire document	Triple-click with the ↗ pointer to the left of any text; press [Ctrl][A]; or click the Select button in the Editing group on the Home tab, and then click Select All

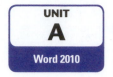

Formatting Text Using the Mini Toolbar

Formatting text is a fast and fun way to spruce up the appearance of a document and highlight important information. You can easily change the font, color, size, style, and other attributes of text by selecting the text and clicking a command on the Home tab. The **Mini toolbar**, which appears faintly above text when you first select it, also includes commonly used text and paragraph formatting commands. You enhance the appearance of the memo by formatting the text using the Mini toolbar. When you are finished, you preview the memo for errors and then print it.

STEPS

TROUBLE
If the Mini toolbar disappears, right-click the selection to display it again.

1. **Double-click Memorandum**

The Mini toolbar appears in ghosted fashion over the selected text. When you point to the Mini toolbar, it becomes solid, as shown in Figure A-9. You click a formatting option on the Mini toolbar to apply it to the selected text. Table A-5 describes the function of the buttons on the Mini toolbar. The buttons on the Mini toolbar are also available on the Ribbon.

2. **Click the Center button ☰ on the Mini toolbar**

The word "Memorandum" is centered between the left and right document margins.

QUICK TIP
Click the Shrink Font button to decrease the font size.

3. **Click the Grow Font button A˙ on the Mini toolbar eight times, then click the Bold button B on the Mini toolbar**

Each time you click the Grow Font button the selected text is enlarged. Applying bold to the text makes it thicker and darker.

4. **Select TO:, click B, select FROM:, click B, select DATE:, click B, select RE:, then click B**
Bold is applied to the heading text.

5. **Click the blank line between the RE: line and the body text, then click the Bottom Border button ⊞ in the Paragraph group**

A single-line border is added between the heading and the body text in the memo.

QUICK TIP
You can customize your Quick Access toolbar to include the Quick Print button, which prints a document using the default print settings.

6. **Save the document, click the File tab, then click Print**

Information related to printing the document appears on the Print tab in Backstage view. Options for printing the document appear on the left side of the Print tab and a preview of the document as it will look when printed appears on the right side, as shown in Figure A-10. Before you print a document, it's a good habit to examine it closely so you can identify and correct any problems.

7. **Click the Zoom In button ⊕ five times, then proofread your document carefully for errors**

The document is enlarged in print preview. If you notice errors in your document, you need to correct them before you print. To do this, press [Esc] or click the Home tab to close Backstage view, correct any mistakes, save your changes, click the File tab, and then click the Print command again to be ready to print the document.

8. **Click the Print button on the Print tab**

A copy of the memo prints using the default print settings. To change the current printer, change the number of copies to print, select what pages of a document to print, or modify another print setting, you simply change the appropriate setting on the Print tab before clicking the Print button.

9. **Click the File tab, then click Close**
The document closes, but the Word program window remains open.

Creating Documents with Word 2010

FIGURE A-9: Mini toolbar

Bold button on Ribbon and Mini toolbar

Mini toolbar

Bottom Border button

Center button on Ribbon and Mini toolbar

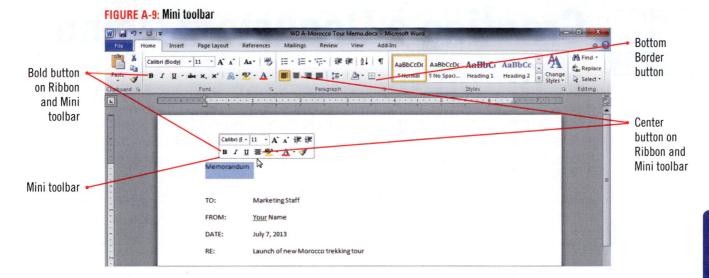

FIGURE A-10: Preview of the completed memo

File tab

Click to print

Print command

Options for changing the default print settings

Preview of how document will look when printed

Text is enlarged, bold, and centered

Bottom border added between heading and body text

Text is bold

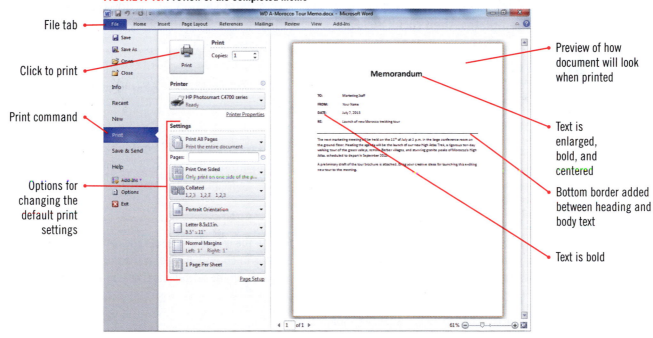

TABLE A-5: Buttons on the Mini toolbar

button	use to	button	use to
Calibri (E ▾)	Change the font of text	*I*	Italicize text
11 ▾	Change the font size of text	U	Underline text
A^	Make text larger	≡	Center text between the margins
A˅	Make text smaller	aby ▾	Apply colored highlighting to text
⇤	Decrease the indent level of a paragraph	A ▾	Change the color of text
⇥	Increase the indent level of a paragraph	✒	Copy the formats applied to text to other text
B	Apply bold to text		

Creating a Document Using a Template

Word includes many templates that you can use to create faxes, letters, reports, brochures, and other professionally designed documents quickly. A **template** is a formatted document that contains place-holder text,which you replace with your own text. To create a document that is based on a template, you use the New command on the File tab, and then select a template to use. You can then customize the document and save it with a new filename. 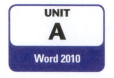 You want to fax a draft of the Morocco tour brochure to Kai Haketa, the tour developer for Africa. You use a template to create a fax cover sheet.

STEPS

1. **Click the File tab, then click New**

    The New tab opens in Backstage view, as shown in Figure A-11.

2. **Click Sample templates in the Available Templates section, scroll down the list of Available Templates, then click Oriel Fax**

    A preview of the Oriel Fax template appears in the preview section.

3. **Click Create**

    The Oriel Fax template opens as a new document in the document window. It contains placeholder text, which you can replace with your own information.

4. **Click [Pick the date]**

    The placeholder text is selected and appears inside a content control. A **content control** is an interactive object that you use to customize a document with your own information. A content control might include placeholder text, a drop-down list of choices, or a calendar. To deselect a content control, you click a blank area of the document.

5. **Click the Pick the date list arrow**

    A calendar opens below the content control. You use the calendar to select the date you want to appear on your document—simply click a date on the calendar to enter that date in the document. You can use the arrows to the left and right of the month and year to scroll the calendar and display a different month.

6. **Click the Today button on the calendar**

    The current date replaces the placeholder text.

7. **Click [TYPE THE RECIPIENT NAME], type Kai Haketa, Guest, click [Type the recipient fax number], then type 1-212-44-555-1510**

    You do not need to drag to select the placeholder text in a content control, you can simply click it. The text you type replaces the placeholder text.

8. **Click [Type the recipient phone number], press [Delete] twice, press [Backspace] seven times, then type HOTEL MARRAKECH, ROOM 1275**

    The recipient phone number content control is removed from the document.

9. **If the text in the From line is not your name, drag to select the text, then type your name**

    When the document is created, Word automatically enters the user name identified in the Word Options dialog box in the From line. This text is not placeholder text, so you have to drag to select it.

10. **Replace the remaining heading placeholder text with the text shown in Figure A-12, delete the CC: content control, click the File tab, click Save As, then save the document as WD A-Kai Fax to the drive and folder where you store your Data Files**

    The document is saved with the filename WD A-Kai Fax.

FIGURE A-11: New tab in Backstage view

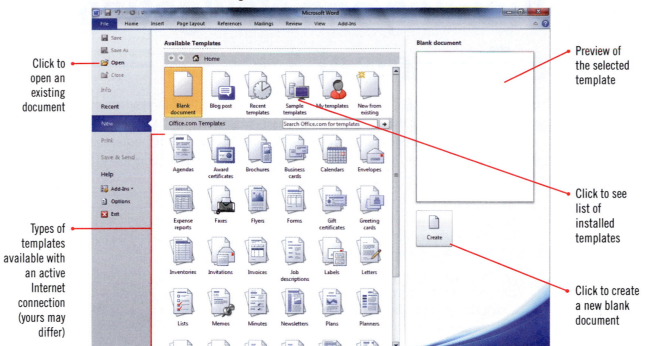

Click to open an existing document

Types of templates available with an active Internet connection (yours may differ)

Preview of the selected template

Click to see list of installed templates

Click to create a new blank document

Word 2010

FIGURE A-12: Document created using the Oriel fax template

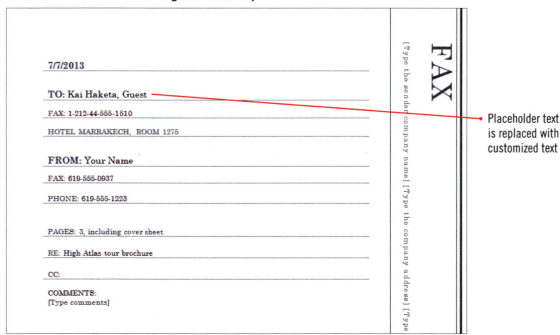

Placeholder text is replaced with customized text

Viewing and Navigating a Document

The Word Zoom feature lets you enlarge a document in the document window to get a close-up view of a detail or reduce the size of the document in the document window for an overview of the layout as a whole. You zoom in and out on a document using the tools in the Zoom group on the View tab and the Zoom level buttons and Zoom slider on the status bar. 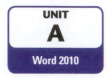 You find it is helpful to zoom in and out on the document as you finalize the fax cover sheet.

STEPS

1. **Click the down scroll arrow** ▼ **at the bottom of the vertical scroll bar until COMMENTS: is near the top of your document window**

   The scroll arrows or scroll bars allow you to **scroll** through a document. You scroll through a document when you want to display different parts of the document in the document window. You can also scroll by clicking the scroll bar above and below the scroll box, or by dragging the scroll box up or down in the scroll bar. In longer documents, you can click the Previous Page button ⬆ or the Next Page button ⬇ on the scroll bar to display the document page by page.

2. **Click [Type comments], then type A draft copy of the High Atlas tour brochure is attached. Please revise the text for accuracy. The photos are for placement only. Have you hired a photographer yet?**

QUICK TIP
You can also click the Zoom button in the Zoom group on the View tab to open the Zoom dialog box.

3. **Click the Zoom level button** `100%` **on the status bar**

   The Zoom dialog box opens. You use the Zoom dialog box to select a zoom level for displaying the document in the document window.

4. **Click the Whole page option button, then click OK**

   The entire document is displayed in the document window.

5. **Click the text at the bottom of the page to move the insertion point to the bottom of the page, click the View tab, then click the Page Width button in the Zoom group**

   The document is enlarged to the width of the document window. When you enlarge a document, the area where the insertion point is located appears in the document window.

6. **Click in the Urgent box, type x, then click the One Page button in the Zoom group**

   The entire document is displayed in the document window.

7. **Click Fax to move the insertion point to the upper-right corner of the page, then move the Zoom slider to the right until the Zoom percentage is 100%, as shown in Figure A-13**

   Moving the Zoom slider to the right enlarges the document in the document window. Moving the zoom slider to the left allows you to see more of the page at a reduced size. You can also move the Zoom slider by clicking a point on the Zoom slide, or by clicking the Zoom Out and Zoom In buttons.

TROUBLE
Your company name content control might include the name of a company, such as Microsoft. Right-click it and then click Remove Content Control, or select the text and press [Delete].

8. **Click the Zoom In button** ⊕ **three times, right-click the vertical placeholder [Type the sender company name], click Remove Content Control, right-click [Type the company address], click Remove Content Control, click [Type the company phone number], then type Quest Specialty Travel, San Diego, CA**

   The text you type replaces the vertical placeholder text. You do not always need to replace the placeholder text with the type of information suggested in the content control.

9. **Click** `130%`, **click the 100% option button, click OK, then save the document**

   The completed fax cover sheet is shown in Figure A-14.

10. **Submit the document to your instructor, close the file, then exit Word**

FIGURE A-13: Zoom slider

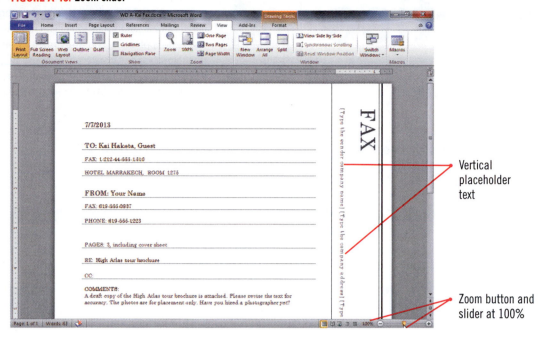

Vertical placeholder text

Zoom button and slider at 100%

FIGURE A-14: Completed fax cover sheet

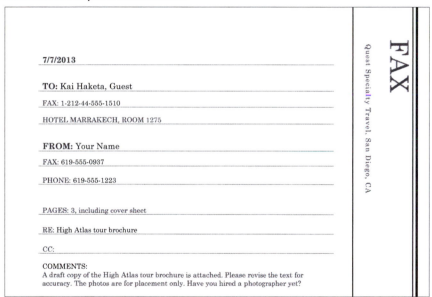

Using Word document views

Document **views** are different ways of displaying a document in the document window. Each Word view provides features that are useful for working on different types of documents. The default view, **Print Layout view**, displays a document as it will look on a printed page. Print Layout view is helpful for formatting text and pages, including adjusting document margins, creating columns of text, inserting graphics, and formatting headers and footers. Also useful is **Draft view**, which shows a simplified layout of a document, without margins, headers and footers, or graphics. When you want to quickly type, edit, and format text, it's often easiest to work in Draft view. Other Word views are helpful for performing specialized tasks. **Full Screen Reading view** displays document text so that it is easy to read and annotate. You can easily highlight content, add comments, and track and review changes in Full Screen Reading view. **Web Layout view** allows you to format Web pages or documents that will be viewed on a computer screen. In Web Layout view, a document appears just as it will when viewed with a Web browser. Finally, **Outline view** is useful for editing and formatting longer documents that include multiple headings. Outline view allows you to reorganize text by moving the headings. You switch between views by clicking the view buttons on the status bar or by using the commands on the View tab. Changing views does not affect how the printed document will appear. It simply changes the way you view the document in the document window.

Practice

Concepts Review

For current SAM information, including versions and content details, visit SAM Central (http://www.cengage.com/samcentral). If you have a SAM user profile, you may have access to hands-on instruction, practice, and assessment of the skills covered in this unit. Since various versions of SAM are supported throughout the life of this text, check with your instructor for the correct instructions and URL/Web site for accessing assignments.

Label the elements of the Word program window shown in Figure A-15.

FIGURE A-15

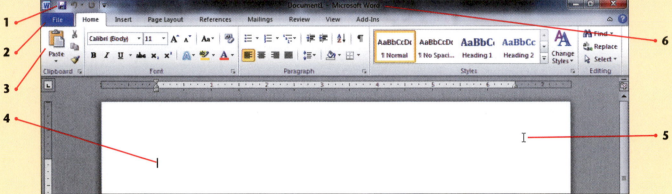

Match each term with the statement that best describes it.

7. **Template**	**a.** Provides access to Word commands
8. **Formatting marks**	**b.** A formatted document that contains placeholder text
9. **Status bar**	**c.** Displays tab settings and paragraph indents
10. **Ribbon**	**d.** Enlarges and reduces the document in the document window
11. **AutoComplete**	**e.** Suggests text to insert into a document
12. **Horizontal ruler**	**f.** Displays the number of pages in the current document
13. **AutoCorrect**	**g.** Fixes certain errors as you type
14. **Zoom slider**	**h.** Special characters that appear on screen but do not print

Select the best answer from the list of choices.

15. **Which tab includes buttons for formatting text?**
    a. View
    b. Page Layout
    c. Insert
    d. Home

16. **Which of the following shows the number of words in the document?**
    a. The status bar
    b. The Mini toolbar
    c. The title bar
    d. The Ribbon

17. **Which element of the Word program window shows the settings for the top and bottom document margins?**
    a. Vertical scroll bar
    b. View tab
    c. Vertical ruler
    d. Status bar

18. **Which of the following is not included in a ScreenTip for a command?**
    a. Description of the function of the command
    b. Link to a help topic on the command
    c. Keyboard shortcut for the command
    d. Alternative location of the command

19. Which view is best for annotating text with comments and highlighting?

    a. Full Screen Reading view   **c.** Print Layout view

    b. Draft view   **d.** Outline view

20. What is the default file extension for a document created in Word 2010?

    a. .dot   **c.** .dotx

    b. .doc   **d.** .docx

Skills Review

1. Explore the Word program window.

  a. Start Word.

  b. Identify as many elements of the Word program window as you can without referring to the unit material.

  c. Click the File tab, then click the Info, Recent, New, Print, Save & Send, and Help commands.

  d. Click each tab on the Ribbon, review the groups and buttons on each tab, then return to the Home tab.

  e. Point to each button on the Home tab and read the ScreenTips.

  f. Click the view buttons to view the blank document in each view, then return to Print Layout view.

  g. Use the Zoom slider to zoom all the way in and all the way out on the document, then return to 100%.

2. Start a document.

  a. In a new blank document, type **FAX** at the top of the page, then press [Enter] two times.

  b. Type the following, pressing [Tab] as indicated and pressing [Enter] at the end of each line:

    To: [Tab] [Tab] **Matthew Donner**

    From: [Tab] [Tab] **Your Name**

    Date: [Tab] [Tab] **Today's date**

    Re: [Tab] [Tab] **Reservation confirmation**

    Pages: [Tab] [Tab] **1**

    Fax: [Tab] [Tab] **(802) 555-5478**

  c. Press [Enter] again, then type **Thank you for your interest in our summer festival weekend package, which includes accommodations for three nights in downtown Toronto, continental breakfast, and a festival pass. Rooms are still available during the following festivals: International Jazz Festival, Comedy Festival, Toronto Fringe Festival, and the Festival of Arts. Please see the attached schedule for festival dates and details.**

  d. Press [Enter], then type **To make a reservation, please call me at (416) 555-7482. I will need payment in full by the 3rd of June to hold a room. No one knows how to celebrate summer like Torontonians!**

  e. Insert **Grand Prix Festival,** before International Jazz Festival.

  f. Using the [Backspace] key, delete **1** in the Pages: line, then type **2**.

  g. Using the [Delete] key, delete **festival** in the last sentence of the first paragraph.

3. Save a document.

  a. Click the Save button on the Quick Access toolbar.

  b. Save the document as **WD A-Donner Fax** with the default file extension to the drive and folder where you store your Data Files.

  c. After your name, type a comma, press [Spacebar], then type **Global Toronto**

  d. Save the document.

4. Select text.

  a. Turn on formatting marks.

  b. Select the **Re:** line, then type **Re:** [Tab] [Tab] **Summer Festival Weekend Package**

  c. Select **three** in the first sentence, then type **two**.

  d. Select **3rd of June** in the second sentence of the last paragraph, type **15th of May**, select **room**, then type **reservation**.

  e. Delete the sentence **No one knows how to celebrate summer like Torontonians!**

  f. Turn off the display of formatting marks, then save the document.

Skills Review (continued)

5. **Format text using the Mini toolbar.**

   a. Select **FAX**, then click the Grow Font button on the Mini toolbar 11 times.

   b. Apply bold to the word **FAX**, then center it on the page.

   c. Apply a bottom border under the word **FAX**.

   d. Apply bold to the following words in the fax heading: **To:**, **From:**, **Date:**, **Re:**, **Pages:**, and **Fax:**.

   e. Preview the document using the Print command.

   f. Zoom in on the document, then proofread the fax.

   g. Correct any typing errors in your document, then save the document. Compare your document to Figure A-16.

   h. Submit the fax to your instructor, then close the document.

6. **Create a document using a template.**

   a. Click the File tab, click New, then click Sample templates.

   b. Create a new document using the Origin Fax template.

   c. Insert today's date using the date content control.

   d. If your name is not on the From line, select the text in the From content control, then type your name.

   e. Click the "Type the sender phone number" placeholder text, press [Delete]; click the "Type the sender fax number" placeholder text, type **555-5748**; click the "Type the sender company name" placeholder text, then type **Global Toronto**.

   f. Type **Janice Richard** to replace the "To:" placeholder text; select "Phone:", type **Re**; type **Sold out summer packages** to replace the "Type the recipient phone number" placeholder text; type **555-1176** to replace the "Type the recipient fax number" placeholder text; then type **Toronto Chamber of Commerce** to replace the "Type the recipient company name" placeholder text.

   g. Save the document with the filename **WD A-Sold Out Fax** to the drive and folder where you store your Data Files.

7. **View and navigate a document.**

   a. Scroll down until Comments is near the top of your document window.

   b. Replace the Comments placeholder text with the following text: **Packages for the following summer festivals are sold out: First Peoples' Festival, Chamber Music Festival, and Dragon Boat Race Festival. We had expected these packages to be less popular than those for the bigger festivals, but interest has been high. Next year, we will increase our bookings for these festivals by 30%.**

   c. Use the Zoom dialog box to view the Whole Page.

   d. Click **Comments** to move the insertion point to the middle of the page, then use the Zoom slider to set the Zoom percentage at approximately 100%.

   e. Scroll to the bottom of the page, click in the Please Recycle box, type **x** if one is not added automatically when you click the box, then save your changes.

   f. Preview the document, then correct any errors, saving changes if necessary. Compare your document to Figure A-17. Submit the document to your instructor, close the file, then exit Word.

FAX

To:	Matthew Donner
From:	Your Name, Global Toronto
Date:	April 3, 2013
Re:	Summer Festival Weekend Package
Pages:	2
Fax:	(802) 555-5478

Thank you for your interest in our summer festival weekend package, which includes accommodations for two nights in downtown Toronto, continental breakfast, and a festival pass. Rooms are still available during the following festivals: Grand Prix Festival, International Jazz Festival, Comedy Festival, Toronto Fringe Festival, and the Festival of Arts. Please see the attached schedule for dates and details.

To make a reservation, please call me at (416) 555-7482. I will need payment in full by the 15th of May to hold a reservation.

▶Fax   4/3/2013

From:	Your Name
Phone:	
Fax:	555-5748
Company Name:	Global Toronto
To:	Janice Richard
Phone:	Sold out summer packages
Fax:	555-1176
Company Name:	Toronto Chamber of Commerce

Comments:

Packages for the following summer festivals are sold out: First Peoples' Festival, Chamber Music Festival, and Dragon Boat Race Festival. We had expected these packages to be less popular than those for the bigger festivals, but interest has been high. Next year we will increase our bookings for these festivals by 30%.

Independent Challenge 1

Yesterday you interviewed for a job as marketing director at Chelsea Design Services. You spoke with several people at the company, including Rena Gupta, chief executive officer, whose business card is shown in Figure A-18. You need to write a follow-up letter to Ms. Gupta, thanking her for the interview and expressing your interest in the company and the position. She also asked you to send her some samples of your marketing work, which you will enclose with the letter.

If you have a SAM 2010 user profile, an autogradable SAM version of this assignment may be available at http://www.cengage.com/sam2010. Check with your instructor to confirm that this assignment is available in SAM. To use the SAM version of this assignment, log into the SAM 2010 Web site and download the instruction and start files.

FIGURE A-18

a. Start Word and save a new blank document as **WD A-Gupta Letter** to the drive and folder where you store your Data Files.

b. Begin the letter by clicking the No Spacing button in the Styles group. You use this button to apply the No Spacing style to the document so that your document does not include extra space between paragraphs.

c. Type a personal letterhead for the letter that includes your name, address, telephone number, and e-mail address. If Word formats your e-mail address as a hyperlink, right-click your e-mail address, then click Remove Hyperlink.
(*Note*: Format the letterhead after you finish typing the letter.)

d. Three lines below the bottom of the letterhead, type today's date.

e. Four lines below the date, type the inside address, referring to Figure A-18 for the address information. Be sure to include the recipient's title, company name, and full mailing address in the inside address.

f. Two lines below the inside address, type **Dear Ms. Gupta:** for the salutation.

g. Two lines below the salutation, type the body of the letter according to the following guidelines:
  - In the first paragraph, thank her for the interview. Then restate your interest in the position and express your desire to work for the company. Add any specific details you think will enhance the power of your letter.
  - In the second paragraph, note that you are enclosing three samples of your work, and explain something about the samples you are enclosing.
  - Type a short final paragraph.

h. Two lines below the last body paragraph, type a closing, then four lines below the closing, type the signature block. Be sure to include your name in the signature block.

i. Two lines below the signature block, type an enclosure notation. (*Hint*: An enclosure notation usually includes the word "Enclosures" or the abbreviation "Enc." followed by the number of enclosures in parentheses.)

j. Format the letterhead with bold, centering, and a bottom border.

k. Save your changes.

l. Preview the letter, submit it to your instructor, then close the document and exit Word.

Independent Challenge 2

Your company has recently installed Word 2010 on its company network. As the training manager, it's your responsibility to teach employees how to use the new software productively. Now that they have begun working with Word 2010, several employees have asked you about sharing documents with colleagues using Windows Live SkyDrive. In response, you wrote a memo to all employees explaining Windows Live SkyDrive, some of its features, and how to register for a Windows Live ID. You now need to format the memo before distributing it.

a. Start Word, open the file **WD A-1.docx** from the drive and folder where you store your Data Files, then read the memo to get a feel for its contents.

b. Save the file as **WD A-SkyDrive Memo** to the drive and folder where you store your Data Files.

Independent Challenge 2 (continued)

c. Replace the information in the memo header with the information shown in Figure A-19. Make sure to include your name in the From line and the current date in the Date line.

d. Apply bold to **To:**, **From:**, **Date:**, and **Re:**.

e. Increase the size of **WORD TRAINING MEMORANDUM** to match Figure A-19, center the text on the page, add a border below it, then save your changes.

FIGURE A-19

> ## WORD TRAINING MEMORANDUM
>
> **To:**   All employees
> **From:**   Your Name, Training Manager
> **Date:**   Today's Date
> **Re:**   Windows Live SkyDrive

Advanced Challenge Exercise

■ Using the Font list on the Mini toolbar, apply a different font to **WORD TRAINING MEMORANDUM**. Make sure to select a font that is appropriate for a business memo.

■ Using the Font Color button on the Mini toolbar, change the color of **WORD TRAINING MEMORANDUM** to an appropriate color.

■ Save a copy of the memo in Word 97-2003 Document (*.doc) format as **WD A-SkyDrive Memo ACE** to the drive or folder where you store your Data Files. (*Hint*: Use the Save as type list arrow in the Save As dialog box.)

f. Preview the memo, submit it to your instructor, then close the document and exit Word.

Independent Challenge 3

You are an expert on global warming. The president of the National Park Association, Nathan Cummings, has asked you to be the keynote speaker at an upcoming conference on the impact of climate change on the national parks, to be held in Glacier National Park. You use one of the Word letter templates to write a letter to Mr. Cummings accepting the invitation and confirming the details. Your letter to Mr. Cummings should reference the following information:

- The conference will be held August 4–6, 2013, at the Many Glacier Hotel in the park.
- You have been asked to speak for an hour on Saturday, August 5, followed by one half hour for questions.
- Mr. Cummings suggested the lecture topic "Melting Glaciers, Changing Ecosystems."
- Your talk will include a 45-minute slide presentation.
- The National Park Association will make your travel arrangements.
- Your preference is to arrive at Glacier Park International Airport in Kalispell on the morning of Friday, August 4, and to depart on Monday, August 7. You would like to rent a car at the airport for the drive to the Many Glacier Hotel.
- You want to fly in and out of the airport closest to your home.

a. Start Word, open the File tab, click New, click Sample templates, and then select an appropriate letter template. Save the document as **WD A-Cummings Letter** to the drive and folder where you store your Data Files.

b. Replace the placeholders in the letterhead with your personal information. Include your name, address, phone number, and e-mail address. Delete any placeholders that do not apply. (*Hints*: Depending on the template you choose, the letterhead might be located at the top or on the side of the document. You can press [Enter] when typing in a horizontal placeholder to add an additional line of text. You can also change the format of text typed in a placeholder. If your e-mail address appears as a hyperlink, right-click the e-mail address and click Remove Hyperlink.)

c. Use the Pick the date content control to select the current date.

d. Replace the placeholders in the inside address. Be sure to include Mr. Cumming's title and the name of the organization. Make up a street address and zip code.

e. Type **Dear Mr. Cummings:** for the salutation.

f. Using the information listed previously, type the body of the letter:
- In the first paragraph, accept the invitation to speak.
- In the second paragraph, confirm the important conference details, confirm your lecture topic, and provide any relevant details.

Independent Challenge 3 (continued)

- In the third paragraph, state your travel preferences.
- Type a short final paragraph.

g. Type **Sincerely,** for the closing, then include your name in the signature block.

h. Adjust the formatting of the letter as necessary. For example, remove bold formatting or change the font color of text to a more appropriate color.

Advanced Challenge Exercise

- Zoom in on the title "Melting Glaciers, Changing Ecosystems", delete the quotation marks, then apply italics to the title.
- Select one word in the letter, such as an adjective, and replace it with another similar word to improve the meaning of the sentence.
- Correct your spelling and grammar errors, if any, by right-clicking any red- or green-underlined text and then choosing from the options on the shortcut menu.
- View the letter in Full Screen Reading view, then click the Close button to return to Print Layout view.

i. Proofread your letter, make corrections as needed, then save your changes.

j. Submit the letter to your instructor, close the document, then exit Word.

Real Life Independent Challenge

This Independent Challenge requires an Internet connection.

The computer keyboard has become as essential an office tool as the pencil. The more adept you become at touch typing—the fastest and most accurate way to type—the more comfortable you will be working with computers and the more saleable your office skills to a potential employer. The Internet is one source of information on touch typing, and many Web sites include free typing tests and online tutorials to help you practice and improve your typing skills. In this independent challenge, you will take an online typing test to check your typing skills. You will then research the fundamentals of touch typing and investigate some of the ergonomic factors important to becoming a productive keyboard typist.

a. Use your favorite search engine to search the Internet for information on typing. Use the keywords **typing** and **typing ergonomics** to conduct your search.

b. Review the Web sites you find. Choose a site that offers a free online typing test, take the test, then print the Web page showing the results of your typing test if requested to do so by your instructor.

c. Start Word and save a new blank document as **WD A-Touch Typing** to the drive and folder where you store your Data Files.

d. Type your name at the top of the document.

e. Type a brief report on the results of your research. Your report should answer the following questions:

- What are the URLs of the Web sites you visited to research touch typing and keyboard ergonomics? (*Hint*: A URL is a Web page's address. An example of a URL is www.course.com.)
- What are some benefits of using the touch typing method?
- Which keys should the fingers of the left and right hands rest on when using the touch typing method?
- What ergonomic factors are important to keep in mind while typing?

f. Save your changes to the document, preview and submit it to your instructor, then close the document and exit Word.

Visual Workshop

Create the cover letter shown in Figure A-20. Before beginning to type, click the No Spacing button in the Styles group on the Home tab. Add the bottom border to the letterhead after typing the letter. Save the document as **WD A-Lee Cover Letter** to the drive and folder where you store your Data Files, submit the letter to your instructor, then close the document and exit Word.

FIGURE A-20

Your Name

682 East 8th Avenue, Portland, ME 04105
Tel: 207-555-7283; Fax: 207-555-1445; E-mail: yourname@gmail.com

July 16, 2013

Ms. Ramona Lee
Lee Associates
657 Harbor Street
Suite 501
Portland, ME 04123

Dear Ms. Lee:

I read of the opening for a public information assistant in the July 13 edition of mainejobs.com, and I would like to be considered for the position. I am a recent graduate of Portland Community College (PCC), and I am interested in pursuing a career in public relations.

My interest in a public relations career springs from my publicly acknowledged writing and journalism abilities. For example, at PCC, I was a reporter for the student newspaper and frequently wrote press releases for campus and community events.

I have a wealth of experience using Microsoft Word in professional settings. Last summer, I worked as an office assistant for the architecture firm Coleman & Greenberg, where I used Word to create newsletters, brochures, and financial reports. During the school year, I also worked part-time in the PCC Office of Community Relations, where I used the Word mail merge feature to create form letters and mailing labels.

My enclosed resume details my skills and experience. I welcome the opportunity to discuss the position and my qualifications with you. I can be reached at 207-555-7283.

Sincerely,

Your Name

Enc.

Editing Documents

Files You Will Need:

WD B-1.docx
WD B-2.docx
WD B-3.docx
WD B-4.docx
WD B-5.docx
WD B-6.docx
WD B-7.docx

The sophisticated editing features in Word make it easy to revise and polish your documents. In this unit, you learn how to revise an existing file by opening it, copying and moving text, and then saving the document as a new file. You also learn how to perfect your documents using proofing tools and how to quickly prepare a document for distribution to the public. You have been asked to edit and finalize a press release for a QST promotional lecture series. The press release should provide information about the series so that newspapers, radio stations, and other media outlets can announce it to the public. QST press releases are disseminated by fax and by e-mail. Before distributing the file electronically to your lists of press contacts and local QST clients, you add several hyperlinks and then strip the file of private information.

OBJECTIVES

- Cut and paste text
- Copy and paste text
- Use the Office Clipboard
- Find and replace text
- Check spelling and grammar
- Research information
- Add hyperlinks
- Work with document properties

Cutting and Pasting Text

The editing features in Word allow you to move text from one location to another in a document. Moving text is often called **cut and paste**. When you **cut** text, it is removed from the document and placed on the **Clipboard**, a temporary storage area for text and graphics that you cut or copy from a document. You can then paste, or insert, text that is stored on the Clipboard in the document at the location of the insertion point. You cut and paste text using the Cut and Paste buttons in the Clipboard group on the Home tab. You also can move selected text by dragging it to a new location using the mouse. This operation is called **drag and drop**. You open the press release that was drafted by a colleague, save it with a new filename, and then reorganize the information in the press release using the cut-and-paste and drag-and-drop methods.

STEPS

1. **Start Word, click the File tab, click Open, navigate to the drive and folder where you store your Data Files, click WD B-1.docx, then click Open**

   The document opens. Once you have opened a file, you can edit it and use the Save or the Save As command to save your changes. You use the **Save** command when you want to save the changes you make to a file, overwriting the file that is stored on a disk. You use the **Save As** command when you want to leave the original file intact and create a duplicate file with a different filename, file extension, or location.

2. **Click the File tab, click Save As, type WD B-Lecture PR in the File name text box, then click Save**

   You can now make changes to the press release file without affecting the original file.

3. **Replace Ron Dawson with your name, scroll down until the headline "Helen Moffit to Speak..." is at the top of your document window, then click the Show/Hide ¶ button ¶ in the Paragraph group on the Home tab to display formatting marks**

4. **Select Alaskan guide Gilbert Coonan, (including the comma and the space after it) in the third body paragraph, then click the Cut button ✂ in the Clipboard group**

   The text is removed from the document and placed on the Clipboard. Word uses two different clipboards: the **system Clipboard** (the Clipboard), which holds just one item, and the **Office Clipboard**, which holds up to 24 items. The last item you cut or copy is always added to both clipboards. You'll learn more about the Office Clipboard in a later lesson.

5. **Place the insertion point before African (but after the space) in the first line of the third paragraph, then click the Paste button in the Clipboard group**

   The text is pasted at the location of the insertion point, as shown in Figure B-1. The Paste Options button appears below text when you first paste it in a document. You'll learn more about the Paste Options button in the next lesson. For now, you can ignore it.

6. **Press and hold [Ctrl], click the sentence Ticket prices include lunch. in the fourth paragraph, then release [Ctrl]**

   The entire sentence is selected.

7. **Press and hold the mouse button over the selected text until the pointer changes to** ▯⃕

   The pointer's vertical line is the insertion point. You drag the pointer to position the insertion point where you want the text to be inserted when you release the mouse button.

TROUBLE
If you make a mistake, click the Undo button ⟲ on the Quick Access toolbar, then try again.

8. **Drag the pointer's vertical line to the end of the fifth paragraph (between the period and the paragraph mark) as shown in Figure B-2, then release the mouse button**

   The selected text is moved to the location of the insertion point. It is convenient to move text using the drag-and-drop method when the locations of origin and destination are both visible on the screen. Text is not placed on the Clipboard when you drag and drop it.

9. **Deselect the text, then click the Save button 🖫 on the Quick Access toolbar**

FIGURE B-1: Moved text with Paste Options button

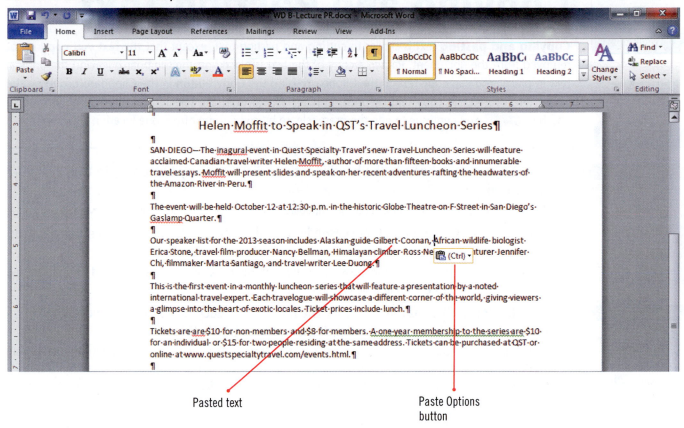

Pasted text

Paste Options
button

FIGURE B-2: Dragging and dropping text in a new location

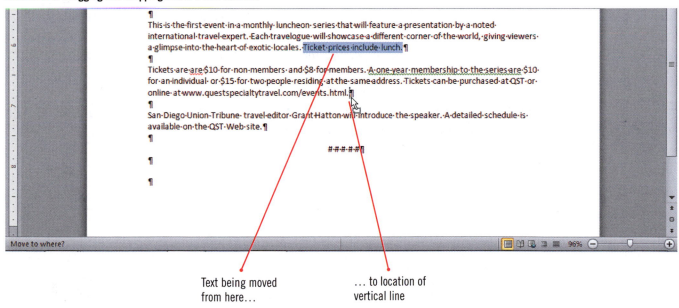

Text being moved
from here…

… to location of
vertical line

Using keyboard shortcuts

A **shortcut key** is a function key, such as [F1], or a combination of keys, such as [Ctrl][S], that you press to perform a command. For example, instead of using the Cut, Copy, and Paste commands on the Ribbon or the Mini toolbar, you can use the **keyboard shortcuts** [Ctrl][X] to cut text, [Ctrl][C] to copy text, and [Ctrl][V] to paste text. You can also press [Ctrl][S] to save changes to a document instead of

clicking the Save button on the Quick Access toolbar or clicking Save on the File tab. Becoming skilled at using keyboard shortcuts can help you quickly accomplish many of the tasks you perform in Word. If a keyboard shortcut is available for a command, then it is listed in the ScreenTip for that command.

Copying and Pasting Text

Copying and pasting text is similar to cutting and pasting text, except that the text you **copy** is not removed from the document. Rather, a copy of the text is placed on the Clipboard, leaving the original text in place. You can copy text to the Clipboard using the Copy button in the Clipboard group on the Home tab, or you can copy text by pressing [Ctrl] as you drag the selected text from one location to another. You continue to edit the press release by copying text from one location to another.

STEPS

1. **Select Travel Luncheon in the headline, then click the Copy button 🗐 in the Clipboard group**

   A copy of the selected text is placed on the Clipboard, leaving the original text you copied in place.

2. **Place the insertion point before season in the third paragraph, then click the Paste button in the Clipboard group**

   "Travel Luncheon" is inserted before "season," as shown in Figure B-3. Notice that the pasted text is formatted differently than the paragraph in which it was inserted.

3. **Click the Paste Options button, move the mouse over each button on the menu that opens to read its ScreenTip, then click the Keep Text Only (T) button**

   The formatting of "Travel Luncheon" is changed to match the rest of the paragraph. The buttons on the Paste Options menu allow you to change the formatting of pasted text. You can choose to keep the original formatting (Keep Source Formatting), match the destination formatting (Merge Formatting), or paste the text unformatted (Keep Text Only).

4. **Select www.questspecialtytravel.com in the fifth paragraph, press and hold [Ctrl], then press and hold the mouse button until the pointer changes to ▯**

5. **Drag the pointer's vertical line to the end of the last paragraph, placing it between site and the period, release the mouse button, then release [Ctrl]**

   The text is copied to the last paragraph. Since the formatting of the text you copied is the same as the formatting of the destination paragraph, you can ignore the Paste Options button. Text is not copied to the Clipboard when you copy it using the drag-and-drop method.

6. **Place the insertion point before www.questspecialtytravel.com in the last paragraph, type at followed by a space, then save the document**

   Compare your document with Figure B-4.

Splitting the document window to copy and move items in a long document

If you want to copy or move items between parts of a long document, it can be useful to split the document window into two panes. This allows you to display the item you want to copy or move in one pane and the destination for the item in the other pane. To split a window, click the Split button in the Window group on the View tab, drag the horizontal split bar that appears to the location you want to split the window, and then click. Once the document window is split into two panes, you can drag the split bar to resize the panes and use the scroll bars in each pane to display different parts of the document. To copy or move an item from one pane to another, you can use the Cut, Copy, and Paste commands, or you can drag the item between the panes. When you are finished editing the document, double-click the split bar to restore the window to a single pane, or click the Remove Split button in the Window group on the View tab.

FIGURE B-3: Text pasted in document

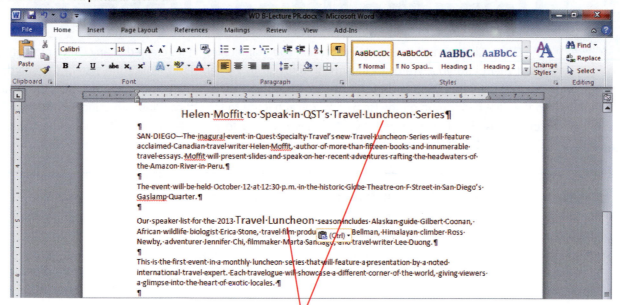

Formatting of the
pasted text matches
the headline text

FIGURE B-4: Copied text in document

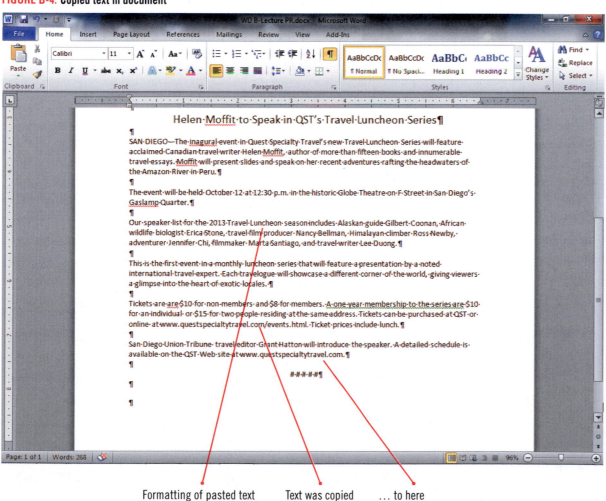

Formatting of pasted text
matches surrounding text

Text was copied
from here…

… to here

Using the Office Clipboard

The Office Clipboard allows you to collect text and graphics from files created in any Office program and insert them into your Word documents. It holds up to 24 items and, unlike the system Clipboard, the items on the Office Clipboard can be viewed. To display the Office Clipboard, you simply click the launcher in the Clipboard group on the Home tab. You add items to the Office Clipboard using the Cut and Copy commands. The last item you collect is always added to both the system Clipboard and the Office Clipboard. You use the Office Clipboard to move several sentences in your press release.

STEPS

QUICK TIP

You can set the Office Clipboard to open automatically when you cut or copy two items consecutively by clicking Options in the Clipboard task pane, and then selecting Show Office Clipboard Automatically.

1. **Click the launcher in the Clipboard group**

   The Office Clipboard opens in the Clipboard task pane. It contains the Travel Luncheon item you copied in the last lesson.

2. **Select the sentence San Diego Union-Tribune travel editor ... (including the space after the period) in the last paragraph, right-click the selected text, then click Cut on the menu that opens**

   The sentence is cut to the Office Clipboard.

3. **Select the sentence A detailed schedule is... (including the ¶ mark), right-click the selected text, then click Cut**

   The Office Clipboard displays the items you cut or copied, as shown in Figure B-5. The icon next to each item indicates the items are from a Word document. The last item collected is displayed at the top of the Clipboard task pane. As new items are collected, the existing items move down the task pane.

4. **Place the insertion point at the end of the second paragraph (after "Quarter." but before the ¶ mark), then click the San Diego Union-Tribune... item on the Office Clipboard**

   Clicking an item on the Office Clipboard pastes the item in the document at the location of the insertion point. Items remain on the Office Clipboard until you delete them or close all open Office programs. Also, if you add a 25th item to the Office Clipboard, the first item you collected is deleted.

5. **Place the insertion point at the end of the third paragraph (after "Duong."), then click the A detailed schedule is... item on the Office Clipboard**

   The sentence is pasted into the document.

6. **Select the fourth paragraph, which begins with the sentence This is the first event... (including the ¶ mark), right-click the selected text, then click Cut**

   The paragraph is cut to the Office Clipboard.

7. **Place the insertion point at the beginning of the third paragraph (before "Our..."), click the Paste button in the Clipboard group on the Home tab, then press [Backspace]**

   The sentences from the "This is the first..." paragraph are pasted at the beginning of the "Our speaker list..." paragraph. You can paste the last item collected using either the Paste command or the Office Clipboard.

8. **Place the insertion point at the end of the third paragraph (after "www.questspecialtytravel. com." and before the ¶ mark), then press [Delete] twice**

   Two ¶ symbols and the corresponding blank lines between the third and fourth paragraphs are deleted.

9. **Click the Show/Hide ¶ button in the Paragraph group**

   Compare your press release with Figure B-6. Note that many Word users prefer to work with formatting marks on at all times. Experiment to see which method you prefer.

QUICK TIP

To delete an individual item from the Office Clipboard, click the list arrow next to the item, then click Delete.

10. **Click the Clear All button on the Clipboard task pane to remove the items from the Office Clipboard, click the Close button on the Clipboard task pane, press [Ctrl][Home], then save the document**

    Pressing [Ctrl][Home] moves the insertion point to the top of the document.

Editing Documents

FIGURE B-5: Office Clipboard in Clipboard task pane

Clipboard
task pane

Items stored on the
Office Clipboard
(yours may include
additional items)

Click to change
display options
for the Office
Clipboard

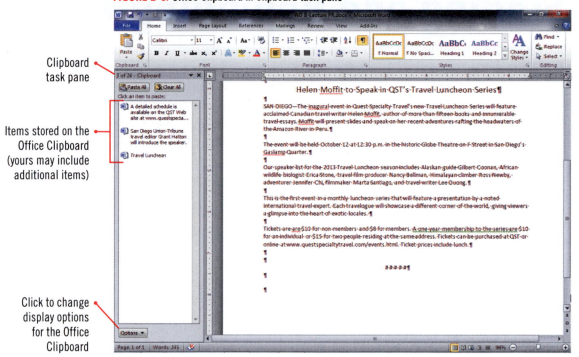

FIGURE B-6: Revised press release

Click to paste all
the items on the
Office Clipboard

Last item
collected

First item moves
down as more
items are collected

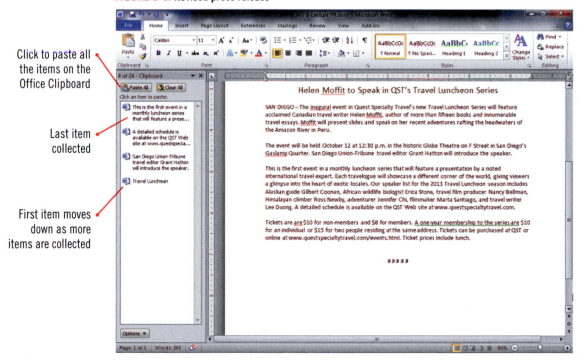

Copying and moving items between documents

You can also use the system and Office Clipboards to copy and move items between documents. To do this, open both documents and the Clipboard task pane in the program window. With multiple documents open, copy or cut an item from one document and then switch to the other document and paste the item. To switch between open documents, point to the Word icon on the taskbar, and then click the document you want to appear in the document window. You can also display more than one document at the same time by clicking the Arrange All button or the View Side by Side button in the Window group on the View tab.

Finding and Replacing Text

The Find and Replace feature in Word allows you to automatically search for and replace all instances of a word or phrase in a document. For example, you might need to substitute "tour" for "trip." To manually locate and replace each instance of "trip" in a long document would be very time-consuming. Using the Replace command you can find and replace all occurrences of specific text at once, or you can choose to find and review each occurrence individually. You also can use the Find command to locate and highlight every occurrence of a specific word or phrase in a document. 🎨 QST has decided to change the name of the lecture series from "Travel Luncheon Series" to "Travel Lecture Series." You use the Replace command to search the document for all instances of "Luncheon" and replace them with "Lecture."

1. **Click the Replace button in the Editing group, then click More in the Find and Replace dialog box**

   The Find and Replace dialog box opens and expands, as shown in Figure B-7.

2. **Type Luncheon in the Find what text box**

   "Luncheon" is the text that will be replaced.

3. **Press [Tab], then type Lecture in the Replace with text box**

   "Lecture" is the text that will replace "Luncheon."

4. **Click the Match case check box in the Search Options section to select it**

   Selecting the Match case check box tells Word to find only exact matches for the uppercase and lowercase characters you entered in the Find what text box. You want to replace all instances of "Luncheon" in the proper name "Travel Luncheon Series." You do not want to replace "luncheon" when it refers to a lunchtime event.

5. **Click Replace All**

   Clicking Replace All changes all occurrences of "Luncheon" to "Lecture" in the press release. A message box reports three replacements were made.

6. **Click OK to close the message box, then click Close in the Find and Replace dialog box**

   Word replaced "Luncheon" with "Lecture" in three locations, but did not replace "luncheon."

7. **Click the Find button in the Editing group**

   Clicking the Find button opens the Navigation pane, which is used to browse a longer document by headings, by pages, or by specific text or objects. The Find command allows you to quickly locate all instances of text in a document. You use it to verify that Word did not replace "luncheon."

8. **Type luncheon in the Search document text box in the Navigation pane, then scroll up until the headline is at the top of the document window**

   The word "luncheon" is highlighted and selected in the document, as shown in Figure B-8.

9. **Click the Close button in the Navigation pane, press [Ctrl][Home], then save the document**

   The highlighting is removed from the text when you close the Navigation pane.

FIGURE B-7: Find and Replace dialog box

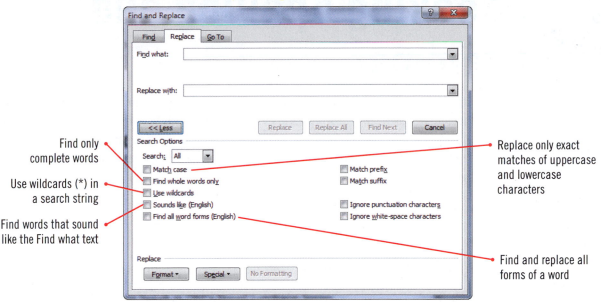

FIGURE B-7: Find and Replace dialog box

Find only complete words

Use wildcards (*) in a search string

Find words that sound like the Find what text

Replace only exact matches of uppercase and lowercase characters

Find and replace all forms of a word

Word 2010

FIGURE B-8: Found text highlighted in document

Navigation pane

Search document text box

List shows each match and its surrounding text

Found text is highlighted

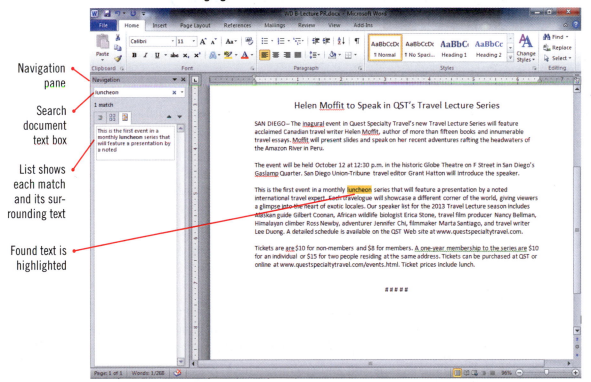

Navigating a document using the Go To command

Rather than scrolling to move to a different place in a longer document, you can use the Go To command to quickly move the insertion point to a specific location. To move to a specific page, section, line, table, graphic, or other item in a document, you use the Go To tab in the Find and Replace dialog box. To open the Find and

Replace dialog box with the Go To tab active, click the Page number button on the status bar. On the Go To tab in the Find and Replace dialog box, select the type of item you want to find in the Go to what list box, enter the relevant information about that item, and then click Go To or Next to move the insertion point to the item.

Checking Spelling and Grammar

When you finish typing and revising a document, you can use the Spelling and Grammar command to search the document for misspelled words and grammar errors. The Spelling and Grammar checker flags possible mistakes, suggests correct spellings, and offers remedies for grammar errors such as subject–verb agreement, repeated words, and punctuation.  You use the Spelling and Grammar checker to search your press release for errors. Before beginning the search, you set the Spelling and Grammar checker to ignore words, such as Moffit, that you know are spelled correctly.

STEPS

1. **Right-click Moffit in the headline**

   A menu that includes suggestions for correcting the spelling of "Moffit" opens. You can correct individual spelling and grammar errors by right-clicking text that is underlined with a red or green wavy line and selecting a correction. Although "Moffit" is not in the Word dictionary, it is spelled correctly in the document.

2. **Click Ignore All**

   Clicking Ignore All tells Word not to flag "Moffit" as misspelled.

3. **Press [Ctrl][Home], click the Review tab, then click the Spelling & Grammar button in the Proofing group**

   The Spelling and Grammar: English (U.S.) dialog box opens, as shown in Figure B-9. The dialog box identifies "inagural" as misspelled and suggests possible corrections for the error. The word selected in the Suggestions box is the correct spelling.

4. **Click Change**

   Word replaces the misspelled word with the correctly spelled word. Next, the dialog box identifies "Gaslamp" as a misspelled word and suggests the correction "Gas lamp." The proper name "Gaslamp Quarter" is spelled correctly in the document.

5. **Click Ignore Once**

   Word ignores the spelling. Next, the dialog box indicates that "are" is repeated in a sentence.

6. **Click Delete**

   Word deletes the second occurrence of the repeated word. Next, the dialog box flags a subject–verb agreement error and suggests using "is" instead of "are," as shown in Figure B-10. The phrase selected in the Suggestions box is correct.

7. **Click Change**

   Word replaces "are" with "is" in the sentence, and the Spelling and Grammar dialog box closes. Keep in mind that the Spelling and Grammar checker identifies many common errors, but you cannot rely on it to find and correct all spelling and grammar errors in your documents. Always proofread your documents carefully.

8. **Click OK to complete the spelling and grammar check, press [Ctrl][Home], then save the document**

Editing Documents

FIGURE B-9: Spelling and Grammar: English (U.S.) dialog box

Word identified as misspelled

Suggested correction

Adds the misspelled word and the correction to the AutoCorrect list

Ignores this occurrence of the word

Ignores all occurrences of the word

Adds the word to the Word dictionary

Changes the word to the selected correction

Changes all occurrences of the word to the selected correction

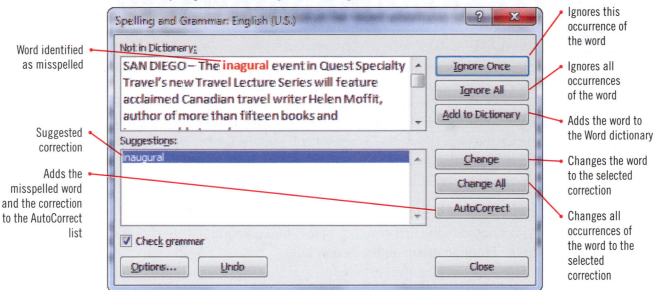

FIGURE B-10: Grammar error identified in Spelling and Grammar dialog box

Grammar error identified

Possible corrections

Check indicates grammar is being checked too

Displays an explanation of the grammar rule used to identify the error

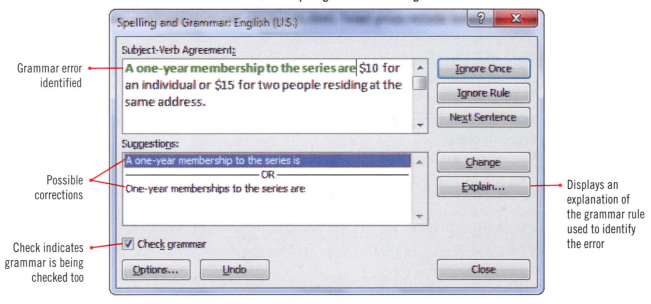

Inserting text with AutoCorrect

As you type, AutoCorrect automatically corrects many commonly misspelled words. By creating your own AutoCorrect entries, you can set Word to insert text that you type often, such as your name or contact information, or to correct words you misspell frequently. For example, you could create an AutoCorrect entry so that the name "Ronald T. Dawson" is automatically inserted whenever you type "rtd" followed by a space. You create AutoCorrect entries and customize other AutoCorrect and AutoFormat options using the AutoCorrect dialog box. To open the AutoCorrect dialog box, click the File tab, click Options, click Proofing in the Word Options dialog box that opens, and then click AutoCorrect Options. On the AutoCorrect tab in the AutoCorrect dialog box, type the text you want to be corrected automatically in the Replace text box (such as

"rtd"), type the text you want to be inserted in its place automatically in the With text box (such as "Ronald T. Dawson"), and then click Add. The AutoCorrect entry is added to the list. Click OK to close the AutoCorrect dialog box, and then click OK to close the Word Options dialog box. Word inserts an AutoCorrect entry in a document when you press [Spacebar] or a punctuation mark after typing the text you want Word to correct. For example, Word inserts "Ronald T. Dawson" when you type "rtd" followed by a space.

If you want to remove an AutoCorrect entry you created, simply open the AutoCorrect dialog box, select the AutoCorrect entry you want to remove in the list, click Delete, click OK, and then click OK to close the Word Options dialog box.

Researching Information

The Word Research feature allows you to quickly search reference sources and the World Wide Web for information related to a word or phrase. Among the reference sources available in the Research task pane is a Thesaurus, which you can use to look up synonyms for awkward or repetitive words. When you are working with an active Internet connection, the Research task pane also provides access to dictionary and translation sources, as well as to Web search engines such as Bing. After proofreading your document for errors, you decide the press release would read better if several adjectives were more descriptive. You use the Thesaurus to find synonyms.

QUICK TIP

You can also click the Research button in the Proofing group to open the Research task pane.

1. **Scroll down until the headline is displayed at the top of your screen**

2. **Select noted in the first sentence of the third paragraph, then click the Thesaurus button in the Proofing group on the Review tab**

   The Research task pane opens, as shown in Figure B-11. "Noted" appears in the Search for text box, and possible synonyms for "noted" are listed under the Thesaurus: English (U.S.) heading in the task pane.

QUICK TIP

To look up synonyms for a different word, type the word in the Search for text box, then click the green Start searching button.

3. **Point to prominent in the list of synonyms**

   A box containing a list arrow appears around the word.

4. **Click the list arrow, click Insert on the menu that opens, then close the Research task pane**

   "Prominent" replaces "noted" in the press release.

5. **Right-click innumerable in the first sentence of the first paragraph, point to Synonyms on the menu that opens, then click numerous**

   "Numerous" replaces "innumerable" in the press release.

6. **Select the four paragraphs of body text, then click the Word Count button in the Proofing group**

   The Word Count dialog box opens, as shown in Figure B-12. The dialog box lists the number of pages, words, characters, paragraphs, and lines included in the selected text. Notice that the status bar also displays the number of words included in the selected text and the total number of words in the entire document. If you want to view the page, character, paragraph, and line count for the entire document, make sure nothing is selected in your document, and then click Word Count in the Proofing group.

QUICK TIP

To add or remove available reference sources, click Research options in the Research task pane.

7. **Click Close, press [Ctrl][Home], then save the document**

8. **Click the File tab, click Save As, type WD B-Lecture PR Public in the File name text box, then click Save**

   The WD B-Lecture PR file closes, and the WD B-Lecture PR Public file is displayed in the document window. You will modify this file to prepare it for electronic release to the public.

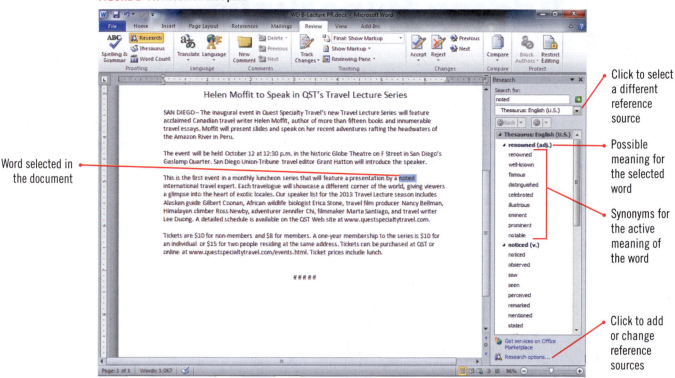

Word selected in the document

Click to select a different reference source

Possible meaning for the selected word

Synonyms for the active meaning of the word

Click to add or change reference sources

Word 2010

FIGURE B-12: Word Count dialog box

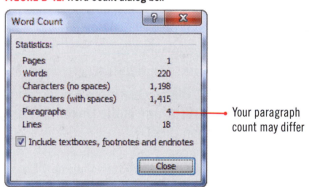

Your paragraph count may differ

Publishing a blog directly from Word

A **blog**, which is short for weblog, is an informal journal that is created by an individual or a group and available to the public on the Internet. A blog usually conveys the ideas, comments, and opinions of the blogger and is written using a strong personal voice. The person who creates and maintains a blog, the **blogger**, typically updates the blog daily. If you have or want to start a blog, you can configure Word to link to your blog site so that you can write, format, and publish blog entries directly from Word.

To create a new blog post, click the File tab, click New, then double-click Blog post to open a predesigned blog post document

that you can customize with your own text, formatting, and images. You can also publish an existing document as a blog post by opening the document, clicking the File tab, clicking Save & Send, and then clicking Publish as Blog Post. In either case, Word prompts you to log onto your personal blog account. To blog directly from Word, you must first obtain a blog account with a blog service provider. Resources, such as the Word Help system and online forums, provide detailed information on obtaining and registering your personal blog account with Word.

Adding Hyperlinks

A **hyperlink** is text or a graphic that, when clicked, "jumps" the viewer to a different location or program. When a document is viewed on screen, hyperlinks allow readers to link (or jump) to a Web page, an e-mail address, a file, or a specific location in a document. When you create a hyperlink in a document, you select the text or graphic you want to use as a hyperlink and then you specify the location you want to jump to when the hyperlink is clicked. You create a hyperlink using the Hyperlink button in the Links group on the Insert tab. Text that is formatted as a hyperlink appears as colored, underlined text. 🎨 Hundreds of people on your lists of press and client contacts will receive the press release by e-mail or Internet fax. To make it easier for these people to access additional information about the series, you add several hyperlinks to the press release.

STEPS

QUICK TIP
By default, Word automatically creates a hyperlink to an e-mail address or URL when you type the address or URL in a document.

1. **Select your name, click the Insert tab, then click the Hyperlink button in the Links group**

   The Insert Hyperlink dialog box opens, as shown in Figure B-13. You use this dialog box to specify the location of the Web page, file, e-mail address, or position in the current document you want to jump to when the hyperlink—in this case, your name—is clicked.

2. **Click E-mail Address in the Link to section**

   The Insert Hyperlink dialog box changes so you can create a hyperlink to your e-mail address.

3. **Type your e-mail address in the E-mail address text box, type Travel Lecture Series in the Subject text box, then click OK**

   As you type, Word automatically adds mailto: in front of your e-mail address. After you close the dialog box, the hyperlink text—your name—is formatted in blue and underlined.

QUICK TIP
To remove a hyperlink, right-click it, then click Remove Hyperlink. Removing a hyperlink removes the link, but the text remains.

4. **Press and hold [Ctrl], then click the your name hyperlink**

   An e-mail message addressed to you with the subject "Travel Lecture Series" opens in the default e-mail program. People can use this hyperlink to send you an e-mail message.

5. **Close the e-mail message window**

   The hyperlink text changes to purple, indicating the hyperlink has been followed.

6. **Scroll down, select Gaslamp Quarter in the second paragraph, click the Hyperlink button, click Existing File or Web Page in the Link to section, type www.gaslamp.org in the Address text box, then click OK**

   As you type the Web address, Word automatically adds "http://" in front of "www." The text "Gaslamp Quarter" is formatted as a hyperlink to the Gaslamp Quarter Association home page at www.gaslamp.org. When clicked, the hyperlink will open the Web page in the default browser window.

7. **Select detailed schedule in the last sentence of the third paragraph, click the Hyperlink button, type www.questspecialtytravel.com in the Address text box, then click OK**

   The text "detailed schedule" is formatted as a hyperlink to the QST Web site. If you point to a hyperlink in Word, the link to location appears in a ScreenTip. You can edit ScreenTip text to make it more descriptive.

QUICK TIP
You can also edit the hyperlink destination or the hyperlink text.

8. **Right-click Quarter in the Gaslamp Quarter hyperlink, click Edit Hyperlink, click ScreenTip in the Edit Hyperlink dialog box, type Map, parking, and other information about the Gaslamp Quarter in the ScreenTip text box, click OK, click OK, save your changes, then point to the Gaslamp Quarter hyperlink in the document**

   The ScreenTip you created appears above the Gaslamp Quarter hyperlink, as shown in Figure B-14.

TROUBLE
If you are not working with an active Internet connection, skip this step.

9. **Press [Ctrl], click the Gaslamp Quarter hyperlink, click the Word icon 🇼 on the taskbar, press [Ctrl], click the detailed schedule hyperlink, verify that the links opened in separate tabs in your browser, close the tabs, then click the Word icon 🇼 on the taskbar to return to the press release document in Word**

   Before distributing a document, it's important to test each hyperlink to verify it works as you intended.

Create a hyperlink to a Web page or file

Create a hyperlink to a location in the current file

Create a hyperlink to a new blank document

Create a hyperlink to an e-mail address

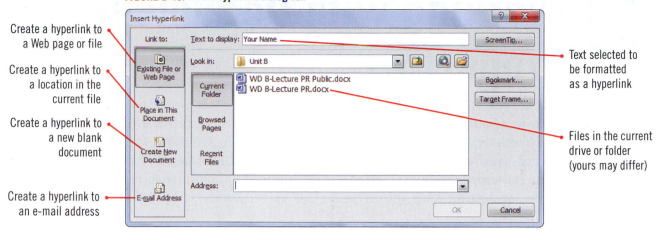

Text selected to be formatted as a hyperlink

Files in the current drive or folder (yours may differ)

Word 2010

FIGURE B-14: Hyperlinks in the document

Purple text indicates the hyperlink has been followed

Hyperlinks are colored and underlined

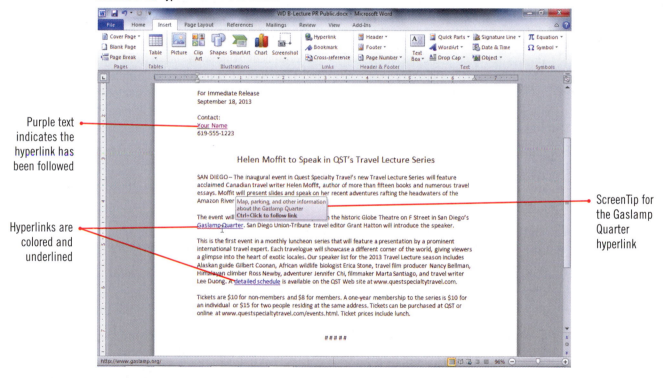

ScreenTip for the Gaslamp Quarter hyperlink

E-mailing and faxing documents directly from Word

Word includes several options for distributing and sharing documents over the Internet directly from within Word, including e-mailing and faxing documents. When you e-mail a document from within Word, the document is sent as an attachment to an e-mail message using your default e-mail program. To e-mail a file, open the file in Word, click the File tab, click Save & Send, and then select one of the options under Send Using E-mail on the Save & Send tab. You can choose to attach the document as a Word file, a .pdf file, or an .xps file, or to send it as an Internet fax. When you click an option, a message window opens that includes the filename of the current file as the message subject and the file as an attachment. Type the e-mail address(es) of the recipient(s) in the To and Cc text boxes, any message you want in the message window, and then click Send on the message window toolbar to send the message. The default e-mail program sends a copy of the document to each recipient. Note that faxing a document directly from Word requires registration with a third-party Internet fax service. Fax services generally charge a monthly or per page fee for sending and receiving faxes.

Working with Document Properties

Before you distribute a document electronically to people outside your organization, it's wise to make sure the file does not include embedded private or confidential information. The Info tab in Backstage view includes tools for stripping a document of sensitive information, for securing its authenticity, and for guarding it from unwanted changes once it is distributed to the public. One of these tools, the Document Inspector, detects and removes unwanted private or confidential information from a document. 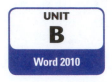 Before sending the press release to the public, you remove all identifying information from the file.

STEPS

QUICK TIP
To create or modify document proper-ties for a file, type in the Document Properties panel text boxes.

1. **Press [Ctrl][Home], then click the File tab**

   Backstage view opens with the Info tab displayed. The Information pane, in the middle of the tab, includes options related to stripping the file of private information. See Table B-1. The preview pane, on the right side of the tab, displays basic information about the document. Notice that the file contains document properties. You might want to remove these before you distribute the press release to the public.

2. **Click the Properties button in the preview pane, then click Show Document Panel**

   The Document Properties panel opens above the document window, as shown in Figure B-15. It shows the standard document properties for the press release. **Document properties** are user-defined details about a file that describe its contents and origin, including the name of the author, the title of the document, and keywords that you can assign to help organize and search your files. You decide to remove this information from the file before you distribute it electronically.

3. **Click the File tab, click the Check for Issues button, then click Inspect Document, clicking Yes if prompted to save changes**

   The Document Inspector dialog box opens. You use this dialog box to indicate which private or identifying information you want to search for and remove from the document.

4. **Make sure all the check boxes are selected, then click Inspect**

   After a moment, the Document Inspector dialog box changes to indicate that the file contains document properties.

QUICK TIP
A document prop-erty, such as author name, might appear automatically in a content control in a document. Stripping a file of document properties does not remove this information from a content control.

5. **Click Remove All next to Document Properties, then click Close**

   The standard document property information is removed from the press release document.

6. **Click the Properties button in the preview pane, then click Show Document Panel**

   The Document Properties panel opens and shows that the document properties have been removed from the file.

7. **Click the Close button ✖ in the Document Properties panel, save the document, submit it to your instructor, close the file, then exit Word**

   The completed press release is shown in Figure B-16.

TABLE B-1: Options on the Info tab

option	use to
Protect Document	Mark a document as final so that it is read-only and cannot be edited; encrypt a document so that a password is required to open it; restrict what kinds of changes can be made to a document and by whom; and add a digital signature to a document to verify its integrity
Check for Issues	Detect and remove unwanted information from a document, including document properties and comments; check for content that people with disabilities might find difficult to read; and check the document for features that are not sup-ported by previous versions of Microsoft Word
Manage versions	Browse through and delete draft versions of unsaved files

FIGURE B-15: Document Properties panel

Document properties assigned by Ron Dawson when the original file was created

Your file location will differ

Document Properties panel

FIGURE B-16: Completed press release for electronic distribution

Viewing and modifying advanced document properties

The Document Properties panel includes summary information about the document that you enter to suit your needs. To view more detailed document properties, including those entered automatically by Word when the document is created, click the Document Properties button in the Document Properties panel, and then click Advanced Properties to open the Properties dialog box. You can also click the Properties button on the Info tab and then click Advanced Properties to open the Properties dialog box. The General, Statistics, and Contents tabs of the Properties dialog box display information about the file that is automatically created and updated by Word. The General tab shows the file type, location, size, and date and time the file was created and last modified; the Statistics tab displays information about revisions to the document along with the number of pages, words, lines, paragraphs, and characters in the file; and the Contents tab shows the title of the document.

You can define other document properties using the Properties dialog box Summary and Custom tabs. The Summary tab shows information similar to the information shown in the Document Properties panel. The Custom tab allows you to create new document properties, such as client, project, or date completed. To create a custom property, select a property name in the Name list box on the Custom tab, use the Type list arrow to select the type of data you want for the property, type the identifying detail (such as a project name) in the Value text box, and then click Add. When you are finished viewing or modifying the document properties, click OK to close the Properties dialog box, then click the Close button on the Document Properties panel.

Practice

Concepts Review

For current SAM information, including versions and content details, visit SAM Central (http://www.cengage.com/samcentral). If you have a SAM user profile, you may have access to hands-on instruction, practice, and assessment of the skills covered in this unit. Since various versions of SAM are supported throughout the life of this text, check with your instructor for the correct instructions and URL/Web site for accessing assignments.

Label the elements of the Word program window shown in Figure B-17.

FIGURE B-17

Match each term with the statement that best describes it.

6. Paste

7. Shortcut key

8. System Clipboard

9. Document properties

10. Office Clipboard

11. Cut

12. Thesaurus

13. Hyperlink

14. Blog

a. Command used to insert text stored on the Clipboard into a document

b. Temporary storage area for up to 24 items collected from Office files

c. Temporary storage area for only the last item cut or copied from a document

d. A function key or a combination of keys that perform a command when pressed

e. Text or a graphic that jumps the reader to a different location or program when clicked

f. An informal journal that is available to the public on the Internet

g. User-defined details about a file that describe its contents and origin

h. Feature used to suggest synonyms for words

i. Command used to remove text from a document and place it on the Clipboard

Select the best answer from the list of choices.

15. **Which of the following statements is *not* true?**
    a. You can view the contents of the Office Clipboard.
    b. The Office Clipboard can hold more than one item.
    c. The last item cut or copied from a document is stored on the system Clipboard.
    d. When you move text by dragging it, a copy of the text you move is stored on the system Clipboard.

16. **What is the keyboard shortcut for the Paste command?**
    a. [Ctrl][P]
    b. [Ctrl][X]
    c. [Ctrl][V]
    d. [Ctrl][C]

17. **Which command is used to display a document in two panes in the document window?**
    a. Split
    b. New Window
    c. Arrange All
    d. Two Pages

18. **To locate and select all instances of a word in a document, which command do you use?**
    a. Find
    b. Search
    c. Highlight
    d. Replace

19. **A hyperlink *cannot* be linked to which of the following?**
    a. ScreenTip
    b. Document
    c. Web page
    d. E-mail address

20. **Which of the following is an example of a document property?**
    a. Permission
    b. URL
    c. Language
    d. Keyword

Skills Review

1. **Cut and paste text.**
   a. Start Word, click the File tab, then open the file WD B-2.docx from the drive and folder where you store your Data Files.
   b. Save the document with the filename **WD B-WAOS 2013 PR**.
   c. Select **Your Name** and replace it with your name.
   d. Display paragraph and other formatting marks in your document if they are not already displayed.
   e. Use the Cut and Paste buttons to switch the order of the two sentences in the fourth paragraph (which begins New group shows...).
   f. Use the drag-and-drop method to switch the order of the second and third paragraphs.
   g. Adjust the spacing if necessary so that there is one blank line between paragraphs, then save your changes.

2. **Copy and paste text.**
   a. Use the Copy and Paste buttons to copy **WAOS 2011** from the headline and paste it before the word **map** in the third paragraph.
   b. Change the formatting of the pasted text to match the formatting of the third paragraph, then insert a space between **2011** and **map** if necessary.
   c. Use the drag-and-drop method to copy **WAOS** from the third paragraph and paste it before the word **group** in the second sentence of the fourth paragraph, then save your changes.

3. **Use the Office Clipboard.**
   a. Use the launcher in the Clipboard group to open the Clipboard task pane.
   b. Scroll so that the first body paragraph is displayed at the top of the document window.
   c. Select the fifth paragraph (which begins Studio location maps...) and cut it to the Office Clipboard.
   d. Select the third paragraph (which begins Wilmington is easily accessible...) and cut it to the Office Clipboard.
   e. Use the Office Clipboard to paste the Studio location maps... item as the new fourth paragraph.
   f. Use the Office Clipboard to paste the Wilmington is easily accessible... item as the new fifth paragraph.
   g. Adjust the spacing if necessary so there is one blank line between each of the six body paragraphs.
   h. Turn off the display of formatting marks, clear and close the Office Clipboard, then save your changes.

Skills Review (continued)

4. **Find and replace text.**

 a. Using the Replace command, replace all instances of **2011** with **2013**.

 b. Replace all instances of **tenth** with **twelfth**.

 c. Replace all instances of the abbreviation **st** with **street**, taking care to replace whole words only when you perform the replace. (*Hint*: Deselect Match case if it is selected.)

 d. Use the Find tab in the Find and Replace dialog box to find all instances of **st** in the document and to make sure no errors occurred when you replaced st with street. (*Hint*: Deselect the Find whole words only check box.)

 e. Save your changes to the press release.

5. **Check spelling and grammar and research information.**

 a. Switch to the Review tab.

 b. Move the insertion point to the top of the document, then use the Spelling and Grammar command to search for and correct any spelling and grammar errors in the press release. (*Hint*: Riverwalk is not misspelled.)

 c. Use the Thesaurus to replace **thriving** in the second paragraph with a different suitable word.

 d. Check the word count of the press release.

 e. Proofread your press release, correct any errors, then save your changes.

6. **Add hyperlinks.**

 a. Save the document as **WD B-WAOS 2013 PR Public**, then switch to the Insert tab.

 b. Select your name, then open the Insert Hyperlink dialog box.

 c. Create a hyperlink to your e-mail address with the subject **WAOS 2013**.

 d. Test the your name hyperlink, then close the message window that opens. (*Hint*: Press [Ctrl], then click the hyperlink.)

 e. Select **NEA** in the last paragraph of the press release, then create a hyperlink to the Web page with the URL **www.nea.gov**.

 f. Right-click the NEA hyperlink, then edit the hyperlink ScreenTip to become **Information on the National Endowment for the Arts**.

 g. Point to the NEA hyperlink to view the new ScreenTip, then save your changes.

 h. If you are working with an active Internet connection, press [Ctrl], click the NEA hyperlink, view the NEA home page in the browser window, then close the browser window.

7. **Work with document properties.**

 a. Click the File tab, click the Properties button on the preview pane, then open the Document Properties panel to view the document properties for the press release.

 b. Click the File tab to return to Backstage view with the Info tab displayed, then use the Check for Issues command to run the Document Inspector.

 c. Remove the document property data, click the Home tab, close the Document Properties panel, then save your changes. The finished press release is shown in Figure B-18.

 d. Save the document, submit it to your instructor, close the file, then exit Word.

FIGURE B-18

PRESS RELEASE

FOR IMMEDIATE RELEASE
September 7, 2013

Contact:
Your Name
910-555-2938

WAOS 2013
Wilmington Artists Open Their Studios to the Public

WILMINGTON, NC -- The fall 2013 Open Studios season kicks off with Wilmington Artists Open Studios on Saturday and Sunday, October 13 and 14, from 11 a.m. to 6 p.m. More than 60 Wilmington artists will open their studios and homes to the public for this annual event, now in its twelfth year.

Wilmington is a historic and diverse city, long home to a flourishing community of artists. Quiet residential streets lined with charming Victorians edge a vibrant commercial and industrial zone, all peppered with the studios of printmakers, sculptors, painters, glass and jewelry makers, illustrators, potters, photographers, watercolorists, and other artists working in a wide range of mediums.

Internationally celebrated sculptor Eva Russo will display her new work in the rotunda of City Hall. New WAOS group shows will open at the Atlantic Gallery and at the Cape Fear Café, both on Front Street.

Studio location maps will be available prior to the opening at businesses and public libraries, and on the days of the event at the Riverwalk. Riverwalk is located at the junction of Water Street and Dock Street in downtown Wilmington.

Wilmington is easily accessible from all points in coastal southeastern North Carolina by car or bus, and from other cities by air. On Saturday, non-Wilmington residents may park in permit-only areas provided they display a copy of the WAOS 2013 map on the dashboard. There are no parking restrictions on Sundays in Wilmington.

WAOS 2013 receives funds from participating artists and from the Wilmington Arts Council, the North Carolina Cultural Council, and the NEA with valuable support from local universities and businesses.

#####

Independent Challenge 1

Because of your success in revitalizing a historic theatre in Wellington, New Zealand, you were hired as the director of The Canberra Lyric Theatre in Canberra, Australia, to breathe life into its theatre revitalization efforts. After a year on the job, you are launching your first major fund-raising drive. You'll create a fund-raising letter for the Lyric Theatre by modifying a letter you wrote for the theatre in Wellington.

If you have a SAM 2010 user profile, an autogradable SAM version of this assignment may be available at http://www.cengage.com/sam2010. Check with your instructor to confirm that this assignment is available in SAM. To use the SAM version of this assignment, log into the SAM 2010 Web site and download the instruction and start files.

a. Start Word, open the file WD B-3.docx from the drive and folder where you store your Data Files, then save it as **WD B-Lyric Fundraising Letter**.

b. Replace the theatre name and address, the date, the inside address, and the salutation with the text shown in Figure B-19.

c. Use the Replace command to replace all instances of **Wellington** with **Canberra**.

d. Use the Replace command to replace all instances of **Town Hall** with **Lyric**.

e. Use the Replace command to replace all instances of **New Zealanders** with **Australians**.

f. Use the Find command to locate the word **considerable**, then use the Thesaurus to replace the word with a synonym.

g. Move the fourth body paragraph so that it becomes the second body paragraph.

FIGURE B-19

The Canberra Lyric Theatre

284 Constitution Avenue, Canberra ACT 2601, Australia

June 5, 2013

Mr. Andrew Davis
45 Robinson St.
O'Connor ACT 2602

Dear Mr. Davis:

h. Create an AutoCorrect entry that inserts **Executive Director** whenever you type **exd**.

i. Replace Your Name with your name in the signature block, select Title, then type **exd** followed by a space.

j. Use the Spelling and Grammar command to check for and correct spelling and grammar errors.

k. Delete the AutoCorrect entry you created for exd. (*Hint*: Open the AutoCorrect dialog box, select the AutoCorrect entry you created, then click [Delete].)

Advanced Challenge Exercise

- Open the Document Properties panel, add your name as the author, change the title to **Canberra Lyric Theatre**, add the keyword **fund-raising**, then add the comment **Letter for the capital campaign**.
- Open the Properties dialog box, review the properties on the Summary tab, then review the paragraph, line, word, and character count on the Statistics tab.
- On the Custom tab, add a property named **Project** with the value **Capital Campaign**, then close the dialog box and the Document Properties panel.

l. Proofread the letter, correct any errors, save your changes, submit a copy to your instructor, close the document, then exit Word.

Independent Challenge 2

An advertisement for job openings in Denver caught your eye and you have decided to apply. The ad, shown in Figure B-20, was printed in last weekend's edition of your local newspaper. Instead of writing a cover letter from scratch, you revise a draft of a cover letter you wrote several years ago for a summer internship position.

a. Read the ad shown in Figure B-20 and decide which position to apply for. Choose the position that most closely matches your qualifications.

b. Start Word, open WD B-4.docx from the drive and folder where you store your Data Files, then save it as **WD B-Cover Letter**.

c. Replace the name, address, telephone number, and e-mail address in the letterhead with your own information.

d. Remove the hyperlink from the e-mail address.

e. Replace the date with today's date, then replace the inside address and the salutation with the information shown in Figure B-20.

f. Read the draft cover letter to get a feel for its contents.

g. Rework the text in the body of the letter to address your qualifications for the job you have chosen to apply for in the following ways:

- Delete the third paragraph.
- Adjust the first sentence of the first paragraph as follows: specify the job you are applying for, including the position code, and indicate where you saw the position advertised.
- Move the first sentence in the last paragraph, which briefly states your qualifications and interest in the position, to the end of the first paragraph, then rework the sentence to describe your current qualifications.
- Adjust the second paragraph as follows: describe your work experience and skills. Be sure to relate your experience and qualifications to the position requirements listed in the advertisement. Add a third paragraph if your qualifications are extensive.
- Adjust the final paragraph as follows: politely request an interview for the position and provide your phone number and e-mail address.

h. Include your name in the signature block.

i. When you are finished revising the letter, check it for spelling and grammar errors, and correct any mistakes. Make sure to remove any hyperlinks.

j. Save your changes to the letter, submit the file to your instructor, close the document, then exit Word.

FIGURE B-20

*Global*Dynamics

Career Opportunities in Denver

Global Dynamics, an established software development firm with offices in North America, Asia, and Europe, is seeking candidates for the following positions in its Denver facility:

Instructor
Responsible for delivering software training to our expanding Rocky Mountain customer base. Duties include delivering hands-on training, keeping up-to-date with product development, and working with the Director of Training to ensure the high quality of course materials. Successful candidate will have excellent presentation skills and be proficient in Microsoft PowerPoint and Microsoft Word. **Position B12C6**

Administrative Assistant
Proficiency with Microsoft Word a must! Administrative office duties include making travel arrangements, scheduling meetings, taking notes and publishing meeting minutes, handling correspondence, and ordering office supplies. Must have superb multitasking abilities, excellent communication, organizational, and interpersonal skills, and be comfortable working with e-mail and the Internet. **Position B16F5**

Copywriter
The ideal candidate will have marketing or advertising writing experience in a high tech environment, including collateral, newsletters, and direct mail. Experience writing for the Web, broadcast, and multimedia is a plus. Fluency with Microsoft Word required. **Position C13D4**

Positions offer salary, excellent benefits, moving expenses, and career growth opportunities.

Send resume and cover letter referencing position code to:

Thomas Finlay
Director of Recruiting
Global Dynamics
330 Fillmore Street
Denver, CO 80206

Independent Challenge 3

As administrative director of continuing education, you drafted a memo to instructors asking them to help you finalize the course schedule for next semester. Today, you'll examine the draft and make revisions before distributing it as an e-mail attachment.

a. Start Word, open the file WD B-5.docx from the drive and folder where you store your Data Files, then save it as **WD B-Business Courses Memo**.

b. Replace Your Name with your name in the From line, then scroll down until the first body paragraph is at the top of the screen.

Advanced Challenge Exercise

- Use the Split command on the View tab to split the window under the first body paragraph, then scroll until the last paragraph of the memo is displayed in the bottom pane.
- Use the Cut and Paste buttons to move the sentence **If you are planning to teach...** from the first body paragraph to become the first sentence in the last paragraph of the memo.
- Double-click the split bar to restore the window to a single pane.

c. Use the [Delete] key to merge the first two paragraphs into one paragraph.

d. Use the Office Clipboard to reorganize the list of twelve-week courses so that the courses are listed in alphabetical order, then clear and close the Office Clipboard.

e. Use the drag-and-drop method to reorganize the list of one-day seminars so that the seminars are listed in alphabetical order.

f. Select the phrase "Web site" in the first paragraph, then create a hyperlink to the URL **www.course.com** with the ScreenTip **Spring 2014 Business Courses**.

g. Select "e-mail me" in the last paragraph, then create a hyperlink to your e-mail address with the subject **Final Business Course Schedule**.

h. Use the Spelling and Grammar command to check for and correct spelling and grammar errors.

i. Use the Document Inspector to strip the document of document property information, ignore any other content that is flagged by the Document Inspector, then close the Document Inspector.

j. Proofread the memo, correct any errors, save your changes, submit a copy to your instructor, close the document, then exit Word.

Real Life Independent Challenge

This Independent Challenge requires an Internet connection.

Reference sources—dictionaries, thesauri, style and grammar guides, and guides to business etiquette and procedure—are essential for day-to-day use in the workplace. Much of this reference information is available on the World Wide Web. In this independent challenge, you will locate reference sources on the Web and use some of them to look up definitions, synonyms, and antonyms for words. Your goal is to familiarize yourself with online reference sources so you can use them later in your work.

a. Start Word, open the file WD B-6.docx from the drive and folder where you store your Data Files, then save it as **WD B-Web Reference Sources**. This document contains the questions you will answer about the Web reference sources you find. You will type your answers to the questions in the document.

b. Replace the placeholder text at the top of the Web Reference Sources document with your name and the date.

c. Use your favorite search engine to search the Web for grammar and style guides, dictionaries, and thesauri. Use the keywords **grammar**, **usage**, **dictionary**, **glossary**, and **thesaurus** to conduct your search.

d. Complete the Web Reference Sources document, then proofread it and correct any mistakes.

e. Save the document, submit a copy to your instructor, close the document, then exit Word.

Visual Workshop

Open WD B-7.docx from the drive and folder where you store your Data Files, then save the document as **WD B-Visa Letter**. Replace the placeholders for the date, letterhead, inside address, salutation, and closing with the information shown in Figure B-21, then use the Office Clipboard to reorganize the sentences to match Figure B-21. Correct spelling and grammar errors, remove the document property information from the file, then submit a copy to your instructor.

FIGURE B-21

Your Name

4637 Baker Street, Chicago, IL 60627; Tel: 630-555-2840

1/3/2013

Embassy of the People's Republic of China
2300 Connecticut Avenue NW
Washington, DC 20008-1724

Dear Sir or Madam:

I am applying for a long-stay tourist visa to China, valid for four years. I am scheduled to depart for Shanghai on March 13, 2013, returning to Chicago on September 8, 2013.

During my stay in China, I will be interviewing musicians and recording footage for a film I am making on contemporary Chinese music. I would like a multiple entry visa valid for four years so I can return to China after this trip to follow up on my initial research. I will be based in Shanghai, but I will be traveling frequently to record performances and to meet with musicians and producers.

Included with this letter are my completed visa application form, my passport, a passport photo, a copy of my return air ticket, and the visa fee. Please contact me if you need further information.

Sincerely,

Your Name

Enc: 5

Formatting Text and Paragraphs

Files You Will Need:

WD C-1.docx
WD C-2.docx
WD C-3.docx
WD C-4.docx
WD C-5.docx
WD C-6.docx

Formatting can enhance the appearance of a document, create visual impact, and help illustrate a document's structure. The formatting of a document can also set a tone, allowing readers to know at a glance if the document is business-like, informal, or fun. In this unit you learn how to format text using fonts and a variety of paragraph-formatting effects, such as borders, shading, and bullets. You also learn how to illustrate a document with clip art.  You have finished drafting the text for a two-page flyer advertising last minute specials for October tours. Now, you need to format the flyer so it is attractive and highlights the significant information.

OBJECTIVES

Format with fonts

Copy formats using the Format Painter

Change line and paragraph spacing

Align paragraphs

Work with tabs

Work with indents

Add bullets and numbering

Add borders and shading

Insert clip art

Formatting with Fonts

Formatting text with fonts is a quick and powerful way to enhance the appearance of a document. A **font** is a complete set of characters with the same typeface or design. Arial, Times New Roman, Courier, Tahoma, and Calibri are some of the more common fonts, but there are hundreds of others, each with a specific design and feel. Another way to change the appearance of text is to increase or decrease its **font size**. Font size is measured in points. A **point** is 1/72 of an inch.  You change the font and font size of the body text, title, and headings in the flyer. You select fonts and font sizes that enhance the sales tone of the document and help to structure the flyer visually for readers.

STEPS

1. **Start Word, open the file WD C-1.docx from the drive and folder where you store your Data Files, then save it as WD C-Last Minute Deals**

   Notice that the name of the font used in the document, Calibri, is displayed in the Font list box in the Font group. The word "(Body)" in the Font list box indicates Calibri is the font used for body text in the current theme, the default theme. A **theme** is a related set of fonts, colors, styles, and effects that is applied to an entire document to give it a cohesive appearance. The font size, 11, appears in the Font Size list box in the Font group.

QUICK TIP

There are two types of fonts: serif fonts have a small stroke, called a serif, at the ends of characters; sans serif fonts do not have a serif. Garamond is a serif font. Trebuchet MS is a sans serif font.

2. **Scroll the document to get a feel for its contents, press [Ctrl][Home], press [Ctrl][A] to select the entire document, then click the Font list arrow in the Font group**

   The Font list, which shows the fonts available on your computer, opens as shown in Figure C-1. The font names are formatted in the font. Font names can appear in more than one location on the font list.

3. **Drag the pointer slowly down the font names in the Font list, drag the scroll box to scroll down the Font list, then click Garamond**

   Dragging the pointer down the font list allows you to preview how the selected text will look in the highlighted font. Clicking a font name applies the font. The font of the flyer changes to Garamond.

QUICK TIP

You can also type a font size in the Font Size text box.

4. **Click the Font Size list arrow in the Font group, drag the pointer slowly up and down the Font Size list, then click 12**

   Dragging the pointer over the font sizes allows you to preview how the selected text will look in the highlighted font size. Clicking 12 increases the font size of the selected text to 12 points.

5. **Select the title Quest Specialty Travel Last Minute Travel Deals, click the Font list arrow, scroll to and click Trebuchet MS, click the Font Size list arrow, click 22, then click the Bold button B in the Font group**

   The title is formatted in 22-point Trebuchet MS bold.

QUICK TIP

To use a different set of theme colors, click the Page Layout tab, click the Theme Colors button in the Themes group, then select a different color set.

6. **Click the Font Color list arrow A in the Font group**

   A gallery of colors opens. It includes the set of theme colors in a range of tints and shades as well as a set of standard colors. You can point to a color in the gallery to preview it applied to the selected text.

7. **Click the Purple, Accent 4, Darker 25% color as shown in Figure C-2, then deselect the text**

   The color of the title text changes to purple. The active color on the Font Color button also changes to purple.

8. **Select the heading Rajasthan Desert Safari, then, using the Mini toolbar, click the Font list arrow, click Trebuchet MS, click the Font Size list arrow, click 14, click A, click B, then deselect the text**

   The heading is formatted in 14-point Trebuchet MS bold with a purple color. Notice that when you use the buttons on the Mini toolbar to format text, you cannot preview the formatting options in the document.

9. **Press [Ctrl][Home], then click the Save button on the Quick Access toolbar**

   Compare your document to Figure C-3.

FIGURE C-1: Font list

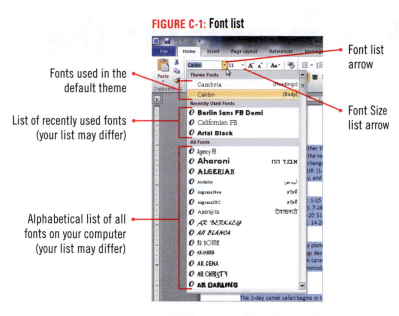

Fonts used in the default theme

Font list arrow

Font Size list arrow

List of recently used fonts (your list may differ)

Alphabetical list of all fonts on your computer (your list may differ)

FIGURE C-2: Font Color Palette

Font Color list arrow

Name of color appears as a ScreenTip

Click to create a custom color

FIGURE C-3: Document formatted with fonts

Title formatted in 22-point Trebuchet MS, bold, purple

Body text formatted in 12-point Garamond

Heading formatted in 14-point Trebuchet MS, bold, purple

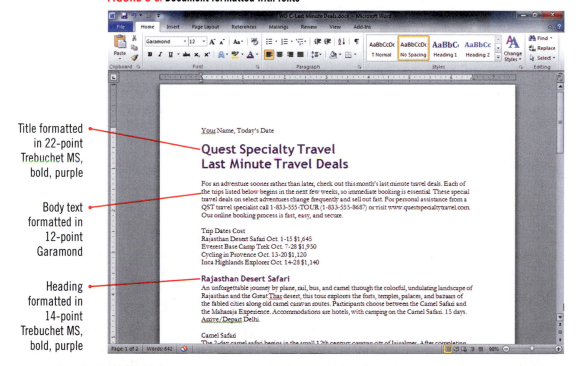

Adding a drop cap

A fun way to illustrate a document with fonts is to add a drop cap to a paragraph. A **drop cap** is a large initial capital letter, often used to set off the first paragraph of an article. To create a drop cap, place the insertion point in the paragraph you want to format, click the Insert tab, and then click the Drop Cap button in the Text group to open a menu of Drop cap options. Preview and select one of the options on the menu, or click Drop Cap Options to open the Drop Cap dialog box, shown in Figure C-4. In the Drop Cap dialog box, select the position, font, number of lines to drop, and the distance you want the drop cap to be from the paragraph text, and then click OK. The drop cap is added to the paragraph as a graphic object.

Once a drop cap is inserted in a paragraph, you can modify it by selecting it and then changing the settings in the Drop Cap dialog box. For even more interesting effects, you can enhance a drop cap with font color, font styles, or font effects. You can also fill the graphic object with shading or add a border around it. To enhance a drop cap, first select it, and then experiment with the formatting options available in the Font dialog box and in the Borders and Shading dialog box.

FIGURE C-4: Drop Cap dialog box

Copying Formats Using the Format Painter

You can dramatically change the appearance of text by applying different font styles, font effects, and character-spacing effects. For example, you can use the buttons in the Font group to make text darker by applying **bold** or to make text slanted by applying *italic*. When you are satisfied with the formatting of certain text, you can quickly apply the same formats to other text using the Format Painter. The **Format Painter** is a powerful Word feature that allows you to copy all the format settings applied to selected text to other text that you want to format the same way.  You spice up the appearance of the text in the document by applying different font styles and effects.

STEPS

1. Select immediate booking is essential in the first body paragraph, click the Bold button **B** on the Mini toolbar, select the entire paragraph, then click the Italic button *I*

   "Immediate booking is essential" is bold, and the entire paragraph is formatted in italic.

QUICK TIP

To change the case of selected text from lowercase to uppercase—and visa versa—click the Change Case button in the Font group, and then select the case style you want to use.

2. Select Last Minute Travel Deals, then click the launcher ⌐ in the Font group

   The Font dialog box opens, as shown in Figure C-5. You can use options on the Font tab to change the font, font style, size, and color of text, and to add an underline and apply font effects to text.

3. Scroll down the Size list, click 48, click the Font color list arrow, click the Olive Green, Accent 3, Darker 25% color in the Theme Colors, then click the Text Effects button

   The Format Text Effects dialog box opens. You use this dialog box to apply text effects, such as shadows, outlines, and reflections, to text.

4. Click Shadow, click the Presets list arrow, click Offset Diagonal Bottom Right in the Outer section, click Close, click OK, then deselect the text

   The text is larger, green, and has a shadow effect.

5. Select Last Minute Travel Deals, right-click, click Font on the menu that opens, click the Advanced tab, click the Scale list arrow, click 80%, click OK, then deselect the text

   You use the Advanced tab in the Font dialog box to change the scale, or width, of the selected characters, to alter the spacing between characters, or to raise or lower the characters. Decreasing the scale of the characters makes them narrower and gives the text a tall, thin appearance, as shown in Figure C-6.

6. Scroll down, select the subheading Camel Safari, then, using the Mini toolbar, click the Font list arrow, click Trebuchet MS, click **B**, click *I*, click the Font Color list arrow **A** ▾, click the Olive Green, Accent 3, Darker 25% color in the Theme Colors, then deselect the text

   The subheading is formatted in Trebuchet MS, bold, italic, and green.

TROUBLE

Move the pointer over the document text to see the pointer.

7. Select Camel Safari, then click the Format Painter button 🖌 in the Clipboard group

   The pointer changes to 🖌I.

8. Scroll down, select Maharaja Experience with the 🖌I pointer, then deselect the text

   The subheading is formatted in Trebuchet MS, bold, italic, and green, as shown in Figure C-7.

9. Scroll up as needed, select Rajasthan Desert Safari, then double-click 🖌

   Double-clicking the Format Painter button allows the Format Painter to remain active until you turn it off. By keeping the Format Painter active, you can apply formatting to multiple items.

QUICK TIP

You can also press [Esc] to turn off the Format Painter.

10. Scroll down, select the headings Everest Base Camp Trek, Cycling in Provence, and Inca Highlands Explorer with the 🖌I pointer, click 🖌 to turn off the Format Painter, then save your changes

    The headings are formatted in 14-point Trebuchet MS bold with a purple font color.

FIGURE C-5: Font tab in Font dialog box

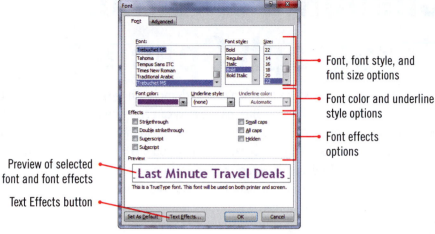

Font, font style, and font size options

Font color and underline style options

Font effects options

Preview of selected font and font effects

Text Effects button

FIGURE C-6: Font and character spacing effects applied to text

Title formatted in 48-point, green, with a shadow effect and a character scale of 80%

Paragraph formatted in italic

FIGURE C-7: Formats copied and applied using the Format Painter

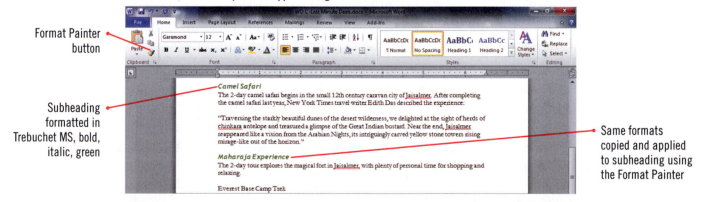

Format Painter button

Subheading formatted in Trebuchet MS, bold, italic, green

Same formats copied and applied to subheading using the Format Painter

Word 2010

Underlining text

Another creative way to call attention to text and to jazz up the appearance of a document is to apply an underline style to words you want to highlight. The Underline list arrow in the Font group displays straight, dotted, wavy, dashed, and mixed underline styles, along with a gallery of colors to choose from. To apply an underline to text, simply select it, click the Underline list arrow, and then select an underline style from the list. For a wider variety of underline styles, click More Underlines in the list, and then select an underline style in the Font dialog box. You can change the color of an underline at any time by selecting the underlined text, clicking the Underline list arrow, pointing to Underline Color, and then choosing from the options in the color gallery. If you want to remove an underline from text, select the underlined text, and then click the Underline button.

Changing Line and Paragraph Spacing

Increasing the amount of space between lines adds more white space to a document and can make it easier to read. Adding space before and after paragraphs can also open up a document and improve its appearance. You use the Line and Paragraph Spacing list arrow in the Paragraph group on the Home tab to quickly change line spacing. To change paragraph spacing, you use the Spacing options in the Paragraph group on the Page Layout tab. Line and paragraph spacing are measured in points. You increase the line spacing of several paragraphs and add extra space under each heading to give the flyer a more open feel. You work with formatting marks turned on, so you can see the paragraph marks (¶).

STEPS

1. **Press [Ctrl][Home], click the Show/Hide ¶ button ¶ in the Paragraph group, place the insertion point in the italicized paragraph under the title, then click the Line and Paragraph Spacing list arrow ≣▾ in the Paragraph group on the Home tab**

   The Line Spacing list opens. This list includes options for increasing the space between lines. The check mark on the Line Spacing list indicates the current line spacing.

2. **Click 1.15**

   The space between the lines in the paragraph increases to 1.15 lines. Notice that you do not need to select an entire paragraph to change its paragraph formatting; simply place the insertion point in the paragraph you want to format.

   > **QUICK TIP**
   > Word recognizes any string of text that ends with a paragraph mark as a paragraph, including titles, headings, and single lines in a list.

3. **Select the five-line list that begins with "Trip Dates Cost", click ≣▾, then click 1.5**

   The line spacing between the selected paragraphs changes to 1.5. To change the paragraph-formatting features of more than one paragraph, you must select the paragraphs.

4. **Scroll down, place the insertion point in the heading Rajasthan Desert Safari, then click the Page Layout tab**

   The paragraph spacing settings for the active paragraph are shown in the Before and After text boxes in the Paragraph group on the Page Layout tab.

   > **QUICK TIP**
   > You can also type a number in the Before and After text boxes.

5. **Click the After up arrow in the Spacing section in the Paragraph group so that 6 pt appears**

   Six points of space are added after the Rajasthan Desert Safari heading paragraph.

   > **TROUBLE**
   > If your [F4] key does not work, use the After up arrow to apply 6 pts of space to the headings listed in Steps 6 and 7, then continue with Step 8.

6. **Scroll down, place the insertion point in the heading Everest Base Camp Trek, then press [F4]**

   Pressing [F4] repeats the last action you took. In this case, six points of space are added after the Everest Base Camp Trek heading. Note that using [F4] is not the same as using the Format painter. Pressing [F4] repeats only the last action. You can use the Format Painter at any time to apply multiple format settings.

7. **Scroll down, select Cycling in Provence, press and hold [Ctrl], select Inca Highlands Explorer, release [Ctrl], then press [F4]**

   When you press [Ctrl] as you select items, you can select and format multiple items at once. Six points of space are added after each heading.

   > **QUICK TIP**
   > Adjusting the space between paragraphs is a more precise way to add white space to a document than inserting blank lines.

8. **Press [Ctrl][Home], place the insertion point in Last Minute Travel Deals, click the Before up arrow in the Spacing section in the Paragraph group twice so that 12 pt appears**

   The second line of the title has 12 points of space before it. Compare your document with Figure C-8.

9. **Click the Home tab, click ¶, then save your changes**

FIGURE C-8: Line and paragraph spacing applied to document

12 points of space added before Last Minute Travel Deals heading

Insertion point (your placement may vary)

6 points of space added after the heading

Spacing section shows paragraph spacing for the paragraph where the insertion point is located

Line spacing is 1.15

Line spacing is 1.5

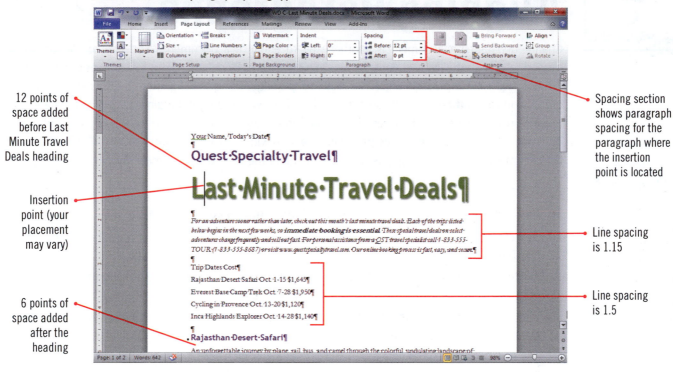

Formatting with Quick Styles

You can also apply multiple format settings to text in one step by applying a style. A **style** is a set of formats, such as font, font size, and paragraph alignment, that are named and stored together. Formatting a document with styles is a quick and easy way to give it a professional appearance. To make it even easier, Word includes sets of styles, called **Quick Styles**, that are designed to be used together in a document to make it attractive and readable. A Quick Style set includes styles for a title, several heading levels, body text, quotes, and lists. The styles in a Quick Style set use common fonts, colors, and formats so that using the styles together in a document gives the document a cohesive look.

To view the active set of Quick Styles, click the More button ⊡ in the Styles group on the Home tab to expand the Quick Styles gallery, shown in Figure C-9. As you move the pointer over each style in the gallery, a preview of the style is applied to the selected text. To apply a style to the selected text, you simply click the style in the Quick Styles gallery. To remove a style from selected text, you click the Clear Formatting button in the Font group or in the Quick Styles gallery.

If you want to change the active set of Quick Styles to a Quick Style set with a different design, click the Change Styles button in the Styles group, point to Style Set, and then select the Quick Style set that best suits your document's content, tone, and audience.

When you change the Quick Style set, a complete set of new fonts and colors is applied to the entire document. You can also change the color scheme or font used in the active Quick Style set by clicking the Change Styles button, pointing to Colors or to Fonts, and then selecting from the available color schemes or font options.

FIGURE C-9: Quick Styles gallery

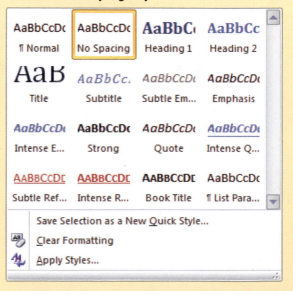

Aligning Paragraphs

Changing paragraph alignment is another way to enhance a document's appearance. Paragraphs are aligned relative to the left and right margins in a document. By default, text is **left-aligned**, which means it is flush with the left margin and has a ragged right edge. Using the alignment buttons in the Paragraph group, you can **right-align** a paragraph—make it flush with the right margin—or **center** a paragraph so that it is positioned evenly between the left and right margins. You can also **justify** a paragraph so that both the left and right edges of the paragraph are flush with the left and right margins. You change the alignment of several paragraphs at the beginning of the flyer to make it more visually interesting.

STEPS

1. **Replace Your Name, Today's Date with your name, a comma, and the date**

TROUBLE

Click the View Ruler button at the top of the vertical scroll bar to display the rulers if they are not already displayed.

2. **Select your name, the comma, and the date, then click the Align Text Right button in the Paragraph group**

   The text is aligned with the right margin. In Page Layout view, the place where the white and shaded sections of the horizontal ruler meet shows the left and right margins.

3. **Place the insertion point between your name and the comma, press [Delete] to delete the comma, then press [Enter]**

   The new paragraph containing the date is also right-aligned. Pressing [Enter] in the middle of a paragraph creates a new paragraph with the same text and paragraph formatting as the original paragraph.

4. **Select the two-line title, then click the Center button in the Paragraph group**

   The two paragraphs that make up the title are centered between the left and right margins.

QUICK TIP

Click the Align Text Left button in the Paragraph group to left-align a paragraph.

5. **Scroll down as needed, place the insertion point in the Rajasthan Desert Safari heading, then click**

   The Rajasthan Desert Safari heading is centered.

6. **Place the insertion point in the italicized paragraph under the title, then click the Justify button in the Paragraph group**

   The paragraph is aligned with both the left and right margins, as shown in Figure C-10. When you justify a paragraph, Word adjusts the spacing between words so that each line in the paragraph is flush with the left and the right margins.

7. **Place the insertion point in Rajasthan Desert Safari, then click the launcher in the Paragraph group**

   The Paragraph dialog box opens, as shown in Figure C-11. The Indents and Spacing tab shows the paragraph format settings for the paragraph where the insertion point is located. You can check or change paragraph format settings using this dialog box.

8. **Click the Alignment list arrow, click Left, click OK, then save your changes**

   The Rajasthan Desert Safari heading is left-aligned.

FIGURE C-10: Modified paragraph alignment

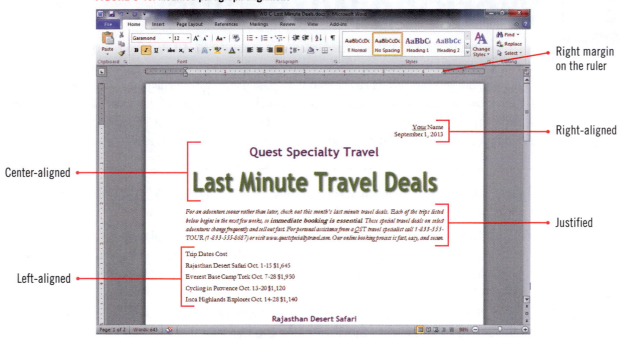

Right margin on the ruler

Center-aligned

Right-aligned

Justified

Left-aligned

FIGURE C-11: Indents and Spacing tab in Paragraph dialog box

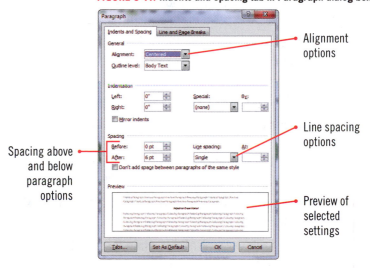

Alignment options

Line spacing options

Spacing above and below paragraph options

Preview of selected settings

Formatting a document using themes

Changing the theme applied to a document is another powerful and efficient way to tailor a document's look and feel, particularly when a document is formatted with a Quick Style set. By default, all documents created in Word are formatted with the default Office theme—which uses Calibri as the font for the body text—but you can change the theme at any time to fit the content, tone, and purpose of a document. When you change the theme for a document, a complete set of new theme colors, fonts, and effects is applied to the whole document.

To preview how various themes look when applied to the current document, click the Themes button in the Themes group on the Page Layout tab, and then move the pointer over each theme in the gallery and notice how the document changes. When you click the theme you like, all document content that uses theme colors, all text

that is formatted with a style, including default body text, and all table styles and graphic effects change to the colors, fonts, and effects used by the theme. In addition, the gallery of colors changes to display the set of theme colors, and the active Quick Style set changes to employ the theme colors and fonts. Note that changing the theme does not affect the formatting of text to which font formatting has already been applied, nor does it change any standard or custom colors used in the document.

If you want to tweak the document design further, you can modify it by applying a different set of theme colors, heading and body text fonts, or graphic effects. To do this, simply click the Theme Colors, Theme Fonts, or Theme Effects button in the Themes group, move the pointer over each option in the gallery to preview it in the document, and then click the option you like best.

Working with Tabs

Tabs allow you to align text at a specific location in a document. A **tab stop** is a point on the horizontal ruler that indicates the location at which to align text. By default, tab stops are located every 1/2" from the left margin, but you can also set custom tab stops. Using tabs, you can align text to the left, right, or center of a tab stop, or you can align text at a decimal point or insert a bar character. Table C-1 describes the different types of tab stops. You set tabs using the horizontal ruler or the Tabs dialog box. You use tabs to format the summary information on last minute tour deals so it is easy to read.

1. **Scroll as needed, then select the five-line list beginning with "Trip Dates Cost"**
   Before you set tab stops for existing text, you must select the paragraphs for which you want to set tabs.

2. **Point to the tab indicator ⌊ at the left end of the horizontal ruler**
   The icon that appears in the tab indicator indicates the active type of tab; pointing to the tab indicator displays a ScreenTip with the name of the active tab type. By default, left tab is the active tab type. Clicking the tab indicator scrolls through the types of tabs and indents.

   > **QUICK TIP**
   > To remove a tab stop, drag it up or down off the ruler.

3. **Click the tab indicator to see each of the available tab and indent types, make Left Tab the active tab type, click the 1" mark on the horizontal ruler, then click the 3½" mark on the horizontal ruler**
   A left tab stop is inserted at the 1" mark and the 3½" on the horizontal ruler. Clicking the horizontal ruler inserts a tab stop of the active type for the selected paragraph or paragraphs.

4. **Click the tab indicator twice so the Right Tab icon ⌋ is active, then click the 5" mark on the horizontal ruler**
   A right tab stop is inserted at the 5" mark on the horizontal ruler, as shown in Figure C-12.

5. **Place the insertion point before Trip in the first line in the list, press [Tab], place the insertion point before Dates, press [Tab], place the insertion point before Cost, then press [Tab]**
   Inserting a tab before "Trip" left-aligns the text at the 1" mark, inserting a tab before "Dates" left-aligns the text at the 3½" mark, and inserting a tab before "Cost" right-aligns "Cost" at the 5" mark.

6. **Insert a tab at the beginning of each remaining line in the list**
   The paragraphs left-align at the 1" mark.

   > **QUICK TIP**
   > Place the insertion point in a paragraph to see the tab stops for that paragraph on the horizontal ruler.

7. **Insert a tab before each Oct. in the list, then insert a tab before each $ in the list**
   The dates left-align at the 3½" mark. The prices right-align at the 5" mark.

8. **Select the five lines of tabbed text, drag the right tab stop to the 5½" mark on the horizontal ruler, then deselect the text**
   Dragging the tab stop moves it to a new location. The prices right-align at the 5½" mark.

   > **QUICK TIP**
   > Double-click a tab stop on the ruler to open the Tabs dialog box.

9. **Select the last four lines of tabbed text, click the launcher ⌐ in the Paragraph group, then click the Tabs button at the bottom of the Paragraph dialog box**
   The Tabs dialog box opens, as shown in Figure C-13. You can use the Tabs dialog box to set tab stops, change the position or alignment of existing tab stops, clear tab stops, and apply tab leaders to tabs. **Tab leaders** are lines that appear in front of tabbed text.

10. **Click 3.5" in the Tab stop position list box, click the 2 option button in the Leader section, click Set, click 5.5" in the Tab stop position list box, click the 2 option button in the Leader section, click Set, click OK, deselect the text, then save your changes**
   A dotted tab leader is added before each 3.5" and 5.5" tab stop in the last four lines of tabbed text, as shown in Figure C-14.

FIGURE C-12: Left and right tab stops on the horizontal ruler

Left tab stops

Right Tab icon in tab indicator

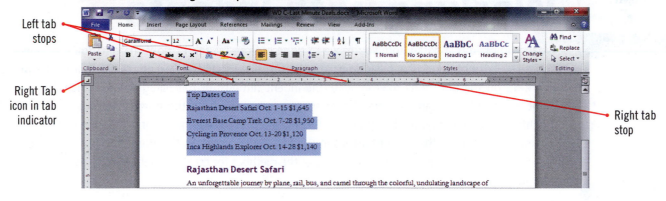

Right tab stop

FIGURE C-13: Tabs dialog box

Click the tab stop you want to modify

Leader options

Apply the selected settings to the selected tab stop

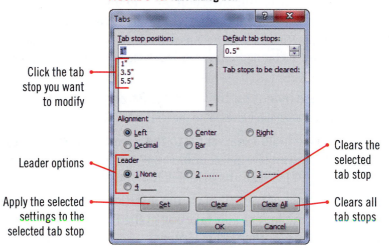

Clears the selected tab stop

Clears all tab stops

FIGURE C-14: Tab leaders

Tab leader

Tabbed text left-aligned with left tab stop

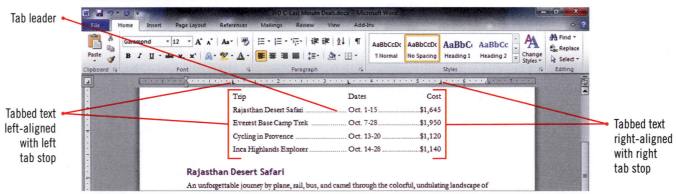

Tabbed text right-aligned with right tab stop

TABLE C-1: Types of tabs

tab	use to
Left tab	Set the start position of text so that text runs to the right of the tab stop as you type
Center tab	Set the center align position of text so that text stays centered on the tab stop as you type
Right tab	Set the right or end position of text so that text moves to the left of the tab stop as you type
Decimal tab	Set the position of the decimal point so that numbers align around the decimal point as you type
Bar tab	Insert a vertical bar at the tab position

Working with Indents

When you **indent** a paragraph, you move its edge in from the left or right margin. You can indent the entire left or right edge of a paragraph, just the first line, or all lines except the first line. The **indent markers** on the horizontal ruler indicate the indent settings for the paragraph in which the insertion point is located. Dragging an indent marker to a new location on the ruler is one way to change the indentation of a paragraph; changing the indent settings in the Paragraph group on the Page Layout tab is another; and using the indent buttons in the Paragraph group on the Home tab is a third. Table C-2 describes different types of indents and some of the methods for creating each.  You indent several paragraphs in the flyer.

STEPS

1. **Press [Ctrl][Home], place the insertion point in the italicized paragraph under the title, then click the Increase Indent button 🔲 in the Paragraph group on the Home tab**

   The entire paragraph is indented ½" from the left margin, as shown in Figure C-15. The indent marker also moves to the ½" mark on the horizontal ruler. Each time you click the Increase Indent button, the left edge of a paragraph moves another ½" to the right.

2. **Click the Decrease Indent button 🔲 in the Paragraph group**

   The left edge of the paragraph moves ½" to the left, and the indent marker moves back to the left margin.

3. **Drag the First Line Indent marker 🔲 to the ¼" mark on the horizontal ruler**

   Figure C-16 shows the First Line Indent marker being dragged. The first line of the paragraph is indented ¼". Dragging the First Line Indent marker indents only the first line of a paragraph.

4. **Scroll to the bottom of page 1, place the insertion point in the quotation, click the Page Layout tab, click the Indent Left text box in the Paragraph group, type .5, click the Indent Right text box, type .5, then press [Enter]**

   The left and right edges of the paragraph are indented ½" from the margins, as shown in Figure C-17.

5. **Press [Ctrl][Home], place the insertion point in the italicized paragraph, then click the launcher 🔲 in the Paragraph group**

   The Paragraph dialog box opens. You can use the Indents and Spacing tab to check or change the alignment, indentation, and paragraph and line spacing settings applied to a paragraph.

6. **Click the Special list arrow, click (none), click OK, then save your changes**

   The first line indent is removed from the paragraph.

Clearing formatting

If you are unhappy with the way text is formatted, you can use the Clear Formatting command to return the text to the default format settings. The default format includes font and paragraph formatting: text is formatted in 11-point Calibri, and paragraphs are left-aligned with 1.15 point line spacing, 10 points of space below, and no indents. To clear formatting from text and return it to the default format, select the text you want to clear, and then click the Clear Formatting button in the Font group on the Home tab. If you prefer to return the text to the default font and remove all paragraph formatting, making the text 11-point Calibri, left-aligned, single spaced, with no paragraph spacing or indents, select the text and then simply click the No Spacing button in the Styles group on the Home tab.

Formatting Text and Paragraphs

FIGURE C-15: Indented paragraph

First Line Indent marker

Increase Indent button

Decrease Indent button

Hanging Indent marker

Right Indent marker

Left Indent marker

Indented paragraph

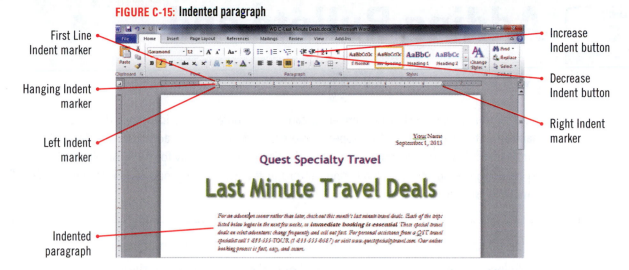

FIGURE C-16: Dragging the First Line Indent marker

First Line Indent marker being dragged to the 1/4" mark

Dotted line shows position of First Line Indent marker

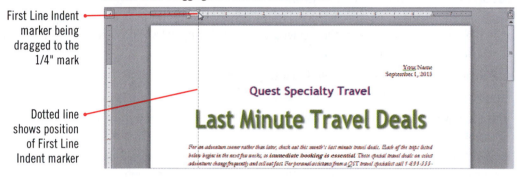

FIGURE C-17: Paragraph indented from the left and right

Paragraph indented ½" from left margin

Paragraph indented ½" from right margin

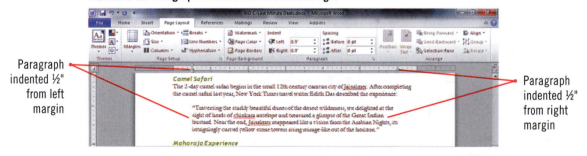

TABLE C-2: Types of indents

indent type: description	to create
Left indent: The left edge of a paragraph is moved in from the left margin	Drag the Left Indent marker ⊡ on the ruler to the right to the position where you want the left edge of the paragraph to align
Right indent: The right edge of a paragraph is moved in from the right margin	Drag the Right Indent marker ⌂ on the ruler to the left to the position where you want the right edge of the paragraph to align
First line indent: The first line of a paragraph is indented more than the subsequent lines	Drag the First Line Indent marker ▽ on the ruler to the right to the position where you want the first line of the paragraph to begin; or activate the First Line Indent marker ▽ in the tab indicator, and then click the ruler at the position where you want the first line of the paragraph to begin
Hanging indent: The subsequent lines of a paragraph are indented more than the first line	Drag the Hanging Indent marker ⊡ on the ruler to the right to the position where you want the hanging indent to begin; or activate the Hanging Indent marker ⊡ in the tab indicator, and then click the ruler at the position where you want the second and remaining lines of the paragraph to begin
Negative indent (or Outdent): The left edge of a paragraph is moved to the left of the left margin	Drag the Left Indent marker ⊡ on the ruler to the left to the position where you want the negative indent to begin

Word 2010

Adding Bullets and Numbering

Formatting a list with bullets or numbering can help to organize the ideas in a document. A **bullet** is a character, often a small circle, that appears before the items in a list to add emphasis. Formatting a list as a numbered list helps illustrate sequences and priorities. You can quickly format a list with bullets or numbering by using the Bullets and Numbering buttons in the Paragraph group on the Home tab.  You format the lists in your flyer with numbers and bullets.

QUICK TIP

To change the style, font, number format, and alignment of the numbers in a list, right-click the list, point to Numbering, then click Define New Number Format.

1. **Scroll until the Everest Base Camp Trek heading is at the top of your screen**

2. **Select the three-line list of 3-day add-ons, click the Home tab, then click the Numbering list arrow** ▤▾ **in the Paragraph group**

   The Numbering Library opens, as shown in Figure C-18. You use this list to choose or change the numbering style applied to a list. You can drag the pointer over the numbering styles to preview how the selected text will look if the numbering style is applied.

3. **Click the numbering style shown in Figure C-18**

   The paragraphs are formatted as a numbered list.

QUICK TIP

To remove a bullet or number, select the paragraph(s), then click ▤ or ▤ .

4. **Place the insertion point after Pokhara — Valley of Lakes, press [Enter], then type Temples of Janakpur**

   Pressing [Enter] in the middle of the numbered list creates a new numbered paragraph and automatically renumbers the remainder of the list. Similarly, if you delete a paragraph from a numbered list, Word automatically renumbers the remaining paragraphs.

5. **Click 1 in the list**

   Clicking a number in a list selects all the numbers, as shown in Figure C-19.

6. **Click the Bold button** ⓑ **in the Font group**

   The numbers are all formatted in bold. Notice that the formatting of the items in the list does not change when you change the formatting of the numbers. You can also use this technique to change the formatting of bullets in a bulleted list.

QUICK TIP

To use a symbol or a picture for a bullet character, click Define New Bullet in the Bullet list, and then select from the options in the Define New Bullet dialog box.

7. **Select the list of items under "Last minute participants in the Everest Base Camp trek...", then click the Bullets button** ▤ **in the Paragraph group**

   The four paragraphs are formatted as a bulleted list using the most recently used bullet style.

8. **Click a bullet in the list to select all the bullets, click the Bullets list arrow** ▤▾ **in the Paragraph group, click the check mark bullet style, click the document to deselect the text, then save your changes**

   The bullet character changes to a check mark, as shown in Figure C-20.

Creating multilevel lists

You can create lists with hierarchical structures by applying a multilevel list style to a list. To create a **multilevel list**, also called an outline, begin by applying a multilevel list style using the Multilevel List list arrow ▤▾ in the Paragraph group on the Home tab, then type your outline, pressing [Enter] after each item. To demote items to a lower level of importance in the outline, place the insertion point in the item, then click the Increase Indent button ▤ in the Paragraph group on the Home tab. Each time you indent a paragraph, the item is demoted to a lower level in the outline. Similarly, you can use the Decrease Indent button ▤ to promote an item to a higher level in the outline. You can also create a hierarchical structure in any bulleted or numbered list by using ▤ and ▤ to demote and promote items in the list. To change the multilevel list style applied to a list, select the list, click ▤▾ , and then select a new style.

FIGURE C-18: Numbering list

Numbering list arrow

Choose this numbering style

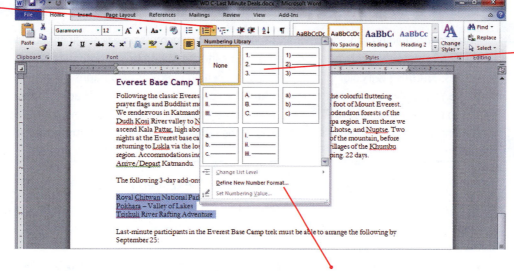

Click to change the style, format, and alignment of the numbers in a list

FIGURE C-19: Numbered list

Bullets button

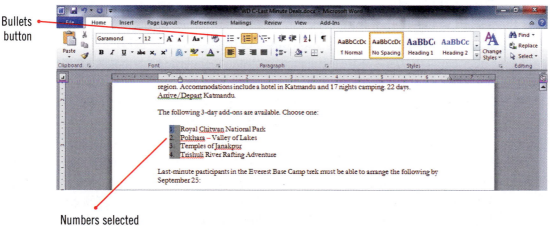

Numbers selected in numbered list

FIGURE C-20: Check mark bullets

Numbers are bold

Check mark bullets applied to list

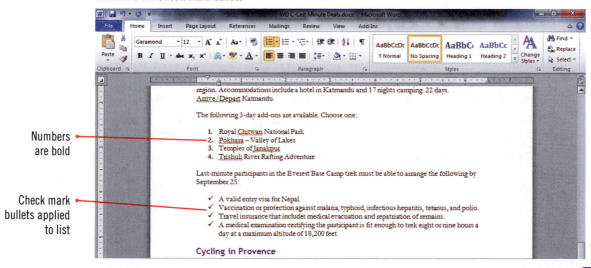

Adding Borders and Shading

Borders and shading can add color and splash to a document. **Borders** are lines you add above, below, to the side, or around words or paragraphs. You can format borders using different line styles, colors, and widths. **Shading** is a color or pattern you apply behind words or paragraphs to make them stand out on a page. You apply borders and shading using the Borders button and the Shading button in the Paragraph group on the Home tab. You enhance the tabbed text of the last minute tours schedule by adding shading to it. You also apply a border around the tabbed text to set it off from the rest of the document.

STEPS

1. **Press [Ctrl][Home], then scroll down until the tabbed text is at the top of your screen**

2. **Select the five paragraphs of tabbed text, click the Shading list arrow 🖍 in the Paragraph group on the Home tab, click the Purple, Accent 4, Lighter 60% color, then deselect the text**

   Light purple shading is applied to the five paragraphs. Notice that the shading is applied to the entire width of the paragraphs, despite the tab settings.

3. **Select the five paragraphs, drag the Left Indent marker 🔲 to the ¾" mark on the horizontal ruler, drag the Right Indent marker 🔺 to the 5¾" mark, then deselect the text**

   The shading for the paragraphs is indented from the left and right, which makes it look more attractive, as shown in Figure C-21.

4. **Select the five paragraphs, click the Bottom Border list arrow ⊞ ▾ in the Paragraph group, click Outside Borders, then deselect the text**

   A black outside border is added around the selected text. The style of the border added is the most recently used border style, in this case the default, a thin black line.

5. **Select the five paragraphs, click the Outside Borders list arrow ⊞ ▾, click No Border, click the No Border list arrow ⊞ ▾, then click Borders and Shading**

   The Borders and Shading dialog box opens, as shown in Figure C-22. You use the Borders tab to change the border style, color, and width, and to add boxes and lines to words or paragraphs.

6. **Click the Box box in the Setting section, scroll down the Style list, click the double-line style, click the Color list arrow, click the Purple, Accent 4, Darker 25% color, click the Width list arrow, click 1½ pt, click OK, then deselect the text**

   A 1½-point dark purple double-line border is added around the tabbed text.

7. **Select the five paragraphs, click the Bold button B in the Font group, click the Font Color list arrow A ▾ in the Font group, click the Purple, Accent 4, Darker 25% color, then deselect the text**

   The text changes to bold dark purple.

8. **Select the first line in the tabbed text, click the launcher 🔲 in the Font group, click the Font tab if it is not the active tab, scroll and click 14 in the Size list, click the Font color list arrow, click the Olive Green, Accent 3, Darker 50% color, click the Small caps check box in the Effects section, click OK, deselect the text, then save your changes**

   The text in the first line of the tabbed text is enlarged and changed to green small caps, as shown in Figure C-23. When you change text to small caps, the lowercase letters are changed to uppercase letters in a smaller font size.

Formatting Text and Paragraphs

FIGURE C-21: Shading applied to the tabbed text

Indent markers show width of the shaded paragraphs

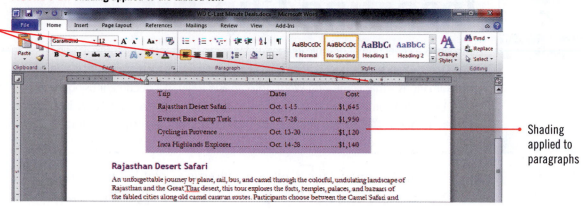

Shading applied to paragraphs

FIGURE C-22: Borders tab in Borders and Shading dialog box

Select border formats before applying them in the Preview area

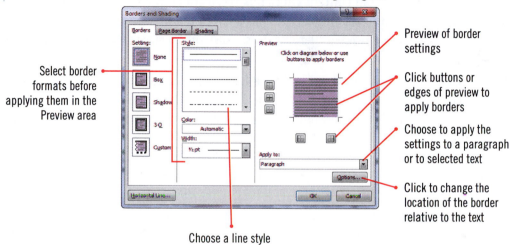

Preview of border settings

Click buttons or edges of preview to apply borders

Choose to apply the settings to a paragraph or to selected text

Click to change the location of the border relative to the text

Choose a line style

FIGURE C-23: Borders and shading applied to the document

Text formatted in green, small caps

Double-line, 1½-point, purple, box border

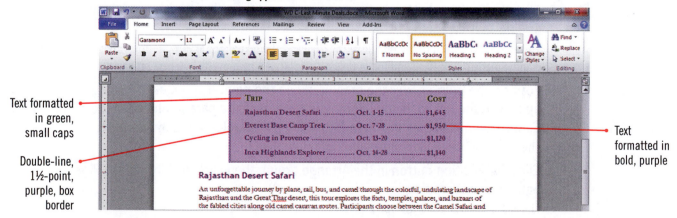

Text formatted in bold, purple

Highlighting text in a document

The Highlight tool allows you to mark and find important text in a document. **Highlighting** is transparent color that is applied to text using the Highlight pointer. To highlight text, click the Text Highlight Color list arrow in the Font group on the Home tab, select a color, then use the I-beam part of the pointer to select the text you want to highlight. Click to turn off the Highlight pointer. To remove highlighting, select the highlighted text, click, then click No Color. Highlighting prints, but it is used most effectively when a document is viewed on screen.

Inserting Clip Art

Clip art is a collection of graphic images that you can insert into a document. Clip art images are stored in the **Clip Organizer**, which is a library of the **clips**—media files such as graphics, photographs, sounds, movies, and animations—that come with Word. You can add a clip to a document using the Clip Art command on the Insert tab. Once you insert a clip art image, you can wrap text around it, resize it, enhance it, and move it to a different location. 🎨 You illustrate the second page of the document with a clip art image.

STEPS

QUICK TIP
You must be working with an active Internet connection to complete this lesson.

1. **Scroll to the top of page 2, place the insertion point before Everest Base Camp Trek, click the Insert tab, then click the Clip Art button in the Illustrations group**
   The Clip Art task pane opens. You can use this task pane to search for clips related to a keyword.

2. **Select the text in the Search for text box if necessary, type Himalayas, make sure the Include Office.com content check box has a check mark, click the Results should be list arrow, make sure All media types has a check mark, then click Go**
   Clips that have the keyword "Himalayas" associated with them appear in the Clip Art task pane, as shown in Figure C-24.

TROUBLE
Select a different clip if the clip shown in Figure C-24 is not available to you. You can also search using the keyword "mountain."

3. **Point to the clip called out in Figure C-24, click the list arrow that appears next to the clip, click Insert on the menu, then close the Clip Art task pane**
   The clip is inserted at the location of the insertion point. When a graphic is selected, the active tab changes to the Picture Tools Format tab. This tab contains commands used to adjust, enhance, arrange, and size graphics. The white circles that appear on the square edges of the graphic are the **sizing handles**.

4. **Type 3.1 in the Shape Height text box in the Size group on the Picture Tools Format tab, then press [Enter]**
   The size of the graphic is reduced. When you decreased the height of the graphic, the width decreased proportionally. You can also resize a graphic proportionally by dragging a corner sizing handle. Now that the graphic is smaller, you can see that it was inserted at the location of the insertion point. Until you apply text wrapping to a graphic, it is part of the line of text in which it was inserted (an **inline graphic**). To move a graphic independently of text, you must make it a **floating graphic**.

QUICK TIP
To position a graphic using precise measurements, click the Position button, click More Layout Options, then adjust the settings on the Position tab in the Layout dialog box.

5. **Click the Position button in the Arrange group, then click Position in Middle Center with Square Text Wrapping**
   The graphic is moved to the middle of the page and the text wraps around it. Applying text wrapping to the graphic made it a floating graphic. A floating graphic can be moved anywhere on a page.

6. **Position the pointer over the graphic, when the pointer changes to ⌖ drag the graphic up and to the left so its top aligns with the top of the paragraph under the Everest Base Camp Trek heading as shown in Figure C-25, then release the mouse button**
   The graphic is moved to the upper-left corner of the page.

7. **Click the Position button in the Arrange group, then click Position in Top Right with Square Text Wrapping**
   The graphic is moved to the upper-right corner of the page.

8. **Click the Picture Effects button in the Picture Styles group, point to Reflection, point to each reflection style to see a preview of the style applied to the graphic, then click Tight Reflection, touching**
   A reflection effect is applied to the graphic.

TROUBLE
If your document is longer than two pages, reduce the size of the clip art graphic by dragging the lower-left corner sizing handle up and to the right.

9. **Click the View tab, then click the Two Pages button**
   The completed document is shown in Figure C-26.

10. **Save your changes, submit the document to your instructor, then close the document and exit Word**

Formatting Text and Paragraphs

FIGURE C-24: Clip Art task pane

Type search keyword here

Select to include content from Office.com

Select type of clips

Select this clip

Clips with the keyword "Himalayas"

Search for clips online

FIGURE C-25: Graphic being moved to a new location

Faded image shows graphic as it is being dragged; position the graphic as shown here

Move pointer

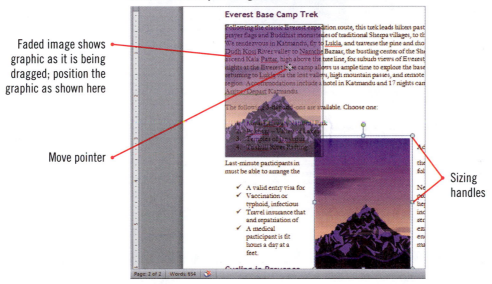

Sizing handles

FIGURE C-26: Completed document

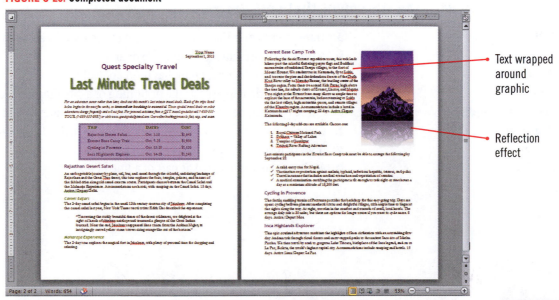

Text wrapped around graphic

Reflection effect

Practice

For current SAM information, including versions and content details, visit SAM Central (http://www.cengage.com/samcentral). If you have a SAM user profile, you may have access to hands-on instruction, practice, and assessment of the skills covered in this unit. Since various versions of SAM are supported throughout the life of this text, check with your instructor for the correct instructions and URL/Web site for accessing assignments.

Concepts Review

Label each element of the Word program window shown in Figure C-27.

FIGURE C-27

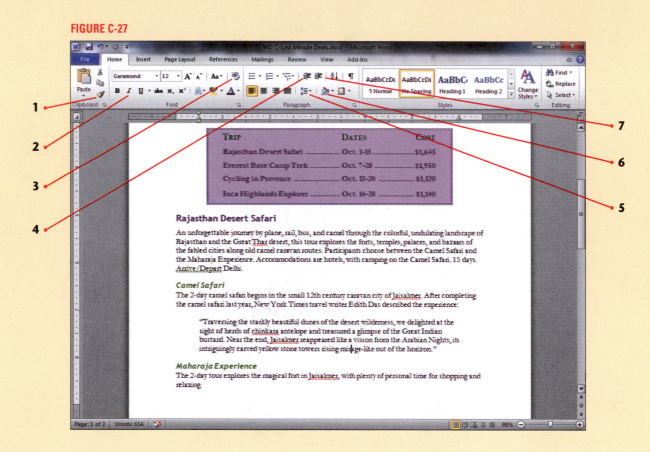

Match each term with the statement that best describes it.

8. **Inline graphic**

9. **Shading**

10. **Point**

11. **Style**

12. **Floating graphic**

13. **Highlight**

14. **Bullet**

15. **Border**

a. Transparent color that is applied to text to mark it in a document

b. A unit of measurement equal to 1/72 of an inch

c. An image that text wrapping has been applied to

d. A character that appears at the beginning of a paragraph to add emphasis

e. A line that can be applied above, below, or to the sides of a paragraph

f. Color or pattern that is applied behind text to make it look attractive

g. A set of format settings

h. An image that is inserted as part of a line of text

Select the best answer from the list of choices.

16. What is Calibri?
- **a.** A character format
- **b.** A style
- **c.** A font
- **d.** A text effect

17. Which type of indent results in subsequent lines of a paragraph being indented more than the first line?
- **a.** Right indent
- **b.** First line indent
- **c.** Negative indent
- **d.** Hanging indent

18. What is the most precise way to increase the amount of white space between two paragraphs?
- **a.** Indent the paragraphs
- **b.** Change the font size
- **c.** Change the before paragraph spacing for the second paragraph
- **d.** Change the line spacing of the paragraphs

19. Which button is used to align a paragraph with both the left and right margins?
- **a.** ☰
- **b.** ☰
- **c.** ☰
- **d.** ☰

20. Which dialog box is used to change the scale of characters?
- **a.** Tabs
- **b.** Font
- **c.** Paragraph
- **d.** Borders and Shading

Skills Review

1. Format with fonts.
- **a.** Start Word, open the file WD C-2.docx from the drive and folder where you store your Data Files, save it as **WD C-Arlington EDA Report**, then scroll through the document to get a feel for its contents.
- **b.** Press [Ctrl][A], then format the text in 12-point Californian FB. Choose a different serif font if Californian FB is not available to you.
- **c.** Press [Ctrl][Home], format the report title **Town of Arlington** in 28-point Berlin Sans FB Demi. Choose a different sans serif font if Berlin Sans FB Demi is not available to you.
- **d.** Change the font color of the report title to Red, Accent 2.
- **e.** Format the subtitle **Economic Development Authority Report Executive Summary** in 16-point Berlin Sans FB Demi, then press [Enter] before Executive in the subtitle.
- **f.** Format the heading **Mission Statement** in 14-point Berlin Sans FB Demi with the Red, Accent 2 font color.
- **g.** Press [Ctrl][Home], then save your changes to the report.

2. Copy formats using the Format Painter.
- **a.** Use the Format Painter to copy the format of the Mission Statement heading to the following headings: **Guiding Principles**, **Issues**, **Proposed Actions**.
- **b.** Show formatting marks, then format the paragraph under the Mission Statement heading in italic.
- **c.** Format **Years Population Growth**, the first line in the four-line list under the Issues heading, in bold, small caps, with Red, Accent 2, Darker 50% font color.
- **d.** Change the font color of the next two lines under Years Population Growth to Red, Accent 2, Darker 50%.
- **e.** Format the line **Source: Office of State Planning** in italic, then save your changes.

3. Change line and paragraph spacing.
- **a.** Change the line spacing of the three-line list under the first body paragraph to 1.5 lines.
- **b.** Add 6 points of space after the title Town of Arlington. Add 18 points of space before and 6 points of space after the Executive Summary line in the subtitle.
- **c.** Add 12 points of space after the Mission Statement heading, then add 12 points of space after each additional heading in the report (Guiding Principles, Issues, Proposed Actions).

    d. Add 6 points of space after each paragraph in the list under the Guiding Principles heading.

    e. Change the line spacing of the four-line list under the Issues heading that begins with Years Population Growth to 1.15.

    f. Add 6 points of space after each paragraph under the Proposed Actions heading.

    g. Press [Ctrl][Home], then save your changes to the report.

4. Align paragraphs.

    a. Press [Ctrl][A] to select the entire document, then justify all the paragraphs.

    b. Center the three-line report title.

    c. Press [Ctrl][End], type your name, press [Enter], type the current date, then right-align your name and the date.

    d. Save your changes to the report.

5. Work with tabs.

    a. Scroll up and select the four-line list of population information under the Issues heading.

    b. Set left tab stops at the 2" mark and the 3¾" mark.

    c. Insert a tab at the beginning of each line in the list.

    d. In the first line, insert a tab before Population. In the second line, insert a tab before 4.5%. In the third line, insert a tab before 53%.

    e. Select the first three lines, then drag the second tab stop to the 3" mark on the horizontal ruler.

    f. Press [Ctrl][Home], then save your changes to the report.

6. Work with indents.

    a. Indent the paragraph under the Mission Statement heading ½" from the left and ½" from the right.

    b. Indent the first line of the paragraph under the Guiding Principles heading ½".

    c. Indent the first line of the three body paragraphs under the Issues heading ½".

    d. Press [Ctrl][Home], then save your changes to the report.

7. Add bullets and numbering.

    a. Apply bullets to the three-line list under the first body paragraph. Change the bullet style to small black circles if that is not the current bullet symbol.

    b. Change the font color of the bullets to Red, Accent 2.

    c. Scroll down until the Guiding Principles heading is at the top of your screen.

    d. Format the six-paragraph list under Guiding Principles as a numbered list.

    e. Format the numbers in 14-point Berlin Sans FB Demi, then change the font color to Red, Accent 2.

    f. Scroll down until the Proposed Actions heading is at the top of your screen, then format the paragraphs under the heading as a bulleted list using check marks as the bullet style.

    g. Change the font color of the bullets to Red, Accent 2, press [Ctrl][Home], then save your changes to the report.

8. Add borders and shading.

    a. Add a 1-point Orange, Accent 6, Darker 25% border below the Mission Statement heading.

    b. Use the Format Painter or the F4 key to add the same border to the other headings in the report (Guiding Principles, Issues, Proposed Actions).

    c. Under the Issues heading, select the first three lines of tabbed text, which are formatted in red, then apply Orange, Accent 6, Lighter 40% shading to the paragraphs.

    d. Select the first three lines of tabbed text again if necessary, then add a 1½ -point Orange, Accent 6, Darker 25% single line box border around the paragraphs.

    e. Indent the shading and border around the paragraphs 1¾" from the left and 1¾" from the right.

    f. Turn off formatting marks, then save your changes.

9. Insert clip art.

    a. Press [Ctrl][Home], then open the Clip Art task pane.

    b. Search for clips related to the keyword **town**.

Skills Review (continued)

c. Insert the clip shown in Figure C-28, then close the Clip Art task pane. (*Note*: An active Internet connection is needed to select the clip shown in the figure. Select a different clip if this one is not available to you. It is best to select a clip that is similar in shape to the clip shown in Figure C-28.)

d. Select the graphic if necessary, then drag the upper-right sizing handle down and to the left so that the graphic is about 3" wide.

e. Use the Position command to position the clip art in the top left with square text wrapping.

f. Use the Shape Width text box in the Size group on the Format tab to change the width of the graphic to 2.2".

g. Apply an Offset Diagonal Bottom Right shadow style to the graphic.

h. Save your changes to the document, submit it to your instructor, close the file, and then exit Word.

FIGURE C-28

Town of Arlington
Economic Development Authority Report

Executive Summary

The Town of Arlington Economic Development Authority (EDA) has written an economic policy plan for the Town of Arlington. The plan is intended to advance dynamic and interactive discussion. It will be used to continuously assess and foster decision-making about the following in the Town of Arlington:

- Development
- Infrastructure
- Quality of life

Mission Statement

The purpose of the EDA is to foster a sustainable economy consistent with the town's planning objectives. The mix of industry, commerce, open space, residential development, and the arts in Arlington results in the town's vitality and an excellent quality of life for its citizens. Maintaining this balance is important.

Guiding Principles

Six basic principles guide Arlington's economic policy. These principles seek to safeguard the special features that give the town its character while embracing appropriate economic opportunities.

1. Arlington should remain a major economic center of the region.
2. Economic activity must respect Arlington's natural, cultural, and historic heritage.
3. A pedestrian-friendly core commercial center is essential.
4. Sustained economic prosperity requires a balance between residential development, industrial/commercial development, and open space.
5. Open space in the rural district must be preserved.
6. Investing in the infrastructure is necessary to maintain and expand the existing tax and job base.

Issues

Of Arlington's approximately 64,000 acres of land, 12% is zoned for business, commercial, or industrial use, and 88% for residential development. Historically the town has relied upon business and industry to provide 35%-40% of the tax base, as well as employment opportunities. Non-residential development has traditionally been the backbone of the Arlington economy. Today, however, Arlington does not have a great deal of non-residential development potential.

The population of Arlington is expected to rise dramatically over the next few decades. The following chart shows the expected change:

Years	Population Growth
1990-2010	4.5%
2010-2030	53% (projected)

Source: *Office of State Planning*

At issue is the town's ability to continue to support increasing public costs (most importantly, education) with a tax base shifting toward residential taxpayers. The EDA believes Arlington should remain the market center of the region and avoid becoming a bedroom community. Arlington has maintained a sense of community in part because more than 50% of working residents are able to earn a living within the town. Jobs must be continuously created to sustain the percentage of residents who live and work in Arlington.

Proposed Actions

- ✓ Implement a business retention program that focuses on the growth and expansion of businesses already operating in Arlington.
- ✓ Build a consortium of technical and skill development resources to assist companies with educational and training needs.
- ✓ Sponsor a green business workshop.
- ✓ Allocate funds for expanded downtown parking.
- ✓ Develop a strategic open space plan.

Your Name
Today's Date

Independent Challenge 1

You are an estimator for GreenHome Construction in Springfield, Illinois. You have drafted an estimate for a home renovation job, and need to format it. It's important that your estimate have a clean, striking design, and reflect your company's professionalism.

a. Start Word, open the file WD C-3.docx from the drive and folder where you store your Data Files, save it as **WD C-GreenHome Construction**, then read the document to get a feel for its contents. Figure C-29 shows how you will format the letterhead.

FIGURE C-29

b. Select the entire document, change the style to No Spacing, then change the font to 12-point Times New Roman.

c. In the first line of the letterhead, format **Green Home** in 30-point Arial Black, then apply all caps. Format **Green** with the Olive Green, Accent 3, Darker 50% font color, format **Home** with the Olive Green, Accent 3 font color, then delete the space between the two words. Format **Construction** in 30-point Arial with an Olive Green, Accent 3, Darker 50% font color, then apply italic. (*Hint*: Type 30 in the Font Size text box, then press [Enter].)

d. Format the next line in 10-point Arial with an Olive Green, Accent 3, Darker 50% font color.

e. Center the two-line letterhead.

f. Add a 2¼-point dotted Olive Green, Accent 3, Darker 50% border below the address line paragraph.

g. With the insertion point in the address line, open the Borders and Shading dialog box, click Options to open the Border and Shading Options dialog box, change the Bottom setting to **5** points, then click OK twice to adjust the location of the border relative to the line of text.

h. Format the title **Proposal of Renovation** in 14-point Arial Black, then center the title.

i. Format the following headings (including the colons) in 11-point Arial Black: **Date**, **Work to be performed for and at**, **Scope of work**, **Payment schedule**, and **Agreement**.

j. Select the 14-line list under **Scope of work** that begins with **Demo of all...**, then change the paragraph spacing to add 4 points of space after each paragraph in the list. (*Hint*: Select 0 pt in the After text box, type 4, then press Enter.)

k. With the list selected, set a right tab stop at the 6¼" mark, insert tabs before every price in the list, then apply dotted line tab leaders.

l. Format the list as a numbered list, then apply bold to the numbers.

m. Apply bold to the two lines, **Total estimated job cost...** and **Approximate job time...** below the list.

n. Replace Your Name with your name in the signature block, select the signature block (Respectfully submitted through your name), set a left tab stop at the 3¼" mark, then indent the signature block using tabs.

o. Examine the document carefully for formatting errors, and make any necessary adjustments.

p. Save the document, submit it to your instructor, then close the file and exit Word.

Independent Challenge 2

Your employer, the Lange Center for Contemporary Arts in Halifax, Nova Scotia, is launching a membership drive. Your boss has written the text for a flyer advertising Lange membership, and asks you to format it so that it is eye catching and attractive.

a. Open the file WD C-4.docx from the drive and folder where you store your Data Files, save it as **WD C-Membership Drive 2013**, then read the document. Figure C-30 shows how you will format the first several paragraphs of the flyer.

FIGURE C-30

b. Select the entire document, change the style to No Spacing, then change the font to 11-point Arial Narrow.

c. Center the first line, **Membership Drive**, and apply shading to the paragraph. Choose a dark custom shading color of your choice for the shading color. (*Hint*: Click More Colors, then select a color from the Standard or Custom tab.) Format the text in 26-point Arial Narrow, bold, with a white font color. Expand the character spacing by 10 points. (*Hint*: Use the Advanced tab in the Font dialog box. Set the Spacing to Expanded, and then type **10** in the By text box.)

d. Format the second line, **2013**, in 36-point Arial Black. Expand the character spacing by 25 points, and change the character scale to 250%. Center the line.

e. Format each **What we do for...** heading in 12-point Arial, bold. Change the font color to the same custom color used for shading the title. (*Note*: The color now appears in the Recent Colors section of the Font Color gallery.) Add a single-line ½-point black border under each heading.

f. Format each subheading (**Gallery**, **Lectures**, **Library**, **All members...**, and **Membership Levels**) in 10-point Arial, bold. Add 3 points of spacing before each paragraph. (*Hint*: Select 0 in the Before text box, type 3, then press Enter.)

g. Indent each body paragraph ¼", except for the lines under the **What we do for YOU** heading.

h. Format the four lines under the **All members...** subheading as a bulleted list. Use a bullet symbol of your choice, and format the bullets in the custom font color.

i. Indent the five lines under the **Membership Levels** heading ¼". For these five lines, set left tab stops at the 1¼" mark and the 2" mark on the horizontal ruler. Insert tabs before the price and before the word All in each of the five lines.

j. Format the name of each membership level (**Artistic**, **Conceptual**, etc.) in 10-point Arial, bold, italic, with the custom font color.

k. Format the **For more information** heading in 14-point Arial, bold, with the custom font color, then center the heading.

l. Center the last two lines, replace Your Name with your name, then apply bold to your name.

Advanced Challenge Exercise

- Change the font color of **2013** to a dark gray, and add a shadow effect.
- Add a shadow effect to each **What we do for...** heading.
- Add a 3-point dotted black border above the **For more information** heading.

m. Examine the document carefully for formatting errors, and make any necessary adjustments.

n. Save the flyer, submit it to your instructor, then close the file and exit Word.

Independent Challenge 3

One of your responsibilities as program coordinator at Solstice Mountain Sports is to develop a program of winter outdoor learning and adventure workshops. You have drafted a memo to your boss to update her on your progress. You need to format the memo so it is professional looking and easy to read.

a. Start Word, open the file WD C-5.docx from the drive and folder where you store your Data Files, then save it as **WD C-Solstice Winter Memo**.

b. Select the heading **Solstice Mountain Sports Memorandum**, apply the Quick Style Title to it, then center the heading. (*Hint*: Open the Quick Style gallery, then click the Title style.)

c. In the memo header, replace Today's Date and Your Name with the current date and your name.

d. Select the four-line memo header, set a left tab stop at the ¾" mark, then insert tabs before the date, the recipient's name, your name, and the subject of the memo.

e. Apply the Quick Style Strong to **Date:**, **To:**, **From:**, and **Re:**.

f. Apply the Quick Style Heading 2 to the headings **Overview**, **Workshops**, **Accommodations**, **Fees**, and **Proposed winter programming**.

g. Under the Fees heading, apply the Quick Style Emphasis to the words **Workshop fees** and **Accommodations fees**.

h. Add a clip art graphic of a snowflake to the first page, wrap text around the graphic, then resize it and position it so it fits into the memo header below the title and aligns with the right margin.

i. On the second page of the document, format the list under the **Proposed winter programming** heading as a multilevel list. Figure C-31 shows the hierarchical structure of the outline. (*Hint*: Apply a multilevel list style, then use the Increase Indent and Decrease Indent buttons to change the level of importance of each item.)

j. Change the outline numbering style to the bullet numbering style shown in Figure C-31 if a different style is used in your outline.

k. Add a clip art graphic of a snowboarder or skier to page 2. Select a graphic that fits the tone of the document. Wrap text around the graphic, then resize it and position it so it aligns with the right margin.

Advanced Challenge Exercise

- Zoom out on the memo so that two pages are displayed in the document window, then, using the Change Styles button, change the style set to Modern.
- Using the Change Case button, change the title Solstice Mountain Sports Memorandum so that only the initial letter of each word is capitalized. Resize and reposition the clip art as needed so that it fits in the memo header and the title still fits on one line.
- Using the Themes button, change the theme applied to the document. Select a theme that works with the clip art graphics you chose.
- Using the Theme Fonts button, change the fonts to a font set of your choice. Choose fonts that allow the document to fit on two pages.
- Using the Theme Colors button, change the colors to a color palette of your choice.
- Apply different styles and adjust other formatting elements as necessary to make the memo attractive, eye catching, and readable. The finished memo should fit on two pages.

l. Save the document, submit it to your instructor, then close the file and exit Word.

FIGURE C-31

Proposed winter programming
- ❖ Skiing, Snowboarding, and Snowshoeing
  - ➢ Skiing and Snowboarding
    - ▪ Cross-country skiing
      - • Cross-country skiing for beginners
      - • Intermediate cross-country skiing
      - • Inn-to-inn ski touring
      - • Moonlight cross-country skiing
    - ▪ Telemarking
      - • Basic telemark skiing
      - • Introduction to backcountry skiing
      - • Exploring on skis
    - ▪ Snowboarding
      - • Backcountry snowboarding
  - ➢ Snowshoeing
    - ▪ Beginner
      - • Snowshoeing for beginners
      - • Snowshoeing and winter ecology
    - ▪ Intermediate and Advanced
      - • Intermediate snowshoeing
      - • Guided snowshoe trek
      - • Above tree line snowshoeing
- ❖ Winter Hiking, Camping, and Survival
  - ➢ Hiking
    - ▪ Beginner
      - • Long-distance hiking
      - • Winter summits
      - • Hiking for women
  - ➢ Winter camping and survival
    - ▪ Beginner
      - • Introduction to winter camping
      - • Basic winter mountain skills
      - • Building snow shelters
    - ▪ Intermediate
      - • Basic winter mountain skills II
      - • Ice climbing
      - • Avalanche awareness and rescue

Real Life Independent Challenge

The fonts you choose for a document can have a major effect on the document's tone. Not all fonts are appropriate for use in a business document, and some fonts, especially those with a definite theme, are appropriate only for specific purposes. In this Independent Challenge, you will use font formatting and other formatting features to design a letterhead and a fax coversheet for yourself or your business. The letterhead and coversheet should not only look professional and attract interest, but also say something about the character of your business or your personality. Figure C-32 shows an example of a business letterhead.

a. Start Word, and save a new blank document as **WD C-Personal Letterhead** to the drive and folder where you store your Data Files.

b. Type your name or the name of your business, your address, your phone number, your fax number, and your Web site or e-mail address.

c. Format your name or the name of your business in a font that expresses your personality or says something about the nature of your business. Use fonts, font colors, font effects, borders, shading, paragraph formatting, and other formatting features to design a letterhead that is appealing and professional.

d. Save your changes, submit the document to your instructor, then close the file.

e. Open a new blank document, and save it as **WD C-Personal Fax Coversheet**. Type FAX, your name or the name of your business, your address, your phone number, your fax number, and your Web site or e-mail address at the top of the document.

f. Type a fax header that includes the following: Date; To; From; Re; Number of pages, including cover sheet; and Comments.

g. Format the information in the fax coversheet using fonts, font effects, borders, shading, paragraph formatting, and other formatting features. Since a fax coversheet is designed to be faxed, all fonts and other formatting elements should be black.

h. Save your changes, submit the document to your instructor, close the file, then exit Word.

FIGURE C-32

Isabella Rodríguez Graphic Design

167 East 12th Street, 4th floor, New York, NY 10003   Tel: 212-555-9767   Fax: 212-555-2992   www.irodriguez.com

Visual Workshop

Open the file WD C-6.docx from the drive and folder where you store your Data Files. Create the menu shown in Figure C-33. (*Hints*: Find the clip art graphic using the keyword **diner**, then use the sizing handles to resize the graphic to be approximately 1.5" tall and 4.4" wide. Choose a different appropriate clip art graphic if the graphic shown in the figure is not available. Use Berlin Sans FB Demi and Calibri, or similar fonts, for the text. Change the font size of the café name to 28 points, the font size of Daily Specials to 18 points, the font size of the days to 14 points, and the font size of the descriptions to 12 points. Format the prices using tabs and leader lines. Use paragraph spacing to adjust the spacing between paragraphs so that all the text fits on one page. Make other adjustments as needed so your menu is similar to the one shown in Figure C-33.) Save the menu as **WD C-Nina's Trackside**, then submit a copy to your instructor.

FIGURE C-33

Nina's Trackside Café

Daily Specials

Monday
Chicken Cajun Bleu: Cajun chicken, chunky blue cheese, cucumbers, leaf lettuce, and tomato on our roasted garlic roll. $6.50

Tuesday
Clam Chowder: Classic New England thick, rich, clam chowder in our peasant French bread bowl. Served with a garden salad. $5.95

Wednesday
Veggie Chili: Hearty veggie chili with melted cheddar in our peasant French bread bowl. Topped with sour cream and scallions. $5.95

Thursday
French Dip: Lean roast beef topped with melted cheddar on our roasted garlic roll. Served with a side of au jus and red bliss mashed potatoes. $6.95

Friday
Turkey-Bacon Club: Double-decker roasted turkey, crisp bacon, leaf lettuce, tomato, and sun-dried tomato mayo on toasted triple seed.. $6.50

Saturday
Greek Salad: Our large garden salad with Kalamata olives, feta cheese, and garlic vinaigrette. Served with an assortment of rolls. $5.95

Sunday
Hot Chicken and Gravy: Delicious chicken and savory gravy served on a thick slice of toasted honest white. Served with a garden salad. $6.95

Chef: Your Name

Formatting Documents

The page-formatting features of Word allow you to lay out and design documents of all types, including reports, brochures, newsletters, and research documents. In this unit, you learn how to change the document margins, add page numbers, insert headers and footers, and format text in columns. You also learn how to work with the Word reference features to add footnotes, insert citations, and create a bibliography.  You have written and formatted the text for an informational report for QST clients about staying healthy while traveling. You are now ready to format the pages. You plan to organize the text in columns, to illustrate the report with a table, and to add footnotes and a bibliography.

OBJECTIVES

Set document margins

Create sections and columns

Insert page breaks

Insert page numbers

Add headers and footers

Insert a table

Add footnotes and endnotes

Insert citations

Manage sources and create a bibliography

Setting Document Margins

Changing a document's margins is one way to change the appearance of a document and control the amount of text that fits on a page. The **margins** of a document are the blank areas between the edge of the text and the edge of the page. When you create a document in Word, the default margins are 1" at the top, bottom, left, and right sides of the page. You can adjust the size of a document's margins using the Margins command on the Page Layout tab or using the rulers. 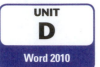 The report should be a four-page document when finished. You begin by reducing the size of the document margins so that more text fits on each page.

STEPS

1. **Start Word, open the file WD D-1.docx from the drive and folder where you store your Data Files, then save it as WD D-Healthy Traveler**

   The report opens in Print Layout view.

2. **Scroll through the report to get a feel for its contents, then press [Ctrl][Home]**

   The report is currently five pages long. Notice that the status bar indicates the page where the insertion point is located and the total number of pages in the document.

3. **Click the Page Layout tab, then click the Margins button in the Page Setup group**

   The Margins menu opens. You can select predefined margin settings from this menu, or you can click Custom Margins to create different margin settings.

4. **Click Custom Margins**

   The Page Setup dialog box opens with the Margins tab displayed, as shown in Figure D-1. You can use the Margins tab to change the top, bottom, left, or right document margin, to change the orientation of the pages from portrait to landscape, and to alter other page layout settings. **Portrait orientation** means a page is taller than it is wide; **landscape orientation** means a page is wider than it is tall. This report uses portrait orientation. You can also use the Orientation button in the Page Setup group on the Page Layout tab to change the orientation of a document.

5. **Click the Top down arrow three times until 0.7" appears, then click the Bottom down arrow until 0.7" appears**

   The top and bottom margins of the report will be .7". Notice that the margins in the Preview section of the dialog box change as you adjust the margin settings.

6. **Press [Tab], type .7 in the Left text box, press [Tab], then type .7 in the Right text box**

   The left and right margins of the report will also be .7". You can change the margin settings by using the arrows or by typing a value in the appropriate text box.

7. **Click OK**

   The document margins change to .7", as shown in Figure D-2. The location of each margin (right, left, top, and bottom) is shown on the horizontal and vertical rulers at the intersection of the white and shaded areas. You can also change a margin setting by using the pointer to drag the intersection to a new location on the ruler.

8. **Click the View tab, then click the Two Pages button in the Zoom group**

   The first two pages of the document appear in the document window.

9. **Scroll down to view all five pages of the report, press [Ctrl][Home], click the Page Width button in the Zoom group, then save your changes**

FIGURE D-1: Margins tab in Page Setup dialog box

Default margin settings

Set gutter margin

Select page orientation

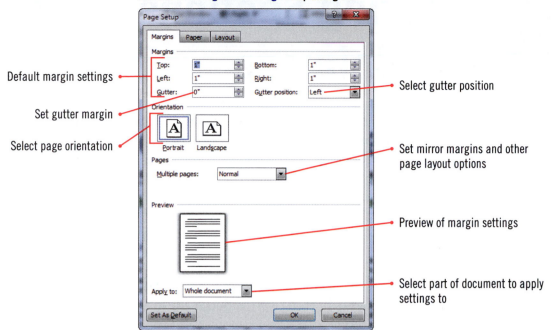

Select gutter position

Set mirror margins and other page layout options

Preview of margin settings

Select part of document to apply settings to

FIGURE D-2: Report with smaller margins

Ruler shows location of left margin

Ruler shows location of top margin

Document is five pages long

Page 1 is the active page

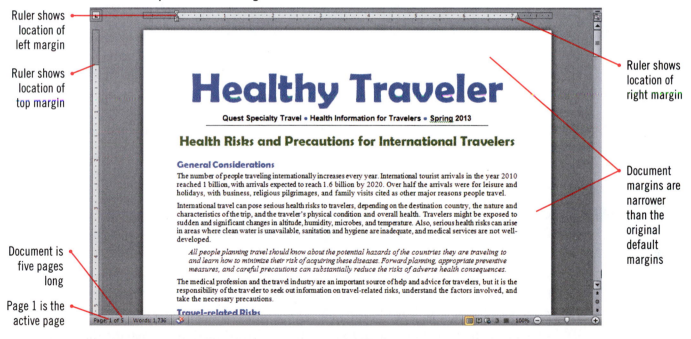

Ruler shows location of right margin

Document margins are narrower than the original default margins

Changing orientation, margin settings, and paper size

By default, the documents you create in Word use an 8½" × 11" paper size in portrait orientation with the default margin settings. You can change the orientation, margin settings, and paper size to common settings using the Orientation, Margins, and Size buttons in the Page Setup group on the Page Layout tab. You can also adjust these settings and others in the Page Setup dialog box. For example, to change the layout of multiple pages, use the Multiple pages list arrow on the Margins tab to create pages that use mirror margins, that include two pages per sheet of paper, or that are formatted using a book fold. **Mirror margins** are used in a document with facing pages, such as a magazine, where the margins on the left page of the document are a mirror image of the margins on the right page. Documents with mirror margins have inside and outside margins, rather than right and left margins. Another type of margin is a gutter margin, which is used in documents that are bound, such as books. A **gutter** adds extra space to the left, top, or inside margin to allow for the binding. Add a gutter to a document by adjusting the setting in the Gutter position text box on the Margins tab. To change the size of the paper used, use the Paper size list arrow on the Paper tab to select a standard paper size, or enter custom measurements in the Width and Height text boxes.

Creating Sections and Columns

Dividing a document into sections allows you to format each section of the document with different page layout settings. A **section** is a portion of a document that is separated from the rest of the document by section breaks. **Section breaks** are formatting marks that you insert in a document to show the end of a section. Once you have divided a document into sections, you can format each section with different column, margin, page orientation, header and footer, and other page layout settings. By default, a document is formatted as a single section, but you can divide a document into as many sections as you like.  You insert a section break to divide the document into two sections, and then format the text in the second section in two columns. First, you customize the status bar to display section information.

STEPS

1. **Right-click the status bar, click Section on the Customize Status Bar menu that opens (if it is not already checked), then click the document to close the menu**
   The status bar indicates the insertion point is located in section 1 of the document.

2. **Click the Home tab, then click the Show/Hide ¶ button ¶ in the Paragraph group**
   Turning on formatting marks allows you to see the section breaks you insert in a document.

3. **Place the insertion point before the heading General Considerations, click the Page Layout tab, then click the Breaks button in the Page Setup group**
   The Breaks menu opens. You use this menu to insert different types of section breaks. See Table D-1.

4. **Click Continuous**
   Word inserts a continuous section break, shown as a dotted double line, above the heading. The document now has two sections. Notice that the status bar indicates the insertion point is in section 2.

5. **Click the Columns button in the Page Setup group**
   The columns menu opens. You use this menu to format text using preset column formats or to create custom columns.

6. **Click More Columns to open the Columns dialog box**

7. **Select Two in the Presets section, click the Spacing down arrow twice until 0.3" appears as shown in Figure D-3, then click OK**
   Section 2 is formatted in two columns of equal width with .3" of spacing between, as shown in Figure D-4. Formatting text in columns is another way to increase the amount of text that fits on a page.

8. **Click the View tab, click the Two Pages button in the Zoom group, scroll down to examine all four pages of the document, press [Ctrl][Home], then save the document**
   The text in section 2—all the text below the continuous section break—is formatted in two columns. Text in columns flows automatically from the bottom of one column to the top of the next column.

TABLE D-1: Types of section breaks

section	function
Next page	Begins a new section and moves the text following the break to the top of the next page
Continuous	Begins a new section on the same page
Even page	Begins a new section and moves the text following the break to the top of the next even-numbered page
Odd page	Begins a new section and moves the text following the break to the top of the next odd-numbered page

FIGURE D-3: Columns dialog box

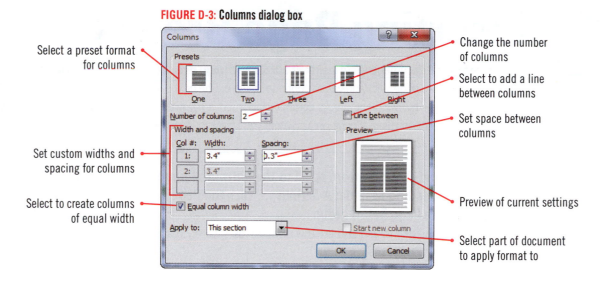

Select a preset format for columns

Change the number of columns

Select to add a line between columns

Set space between columns

Set custom widths and spacing for columns

Preview of current settings

Select to create columns of equal width

Select part of document to apply format to

FIGURE D-4: Continuous section break and columns

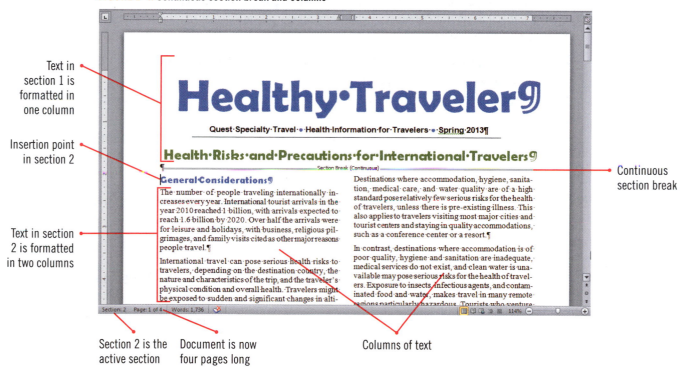

Text in section 1 is formatted in one column

Insertion point in section 2

Text in section 2 is formatted in two columns

Continuous section break

Columns of text

Section 2 is the active section

Document is now four pages long

Changing page layout settings for a section

Dividing a document into sections allows you to vary the layout of a document. In addition to applying different column settings to sections, you can apply different margins, page orientation, paper size, vertical alignment, header and footer, page numbering, footnotes, endnotes, and other page layout settings. For example, if you are formatting a report that includes a table with many columns, you might want to change the table's page orientation to landscape so that it is easier to read. To do this, you would insert a section break before and after the table to create a section that contains only the table, and then you would change the page orientation of the section that contains the table to landscape. If the table does not fill the page, you could also change the vertical alignment of the table

so that it is centered vertically on the page. To do this, use the Vertical alignment list arrow on the Layout tab of the Page Setup dialog box.

To check or change the page layout settings for an individual section, place the insertion point in the section, then open the Page Setup dialog box. Select any options you want to change, click the Apply to list arrow, click This section, then click OK. When you select This section in the Apply to list box, the settings are applied to the current section only. If you select Whole document in the Apply to list box, the settings are applied to all the sections in the document. Use the Apply to list arrow in the Columns dialog box or the Footnote and Endnote dialog box to change those settings for a section.

Formatting Documents

Word 81

Word 2010

Inserting Page Breaks

As you type text in a document, Word inserts an **automatic page break** (also called a soft page break) when you reach the bottom of a page, allowing you to continue typing on the next page. You can also force text onto the next page of a document by using the Breaks command to insert a **manual page break** (also called a hard page break). 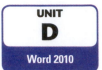 You insert manual page breaks where you know you want to begin each new page of the report.

STEPS

1. **Click the Page Width button, scroll to the bottom of page 1, place the insertion point before the heading Malaria: A Serious ..., click the Page Layout tab, then click the Breaks button in the Page Setup group**

   The Breaks menu opens. You also use this menu to insert page, column, and text-wrapping breaks. Table D-2 describes these types of breaks.

QUICK TIP
To control the flow of text between columns, insert a column break to force the text after the break to the top of the next column.

2. **Click Page**

   Word inserts a manual page break before "Malaria: A Serious Health Risk for Travelers" and moves all the text following the page break to the beginning of the next page, as shown in Figure D-5. The page break appears as a dotted line in Print Layout view when formatting marks are displayed. Page break marks are visible on the screen but do not print.

3. **Scroll down, place the insertion point before the heading Preventive Options... on page 2, press and hold [Ctrl], then press [Enter]**

   Pressing [Ctrl][Enter] is a fast way to insert a manual page break. The heading is forced to the top of the third page.

QUICK TIP
You can also double-click a page break to select it, and then press [Delete] to delete it. You know the page break is selected when both the words and the paragraph mark at the end of the page break are selected.

4. **Scroll to the bottom of page 3, place the insertion point before the heading Insurance for Travelers on page 3, then press [Ctrl][Enter]**

   The heading is forced to the top of the fourth page.

5. **Scroll up, click to the left of the page break on page 2 with the selection pointer ⬔ to select the page break, then press [Delete]**

   The manual page break is deleted and the text from pages 2 and 3 flows together. You can also use the selection pointer to click to the left of a section or a column break to select it.

QUICK TIP
You can balance columns of unequal length on a page by inserting a continuous section break at the end of the last column on the page.

6. **Place the insertion point before the heading Medical Kit.... on page 2, then press [Ctrl][Enter]**

   The heading is forced to the top of the third page.

7. **Click the View tab, click the Two Pages button in the Zoom group, scroll to view all four pages of the document, then save your changes**

   Pages 3 and 4 are shown in Figure D-6.

Controlling automatic pagination

Another way to control the flow of text between pages (or between columns) is to apply pagination settings to specify where Word positions automatic page breaks. For example, you might want to make sure an article appears on the same page as its heading, or you might want to prevent a page from breaking in the middle of the last paragraph of a report. To manipulate automatic pagination, simply select the paragraphs(s) or line(s) you want to control, click the launcher in the Paragraph group on the Home or Page Layout tab, click the Line and Page Breaks tab in the Paragraph dialog box, select one or more of the following settings in the Pagination section, and then click OK. Pagination settings include the following:

- Keep with next setting—apply to any paragraph you want to appear together with the next paragraph on a single page in

order to prevent the page from breaking between the paragraphs.

- Keep lines together setting—apply to selected paragraph or lines to prevent a page from breaking in the middle of a paragraph or between certain lines.
- Page break before setting—apply to specify that a selected paragraph follows an automatic page break.
- Widow/Orphan control setting—turned on by default in the Pagination section of the dialog box. This setting ensures that at least two lines of a paragraph appear at the top and bottom of every page. In other words, it prevents a page from beginning with just the last line of a paragraph (a **widow**), and prevents a page from ending with only the first line of a new paragraph (an **orphan**).

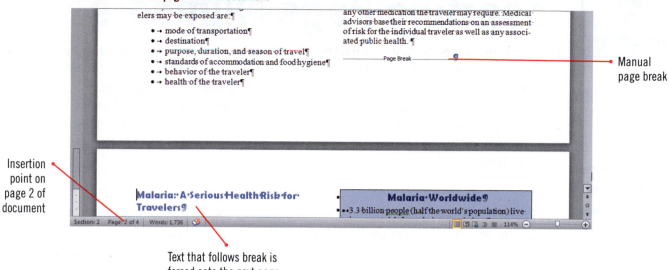

Manual page break

Insertion point on page 2 of document

Text that follows break is forced onto the next page

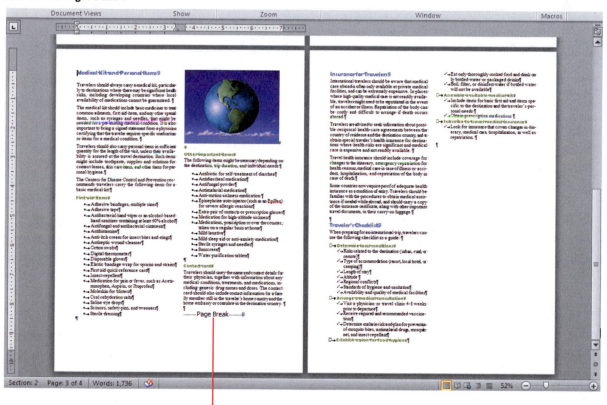

Manual page break

TABLE D-2: Types of breaks

break	function
Page	Forces the text following the break to begin at the top of the next page
Column	Forces the text following the break to begin at the top of the next column
Text Wrapping	Forces the text following the break to begin at the beginning of the next line

Inserting Page Numbers

If you want to number the pages of a multiple-page document, you can insert a page number field to add a page number to each page. A **field** is a code that serves as a placeholder for data that changes in a document, such as a page number or the current date. When you use the Page Number button on the Insert tab to add page numbers to a document, you insert the page number field at the top, bottom, or side of any page, and Word automatically numbers all the pages in the document for you. 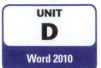 You insert a page number field so that page numbers will appear centered between the margins at the bottom of each page in the document.

STEPS

QUICK TIP

Point to Current Position to insert a page number field at the location of the insertion point.

1. **Press [Ctrl][Home], click the** Page Width button **in the Zoom group on the View tab, click the** Insert tab, **then click the** Page Number button **in the Header & Footer group**

   The Page Number menu opens. You use this menu to select the position for the page numbers. If you choose to add a page number field to the top, bottom, or side of a document, a page number will appear on every page in the document. If you choose to insert it in the document at the location of the insertion point, the field will appear on that page only.

2. **Point to** Bottom of Page

   A gallery of formatting and alignment options for page numbers to be inserted at the bottom of a page opens, as shown in Figure D-7.

QUICK TIP

To change the location or formatting of page numbers, click the Page Number button, point to a page number location, then select a format from the gallery.

3. **Scroll down the gallery to view the options, scroll to the top of the gallery, then click** Plain Number 2 **in the Simple section**

   A page number field containing the number 1 is centered in the Footer area at the bottom of page 1 of the document, as shown in Figure D-8. The document text is gray, or dimmed, because the Footer area is open. Text that is inserted in a Footer area appears at the bottom of every page in a document.

4. **Double-click the** document text, **then scroll to the bottom of page 1**

   Double-clicking the document text closes the Footer area. The page number is now dimmed because it is located in the Footer area, which is no longer the active area. When the document is printed, the page numbers appear as normal text. You will learn more about working with the Footer area in the next lesson.

5. **Scroll down the document to see the page number at the bottom of each page**

   Word numbered each page of the report automatically, and each page number is centered at the bottom of the page. If you want to change the numbering format or start page numbering with a different number, you can simply click the Page Number button, click Format Page Numbers, and then choose from the options in the Page Number Format dialog box.

QUICK TIP

To remove page numbers from a document, click the Page Number button, then click Remove Page Numbers.

6. **Press [Ctrl][Home], then save the document**

Moving around in a long document

Rather than scrolling to move to a different place in a long document, you can use the Browse by Object feature to move the insertion point to a specific location quickly. Browse by Object allows you to browse to the next or previous page, section, line, table, graphic, or other item of the same type in a document. To do this, first click the Select Browse Object button ◎ below the vertical scroll bar to open a palette of object types. On this palette, click the button for the type of item you want to browse through, and then click the Next ▼ or Previous ▲ buttons to scroll through the items of that type in the document.

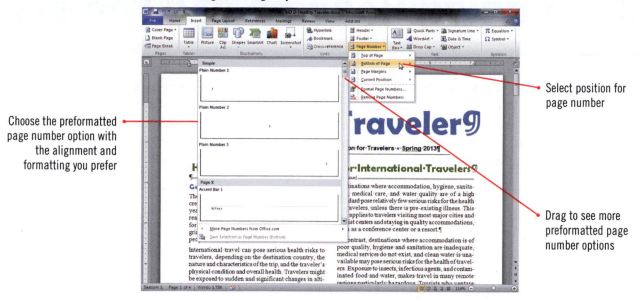

Choose the preformatted page number option with the alignment and formatting you prefer

Select position for page number

Drag to see more preformatted page number options

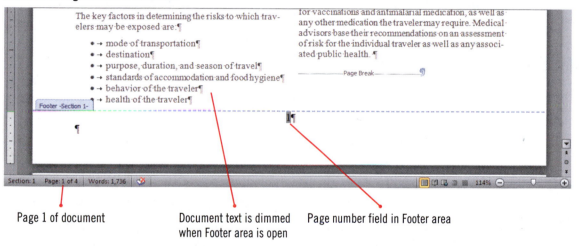

Page 1 of document

Document text is dimmed when Footer area is open

Page number field in Footer area

Inserting Quick Parts

The Word Quick Parts feature makes it easy to insert reusable pieces of content into a document quickly. The **Quick Parts** items you can insert include fields, such as for the current date or the total number of pages in a document; document property information, such as the author and title of a document; and building blocks, which are customized content that you create, format, and save for future use.

To insert a Quick Part into a document at the location of the insertion point, click the Quick Parts button in the Text group on the Insert tab (or, if headers and footers are open, click the Quick Parts button in the Insert group on the Header & Footer Tools Design tab), and then select the type of Quick Part you want to insert. To insert a field into a document, click Field on the Quick Parts menu that opens, click the name of the field you want to insert in the Field dialog box, and then click OK. Field information is updated automatically each time the document is opened or saved.

To insert a document property, point to Document Property on the Quick Parts menu, and then click the property you want to insert. The property is added to the document as a content control and contains the document property information you entered in the Document panel. If you did not assign a document property, the content control contains a placeholder, which you can replace with your own text. Once you replace the placeholder text—or edit the document property information that appears in the content control—this text replaces the document property information in the Document panel.

To insert a building block, click Building Blocks Organizer on the Quick Parts menu, select the building block you want, and then click Insert. You will learn more about working with building blocks in later lessons.

Adding Headers and Footers

A **header** is text or graphics that appears at the top of every page of a document. A **footer** is text or graphics that appears at the bottom of every page. In longer documents, headers and footers often contain the title of the publication or chapter, the name of the author, or a page number. You can add headers and footers to a document by double-clicking the top or bottom margin of a document to open the Header and Footer areas, and then inserting text and graphics into them. You can also use the Header or Footer command on the Insert tab to insert predesigned headers and footers that you can modify to include your information. 🎨 You create a header that includes the name of the report.

STEPS

QUICK TIP

Unless you set different headers and footers for different sections, the information you insert in any Header or Footer area appears on every page in the document.

1. **Click the Insert tab, then click the Header button in the Header & Footer group**

   A gallery of built-in header designs opens.

2. **Scroll down the gallery to view the header designs, scroll to the top of the gallery, then click Blank**

   The Header and Footer areas open, and the document text is dimmed. When the document text is dimmed, it cannot be edited. The Header & Footer Tools Design tab also opens and is the active tab, as shown in Figure D-9. This tab is available whenever the Header and Footer areas are open.

3. **Type Healthy Traveler: Travel and Health Information from Quest Specialty Travel in the content control in the Header area**

   This text will appear at the top of every page in the document.

QUICK TIP

You can also use the Insert Alignment Tab button in the Position group to left-, center-, and right-align text in the Header and Footer areas.

4. **Select the header text, click the Home tab, click the Font list arrow in the Font group, click Berlin Sans FB Demi, click the Font Color list arrow 🅰▾, click Olive Green, Accent 3, Darker 25%, click the Center button ▦ in the Paragraph group, click the Bottom Border button ▥, then click in the Header area to deselect the text**

   The text is formatted in olive green Berlin Sans FB Demi and centered in the Header area with a bottom border.

5. **Click the Header & Footer Tools Design tab, then click the Go to Footer button in the Navigation group**

   The insertion point moves to the Footer area, where a page number field is centered in the Footer area.

QUICK TIP

To change the distance between the header and footer and the edge of the page, change the Header from Top and Footer from Bottom settings in the Position group.

6. **Select the page number field in the footer, change the formatting to Berlin Sans FB Demi and Olive Green, Accent 3, Darker 25%, then click in the Footer area to deselect the text and field**

   The footer text is formatted in olive green Berlin Sans FB Demi.

7. **Click the Close Header and Footer button in the Close group, then scroll down until the bottom of page 1 and the top of page 2 appear in the document window**

   The Header and Footer areas close, and the header and footer text is dimmed, as shown in Figure D-10.

8. **Press [Ctrl][Home]**

   The report already includes the name of the document at the top of the first page, making the header information redundant. You can modify headers and footers so that the header and footer text does not appear on the first page of a document or a section.

9. **Position the pointer over the header text at the top of page 1, then double-click**

   The Header and Footer areas open. The Options group on the Header & Footer Tools Design tab includes options for creating a different header and footer for the first page of a document or a section, and for creating different headers and footers for odd- and even-numbered pages.

QUICK TIP

To remove headers or footers from a document, click the Header or Footer button, and then click Remove Header or Remove Footer.

10. **Click the Different First Page check box to select it, click the Close Header and Footer button, scroll to see the header and footer on pages 2, 3, and 4, then save the document**

    The header and footer text is removed from the Header and Footer areas on the first page.

FIGURE D-9: Header area

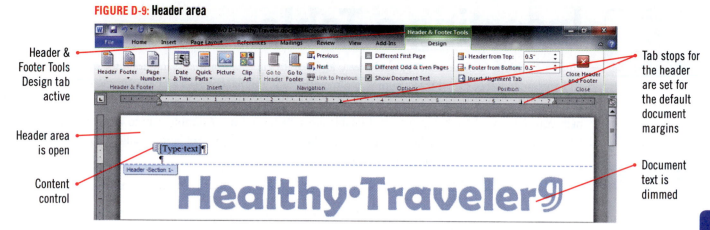

Header & Footer Tools Design tab active

Header area is open

Content control

Tab stops for the header are set for the default document margins

Document text is dimmed

FIGURE D-10: Header and footer in document

Page number appears in footer on every page

Header text appears centered in the header on every page

Adding a custom header or footer to the gallery

When you design a header that you want to use again in other documents, you can add it to the Header gallery by saving it as a building block. **Building blocks** are reusable pieces of formatted content or document parts, including headers and footers, page numbers, and text boxes, that are stored in galleries. Building blocks include predesigned content that comes with Word, as well as content that you create and save for future use. For example, you might create a custom header that contains your company name and logo and is formatted using the fonts, border, and colors you use in all company documents.

To add a custom header to the Header gallery, select all the text in the header, including the last paragraph mark, click the Header button, and then click Save Selection to Header Gallery. In the

Create New Building Block dialog box that opens, type a unique name for the header in the Name text box, click the Gallery list arrow and select the appropriate gallery, verify that the Category is General, and then type a brief description of the new header design in the Description text box. This description appears in a ScreenTip when you point to the custom header in the gallery. When you are finished, click OK. The new header appears in the Header gallery under the General category.

To remove a custom header from the Header gallery, right-click it, click Organize and Delete, make sure the appropriate building block is selected in the Building Blocks Organizer that opens, click Delete, click Yes, and then click Close. You can follow the same process to add or remove a custom footer to the Footer gallery.

Inserting a Table

Adding a table to a document is a useful way to illustrate information that is intended for quick reference and analysis. A **table** is a grid of columns and rows that you can fill with text and graphics. A **cell** is the box formed by the intersection of a column and a row. The lines that divide the columns and rows of a table and help you see the grid-like structure of the table are called **borders**. A simple way to insert a table into a document is to use the Insert Table command on the Insert tab. 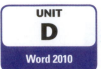 You add a table to page 2 showing the preventive options for serious travel health diseases.

STEPS

1. **Scroll until the heading Preventive Options ... is at the top of your document window**

2. **Select the heading Preventive Options... and the two paragraph marks below it, click the Page Layout tab, click the Columns button in the Page Setup group, click One, click the heading to deselect the text, then scroll down to see the bottom half of page 2**

   A continuous section break is inserted before the heading and after the second paragraph mark, creating a new section, section 3, as shown in Figure D-11. The document now includes four sections, with the heading Preventive Options... in Section 3. Section 3 is formatted as a single column.

3. **Place the insertion point before the first paragraph mark below the heading, click the Insert tab, click the Table button in the Tables group, then click Insert Table**

   The Insert Table dialog box opens. You use this dialog box to create a blank table.

   QUICK TIP
   To delete a table, click in the table, click the Table Tools Layout tab, click the Delete button in the Rows & Columns group, then click Delete Table.

4. **Type 5 in the Number of columns text box, press [Tab], type 6 in the Number of rows text box, make sure the Fixed column width option button is selected, then click OK**

   A blank table with five columns and six rows is inserted in the document. The insertion point is in the upper-left cell of the table, and the Table Tools Design tab becomes the active tab.

5. **Click the Home tab, click the Show/Hide ¶ button ¶ in the Paragraph group, type Disease in the first cell in the first row, press [Tab], type Vaccine, press [Tab], type Prophylaxis Drug, press [Tab], type Eat and Drink Safely, press [Tab], type Avoid Insects, then press [Tab]**

   Pressing [Tab] moves the insertion point to the next cell in the row or to the first cell in the next row.

   QUICK TIP
   You can also click in a cell to move the insertion point to it.

6. **Type Malaria, press [Tab][Tab], click the Bullets list arrow ▤▾ in the Paragraph group, click the check mark style, press [Tab][Tab], then click the Bullets button ▤**

   The active bullet style changes to a check mark. A check mark is added to a cell when you click the Bullets button.

   TROUBLE
   If you pressed [Tab] after the last row, click the Undo button ↺ on the Quick Access toolbar to remove the blank row.

7. **Type the text shown in Figure D-12 in the table cells**

   Don't be concerned if the text wraps to the next line in a cell as you type because you will adjust the width of the columns later.

8. **Click the Table Tools Layout tab, click the AutoFit button in the Cell Size group, click AutoFit Contents, click the AutoFit button again, then click AutoFit Window**

   The width of the table columns is adjusted to fit the text and then the window.

   QUICK TIP
   You can also format table text using the buttons on the Mini toolbar or the Home tab.

9. **Click the Select button in the Table group, click Select Table, click the Align Center button ▤ in the Alignment group, click Disease in the table, click the Select button, click Select Column, click the Align Center Left button ▤, then click in the table to deselect the column**

   The text in the table is centered in each cell, and then the text in the first column is left-aligned.

10. **Click the Table Tools Design tab, click the More button ▾ in the Table Styles group to expand the Table Styles gallery, click the Light List – Accent 3 style, then save your changes**

    The Light List - Accent 3 table style is applied to the table, as shown in Figure D-13. A **table style** includes format settings for the text, borders, and shading in a table.

FIGURE D-11: New section

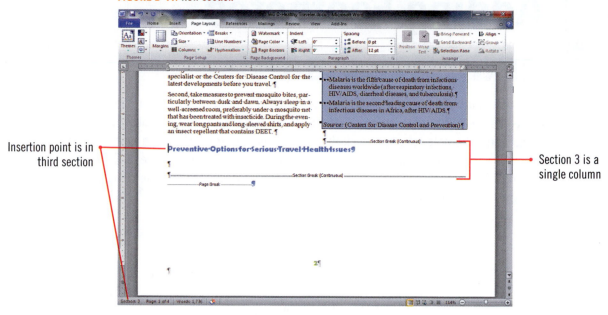

Insertion point is in third section

Section 3 is a single column

FIGURE D-12: Text in table

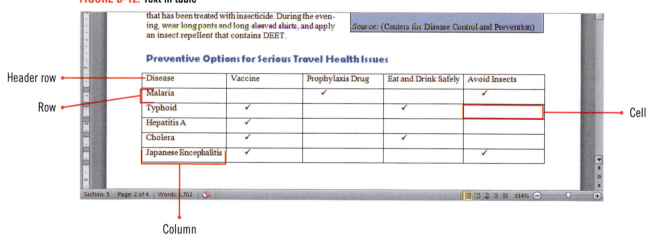

Header row

Row

Cell

Column

FIGURE D-13: Completed table

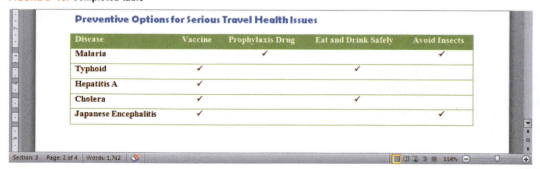

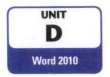

Adding Footnotes and Endnotes

Footnotes and endnotes are used in documents to provide further information, explanatory text, or references for text in a document. A **footnote** or **endnote** is an explanatory note that consists of two linked parts: the note reference mark that appears next to text to indicate that additional information is offered in a footnote or endnote, and the corresponding footnote or endnote text. Word places footnotes at the end of each page and endnotes at the end of the document. You insert and manage footnotes and endnotes using the tools in the Footnotes group on the References tab. You add several footnotes to the report.

STEPS

TROUBLE
Scroll up as needed to see the note reference mark; then scroll down to see the footnote.

1. **Press [Ctrl][Home], place the insertion point at the end of the first body paragraph in the second column of text (after "resort."), click the References tab, then click the Insert Footnote button in the Footnotes group**

   A note reference mark, in this case a superscript 1, appears after "resort.", and the insertion point moves below a separator line at the bottom of the page. A note reference mark can be a number, a symbol, a character, or a combination of characters.

2. **Type Behavior is a critical factor, regardless of the quality of accommodations. For example, going outdoors in a malaria-endemic area could result in becoming infected with malaria.**

   The footnote text appears below the separator line at the bottom of page 1, as shown in Figure D-14.

QUICK TIP
To change the number format of the note reference mark or to use a symbol instead of a character, click the launcher in the Footnotes group, select from the options in the Footnote and Endnote dialog box, then click Apply.

3. **Scroll down until the bottom half of page 3 appears in the document window, place the insertion point at the end of "Medications taken on a regular basis at home" in the second column, click the Insert Footnote button, then type All medications should be stored in carry-on luggage, in their original containers with clear labels. Carry a duplicate supply in checked luggage.**

   The footnote text for the second footnote appears at the bottom of the second column on page 3.

4. **Place the insertion point at the end of "Sunscreen" in the bulleted list in the second column, click the Insert Footnote button, then type SPF 15 or greater.**

   The footnote text for the third footnote appears under the second footnote text at the bottom of page 3.

5. **Place the insertion point after "Disposable gloves" in the first column, click the Insert Footnote button, type At least two pairs., place the insertion point after "Scissors, safety pins, and tweezers" in the first column, click the Insert Footnote button, then type Pack these items in checked luggage.**

   Notice that when you inserted new footnotes between existing footnotes, Word automatically renumbered the footnotes. The new footnotes appear at the bottom of the first column on page 3, as shown in Figure D-15.

6. **Press [Ctrl][Home], then click the Next Footnote button in the Footnotes group**

   The insertion point moves to the first reference mark in the document.

QUICK TIP
To convert all footnotes to endnotes, click the launcher in the Footnotes group, click Convert, click OK, then click Close.

7. **Click the Next Footnote button, press [Delete] to select the number 2 reference mark, then press [Delete] again**

   The second reference mark and associated footnote are deleted from the document and the footnotes are renumbered automatically. You must select a reference mark to delete a footnote; you can not simply delete the footnote text itself.

8. **Press [Ctrl][Home], then save your changes**

FIGURE D-14: Footnote in the document

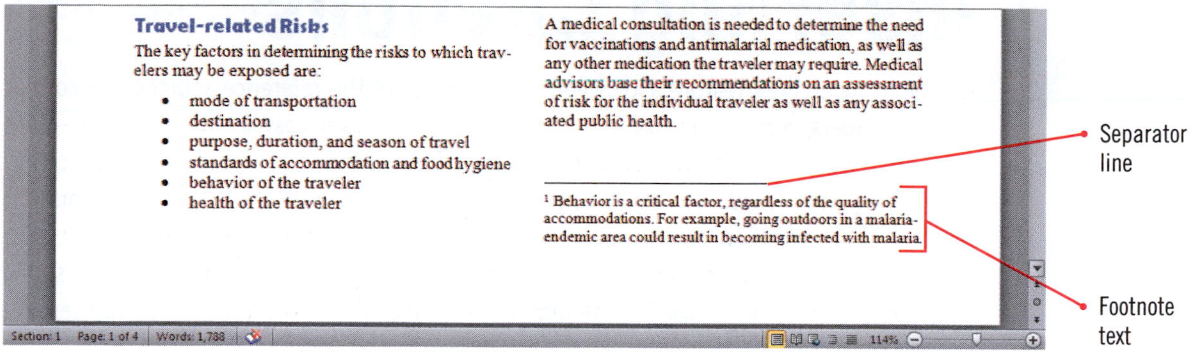

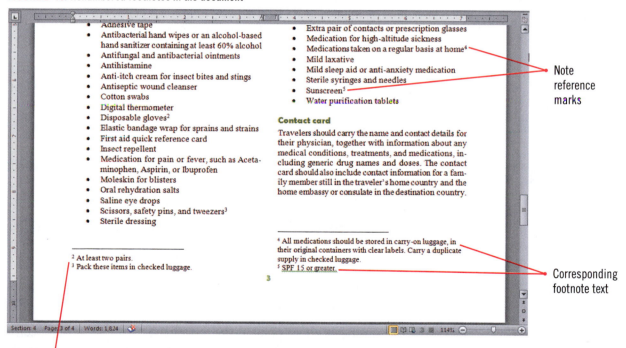

Separator line

Footnote text

FIGURE D-15: Renumbered footnotes in the document

Note reference marks

Corresponding footnote text

Notes are renumbered when a new note is added

Inserting Citations

The Word References feature allows you to keep track of the reference sources you consult when writing research papers, reports, and other documents, and makes it easy to insert a citation in a document. A **citation** is a parenthetical reference in the document text that gives credit to the source for a quotation or other information used in a document. Citations usually include the name of the author and, for print sources, a page number. When you insert a citation you can use an existing source or create a new source. Each time you create a new source, the source information is saved on your computer so that it is available for use in any document.  The report already includes two citations. You add several more citations to the report.

STEPS

1. **Place the insertion point after "people travel" but before the period at the end of the first paragraph in the first column of text, click the Style list arrow in the Citations & Bibliography group, then click MLA Sixth Edition**

   You will format the sources and citations in the report using the style recommended by the Modern Language Association (MLA).

   QUICK TIP

   When you create a new source for a document, it appears automatically in the bibliography when you generate it.

2. **Click the Insert Citation button in the Citations & Bibliography group**

   A list of the sources already used in the document opens. You can choose to cite one of these sources, create a new source, or add a placeholder for a source. When you add a new citation to a document, the source is added to the list of master sources that is stored on the computer. The new source is also associated with the document.

3. **Click Add New Source, click the Type of Source list arrow in the Create Source dialog box, scroll down to view the available source types, click Report, then click the Corporate Author check box**

   You select the type of source and enter the source information in the Create Source dialog box. The fields available in the dialog box change, depending on the type of source selected.

   QUICK TIP

   Only sources that you associate with a document stay with the document when you move it to another computer. The master list of sources remains on the computer where it was created.

4. **Enter the data shown in Figure D-16 in the Create Source dialog box, then click OK**

   The citation (World Tourism Organization) appears at the end of the paragraph. Because the source is a print publication, it needs to include a page number.

5. **Click the citation to select it, click the Citation Options list arrow on the right side of the citation, then click Edit Citation**

   The Edit Citation dialog box opens, as shown in Figure D-17.

   QUICK TIP

   You can also choose to add or remove the author, year, or title from a citation.

6. **Type 19 in the Pages text box, then click OK**

   The page number 19 is added to the citation.

7. **Scroll down, place the insertion point at the end of the quotation (after ...consequences.), click the Insert Citation button, click Add New Source, enter the information shown in Figure D-18, then click OK**

   A citation for the Web publication that the quotation was taken from is added to the report. No page number is used in this citation because the source is a Web site.

8. **Scroll to the bottom of page 2, click under the table, type Source:, italicize Source:, click after Source:, click the Insert Citation button, then click Johnson, Margaret in the list of sources**

   The citation (Johnson) appears under the table.

9. **Click the citation, click the Citation Options list arrow, click Edit Citation, type 55 in the Pages text box, click OK, then save your changes**

   The page number 55 is added to the citation.

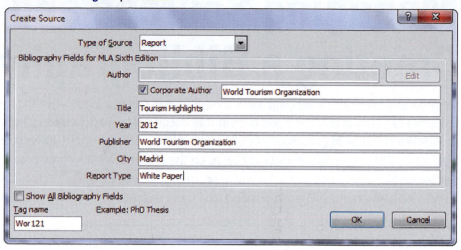

FIGURE D-16: Adding a Report source

FIGURE D-17: Edit Citation dialog box

Citation selected in the content control

Citation Options list arrow

FIGURE D-18: Adding a Web publication source

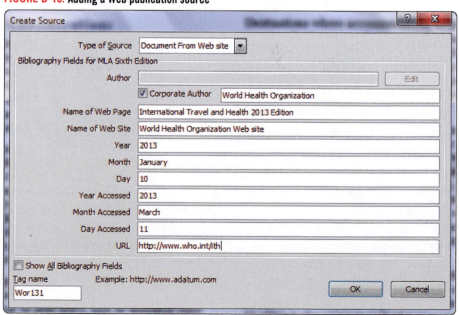

Managing Sources and Creating a Bibliography

Many documents require a **bibliography**, a list of sources that you used in creating the document. The list of sources can include only the works cited in your document (a **works cited** list) or both the works cited and the works consulted (a bibliography). The Bibliography feature in Word allows you to generate a works cited list or a bibliography automatically based on the source information you provide for the document. The Source Manager dialog box helps you to organize your sources. 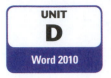 You add a bibliography to the report. The bibliography is inserted as a field, and it can be formatted any way you choose.

STEPS

1. **Press [Ctrl][End] to move the insertion point to the end of the document, then click the Manage Sources button in the Citations & Bibliography group**

   The Source Manager dialog box opens, as shown in Figure D-19. The Master List shows the sources available on your computer. The Current List shows the sources available in the current document. A check mark next to a source indicates the source is cited in the document. You use the tools in the Source Manager dialog box to add, edit, and delete sources from the lists, and to copy sources between the Master List and the Current List. The sources that appear in the Current List are the sources that will appear in the bibliography.

2. **Click the Baker, Mary source in the Current List**

   A preview of the citation and bibliographical entry for the source in MLA style appears in the Preview box. You do not want this source to be included in your bibliography for the report.

3. **Click Delete**

   The source is removed from the Current List.

4. **Click Close, click the Bibliography button in the Citations & Bibliography group, click Bibliography, then scroll up to see the heading Bibliography at the top of the field**

   A Bibliography field is added at the location of the insertion point. The bibliography includes all the sources associated with the document, formatted in the MLA style for bibliographies. The text in the Bibliography field is formatted with the default styles. You want to format the text to match the rest of the report.

5. **Select Bibliography; apply the following formats: Berlin Sans FB Demi, bold, and the Blue, Accent 1 font color; drag down the list of sources to select the entire list and change the font size to 11; then click outside the bibliography to deselect it**

   The format of the bibliography text now matches the rest of the report.

6. **Press [Ctrl][End], type your name, click the View tab, then click Two Pages**

   Completed pages 3 and 4 of the report are shown in the document window, as shown in Figure D-20.

7. **Scroll up to view pages 1 and 2**

   Completed pages 1 and 2 are shown in Figure D-21.

8. **Save your changes, submit your document, close the file, then exit Word**

Working with Web sources

Publications found on the Web can be challenging to document. Many Web sites can be accessed under multiple domains, and URLs change frequently or are so long that they cannot be typed easily. In addition, electronic publications are often updated frequently, making each visit to a Web site potentially unique. For these reasons, it's best to rely on the author, title, and publication information for a Web publication when citing it as a source in a research document. If possible, you can include a URL as supplementary information only, along with the date the Web site was last updated and the date you accessed the site. Whatever format you use for citing Web publications, it's important to be consistent throughout your document. Since Web sites are often removed, it's also a good idea to download or print any Web source you use so that it can be verified later.

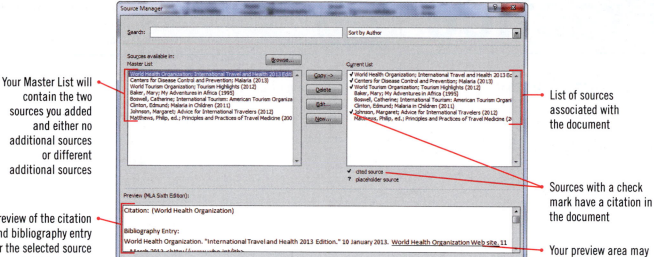

Your Master List will contain the two sources you added and either no additional sources or different additional sources

List of sources associated with the document

Sources with a check mark have a citation in the document

Preview of the citation and bibliography entry for the selected source in MLA style (as defined by Word)

Your preview area may show a different source

Word 2010

FIGURE D-20: **Completed pages 3 and 4**

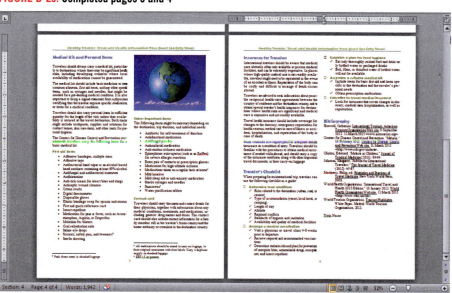

FIGURE D-21: **Completed pages 1 and 2**

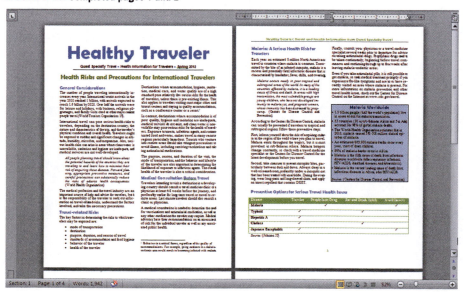

Practice

For current SAM information, including versions and content details, visit SAM Central (http://www.cengage.com/samcentral). If you have a SAM user profile, you may have access to hands-on instruction, practice, and assessment of the skills covered in this unit. Since various versions of SAM are supported throughout the life of this text, check with your instructor for the correct instructions and URL/Web site for accessing assignments.

Concepts Review

Label each element shown in Figure D-22.

FIGURE D-22

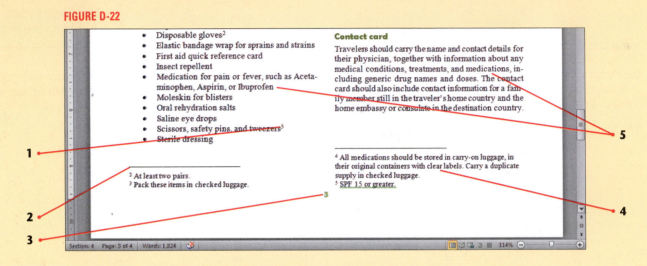

Match each term with the statement that best describes it.

6. **Table**

7. **Manual page break**

8. **Section break**

9. **Footer**

10. **Header**

11. **Citation**

12. **Field**

13. **Margin**

14. **Bibliography**

a. A parenthetical reference in the document text that gives credit to a source

b. The blank area between the edge of the text and the edge of the page

c. A formatting mark that divides a document into parts that can be formatted differently

d. Text or graphics that appear at the bottom of every page in a document

e. A placeholder for information that changes

f. A formatting mark that forces the text following the mark to begin at the top of the next page

g. Text or graphics that appear at the top of every page in a document

h. A list of the sources used to create a document

i. A grid of columns and rows that you can fill with text and graphics

Select the best answer from the list of choices.

15. **Which type of break do you insert if you want to balance the columns in a section?**

    a. Manual page break

    b. Text wrapping break

    c. Column break

    d. Continuous section break

16. **Which type of break can you insert if you want to force text to begin on the next page?**

    a. Text wrapping break

    b. Next page section break

    c. Automatic page break

    d. Continuous section break

17. **Which of the following cannot be inserted using the Quick Parts command?**

    a. Document property

    b. AutoText building block

    c. Page break

    d. Page number field

18. **Which of the following do documents with mirror margins always have?**

    a. Inside and outside margins

    b. Different first page headers and footers

    c. Gutters

    d. Landscape orientation

19. **What name describes formatted pieces of content that are stored in galleries?**

    a. Field

    b. Header

    c. Property

    d. Building Block

20. **Which appears at the end of a document?**

    a. Citation

    b. Endnote

    c. Footnote

    d. Page break

Skills Review

1. **Set document margins.**

   a. Start Word, open the file WD D-2.docx from the drive and folder where you store your Data Files, then save it as **WD D-Elmwood Fitness**.

   b. Change the top and bottom margin settings to Moderate: 1" top and bottom, and .75" left and right.

   c. Save your changes to the document.

2. **Create sections and columns.**

   a. Turn on the display of formatting marks, then customize the status bar to display sections if they are not displayed already.

   b. Insert a continuous section break before the **Welcome to the Elmwood Fitness Center** heading.

   c. Format the text in section 2 in two columns, then save your changes to the document.

3. **Insert page breaks.**

   a. Scroll to page 3, then insert a manual page break before the heading **Facilities and Services**.

   b. Scroll down and insert a manual page break before the heading **Membership**, then press [Ctrl][Home].

   c. On page 1, select the heading **Welcome to the Elmwood Fitness Center** and the paragraph mark below it, use the Columns button to format the selected text as one column, then center the heading on the page.

   d. Follow the direction in step c to format the heading **Facilities and Services** and the paragraph mark below it on page 3, and the heading **Membership** and the paragraph mark below it on page 4, as one column, with centered text, then save your changes to the document

4. **Insert page numbers.**

   a. Insert page numbers in the document at the bottom of the page. Select the Plain Number 2 page number style from the gallery.

   b. Close the Footer area, scroll through the document to view the page number on each page, then save your changes to the document.

5. **Add headers and footers.**

   a. Double-click the margin at the top of a page to open the Header and Footer areas.

   b. With the insertion point in the Header area, click the Quick Parts button in the Insert Group on the Header & Footer Tools Design tab, point to Document Property, then click Author.

Skills Review (continued)

c. Replace the text in the Author content control with your name, press [End] to move the insertion point out of the content control, then press [Spacebar]. (*Note*: If your name does not appear in the header, right-click the Author content control, click Remove Content Control, then type your name in the header.)

d. Click the Insert Alignment Tab button in the Position group, select the Right option button and keep the alignment relative to the margin, then click OK in the dialog box to move the insertion point to the right margin.

e. Use the Insert Date and Time command in the Insert group to insert the current date using a format of your choice as static text. (*Hint*: Be sure the Update Automatically check box is not checked.)

f. Apply italic to the text in the header.

g. Move the insertion point to the Footer area.

h. Double-click the page number to select it, then format the page number in bold and italic.

i. Move the insertion point to the header on page 1 if it is not already there, use the Header & Footer Tools Design tab to create a different header and footer for the first page of the document, type your name in the First Page Header area, then apply italic to your name.

j. Close headers and footers, scroll to view the header and footer on each page, then save your changes to the document.

6. Insert a table.

a. On page 4, double-click the word **Table** to select it at the end of the Membership Rates section, press [Delete], open the Insert Table dialog box, then create a table with two columns and five rows.

b. Apply the purple Light List - Accent 4 table style to the table.

c. Press [Tab] to leave the first cell in the header row blank, then type **Rate**.

d. Press [Tab], then type the following text in the table, pressing [Tab] to move from cell to cell.

Enrollment/Individual	**$100**
Enrollment/Couple	**$150**
Monthly membership/Individual	**$35**
Monthly membership/Couple	**$60**

e. With the insertion point in the table, right-click the table, use the AutoFit command to select the AutoFit to Contents option, and then select the AutoFit to Window option. (*Note*: In this case AutoFit to Window fits the table to the width of the column of text.)

f. Save your changes to the document.

7. Add footnotes and endnotes.

a. Press [Ctrl[Home], scroll down, place the insertion point at the end of the first body paragraph, insert a footnote, then type **People who are active live longer and feel better.**

b. Place the insertion point at the end of the first paragraph under the Benefits of Exercise heading, insert a footnote, then type **There are 1,440 minutes in every day. Schedule 30 of them for physical activity.**

c. Place the insertion point at the end of the first paragraph under the Tips for Staying Motivated heading, insert a footnote, type **Always consult your physician before beginning an exercise program.**, then save your changes.

8. Insert citations.

a. Place the insertion point at the end of the second paragraph under the Benefits of Exercise heading (after "down from 52% in 2010" but before the period), then change the style for citations and bibliography to MLA Sixth Edition.

b. Insert a citation, add a new source, enter the source information shown in the Create Source dialog box in Figure D-23, then click OK.

FIGURE D-23

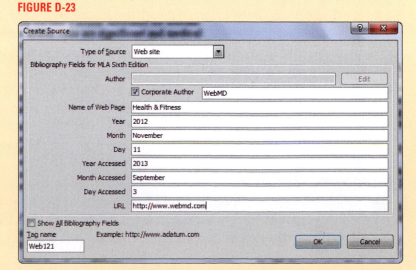

Skills Review (continued)

c. Place the insertion point at the end of the italicized quotation in the second column of text, insert a citation, then select Jason, Laura from the list of sources.

d. Edit the citation to include the page number **25**.

e. Scroll to page 2, place the insertion point at the end of the "Be a morning exerciser" paragraph but before the ending period, insert a citation for WebMD, then save your changes.

9. **Manage sources and create a bibliography.**

a. Press [Ctrl][End], then open the Source Manager dialog box.

b. Select the source Health, National Institute of in the Current List, click Edit, click the Corporate Author check box, edit the entry so it reads **National Institute of Health**, click OK, click Yes if prompted, then click Close.

c. Insert a bibliography.

d. Select Bibliography, then change the font to 14-point Tahoma with a black font color. Pages 1 and 4 of the formatted document are shown in Figure D-24.

e. Save your changes to the document, submit it to your instructor, then close the document and exit Word.

FIGURE D-24

Page 1

Your Name

The Elmwood Fitness Center
A Rehabilitation and Exercise Facility

245 Mountain Avenue, Elmwood, CA • Tel: 415-555-3242 • www.elmwoodfitness.com

Welcome to the Elmwood Fitness Center

The Elmwood Fitness Center's goal is simple: to provide a state-of-the-art exercise facility staffed by highly-skilled professionals in a supportive, healthful environment. By making a commitment to a healthier lifestyle, we believe members will experience an enriched quality of life. Our professional and compassionate staff looks forward to helping you reach your goals and realize the positive results of improving your health.[1]

Benefits of Exercise

Study after study shows that regular physical activity – even at moderate levels – reduces the risk of heart disease, cancer, high blood pressure and obesity, and enhances physical and mental functioning.[2]

Despite this, a report from the Centers for Disease Control and Prevention (CDC) showed that 55% of American adults didn't move enough in 2010 to meet the minimum recommendation of 30 minutes of moderate physical activity on most days of the week. And a Gallup Health and Healthcare Survey found that just 45% of Americans regularly engaged in vigorous exercise in 2012 – down from 52% in 2010 (WebMD).

We believe the key is to find the right exercise for you. If it is fun, you are more likely to stay motivated.

Getting Started

The path to a regular exercise routine has great rewards as well as roadblocks. Our goal is to help make it simple and safe – and give you motivation to push on. According to medical experts:

Most adults need at least 30 minutes of moderate physical activity at least five days per week. Examples include walking briskly, mowing the lawn, dancing, swimming for recreation, or bicycling. Stretching and weight training can also strengthen your body and improve your fitness level. If you've been inactive for a while, use a sensible approach and start out slowly. (Jason 25)

Our staff is here to help you establish a safe, healthy, and fun fitness routine that meets your individual needs and goals.

Tips for Staying Motivated

It seems that the most difficult part of starting or sticking to a fitness plan is just that, starting and sticking to it. Here are our tips for starting and maintaining a healthy exercise routine:[3]

- **Find something you enjoy.** Take a dance class, learn to ski or swim, or try yoga or hiking. Try them all. Keep experimenting until you find an activity that moves you, mentally and physically.

---
[1] People who are active live longer and feel better.
[2] There are 1,440 minutes in every day. Schedule 30 of them for physical activity.

[3] Always consult your physician before beginning an exercise program.

Page 4

Your Name   9/20/2013

Membership

Membership Rates

Membership in Elmwood Fitness requires payment of a one-time enrollment fee, plus a monthly membership fee. Enrollment includes:
- One hour assessment appointment
- Individualized fitness plan
- Facility orientation

	Rate
Enrollment/Individual	$100
Enrollment/Couple	$150
Monthly membership/Individual	$35
Monthly membership/Couple	$60

Billing

For your convenience, we can automatically deduct membership dues from a credit or checking account on a monthly basis. Funds are withdrawn electronically on the third day of each month. A penalty is incurred for accounts with insufficient funds. Members who opt for statement billing will be billed every three months.

Vacation Rates

Going away for several months? No problem. All we ask is that you let us know thirty days in advance. For 50% of your normal monthly rate, we will hold your membership in good standing. Memberships can be held for a minimum of one month and a maximum of three months.

Membership Cards

Please be prepared to present your membership card to the reception desk when entering the Elmwood Fitness Center. If your card is lost, please notify the reception desk as soon as possible. Lost or stolen cards can be replaced with proper identification. Membership cards are not transferable.

Guest Policies

We welcome member guests at any time. Please register your guests at the reception desk and allow a few extra minutes for your guest to complete a registration card. Each guest can access the facility twice in a six-month period. The charge for guests is $10 per visit.

Cancellation of Membership

We request written notice of membership cancellation at least thirty days prior to the effective cancellation date. Though we'll be sorry to see you go, we will cheerfully assist you with the cancellation process.

Bibliography
Jason, Laura. "Establishing a Fitness Routine." Health Times 6 June 2011: 23-31.
Marly, John. Fitness in the 21st Century. Cambridge: Wellness Press, 2009.
National Heart Lung and Blood Institute. Health Information for the Public. 6 June 2012. 3 September 2013 <http://www.nhlbi.nih.gov/>.
National Institute of Health. Medline Plus: Fitness and Exercise. 7 January 2013. 3 September 2013 <http://www.nlm.nih.gov>.
WebMD. Health & Fitness. 11 November 2012. 3 September 2013 <http://www.webmd.com>.

4

Independent Challenge 1

You are the owner of a small business called Harvest Catering. You have begun work on the text for a brochure advertising your business and are now ready to lay out the pages and prepare the final copy. The brochure will be printed on both sides of an 8½" × 11" sheet of paper, and folded in thirds.

If you have a SAM 2010 user profile, an autogradable SAM version of this assignment may be available at http://www.cengage.com/sam2010. Check with your instructor to confirm that this assignment is available in SAM. To use the SAM version of this assignment, log into the SAM 2010 Web site and download the instruction and start files.

a. Start Word, open the file WD D-3.docx from the drive and folder where you store your Data Files, then save it as **WD D-Harvest Catering**. Read the document to get a feel for its contents.

b. Change the page orientation to landscape, and change all four margins to .6".

c. Format the document in three columns of equal width.

d. Insert a next page section break before the heading **Catering Services**.

e. On page 1, insert column breaks before the headings **Sample Tuscan Banquet Menu** and **Sample Indian Banquet Menu**.

f. Change the column spacing in section 1 (which is the first page) to .4", add lines between the columns on the first page, then center the text in the columns.

FIGURE D-25

g. Double-click the bottom margin to open the footer area, create a different header and footer for the first page, then type **Call for custom menus designed to your taste and budget.** in the First Page Footer -Section 1- area.

h. Center the text in the footer area, format it in 20-point Papyrus, bold, with a Red, Accent 2 font color, then close headers and footers.

i. On page 2, insert a column break before Your Name, then press [Enter] 22 times to move the contact information to the bottom of the second column.

j. Replace Your Name with your name, then center the contact information in the column.

k. Insert a column break at the bottom of the second column. Type the text shown in Figure D-25 in the third column, then apply the No Spacing style to the text. Refer to the figure as you follow the instructions for formatting the text in the third column.

l. Format Harvest Catering in 28-point Papyrus, bold.

m. Format the remaining text in 12-point Papyrus. Center the text in the third column.

n. Insert the clip art graphic shown in Figure D-25 or another appropriate clip art graphic. Do not wrap text around the graphic. (*Hint*: Use the search terms fruits and women.)

o. Resize the graphic and add or remove blank paragraphs in the third column of your brochure so that the spacing between elements roughly matches the spacing shown in Figure D-25.

Harvest Catering

Complete catering services available for all types of events. Menus and estimates provided upon request.

Advanced Challenge Exercise

■ Insert a different appropriate clip art graphic at the bottom of the first column on page 2.

■ Apply text wrapping to the graphic, then resize the graphic and position it so it enhances the design of the brochure.

■ Apply a suitable picture style or picture effect to the graphic.

p. Save your changes, then submit a copy to your instructor. If possible, you can print the brochure with the two pages back to back so that the brochure can be folded in thirds.

q. Close the document and exit Word.

Independent Challenge 2

You work in the Campus Safety Department at Pacific State College. You have written the text for an informational flyer about parking regulations on campus, and now you need to format the flyer so it is attractive and readable.

a. Start Word, open the file WD D-4.docx from the drive and folder where you store your Data Files, then save it as **WD D-Parking FAQ**. Read the document to get a feel for its contents.

b. Change all four margins to .7".

c. Insert a continuous section break before **1. May I bring a car to school?** (*Hint:* Place the insertion point before May.)

d. Scroll down and insert a next page section break before **Sample Parking Permit**.

e. Format the text in section 2 in three columns of equal width with .3" of space between the columns.

f. Hyphenate the document using the automatic hyphenation feature. (*Hint:* Use the Hyphenation button in the Page Setup group on the Page Layout tab.)

g. Add a 3-point dotted-line bottom border to the blank paragraph under Pacific State College Department of Campus Safety. (*Hint:* Place the insertion point before the paragraph mark under Pacific State College...)

h. Open the Header area, and insert your name in the header. Right-align your name, and format it in 10-point Arial.

i. Add the following text to the footer, inserting symbols between words as indicated: **Parking and Shuttle Service Office • 54 Buckley Street • Pacific State College • 942-555-2227**. (*Hint:* Click the Symbol command in the Symbols group on the Insert tab to insert a symbol.)

j. Format the footer text in 9-point Arial Black, and center it in the footer. If necessary, adjust the font and font size so that the entire contact information fits on one line.

k. Apply a 3-point dotted-line border above the footer text. Make sure to apply the border to the paragraph.

l. Add a continuous section break at the end of section 2 to balance the columns in section 2.

m. Add the clip art graphic shown in Figure D-26 (or another appropriate clip art graphic) to the upper-right corner of the document, above the border. Make sure the graphic does not obscure the border. (*Hint:* Apply text wrapping to the graphic before positioning it.)

n. Place the insertion point on page 2 (which is section 4). Change the left and right margins in section 4 to 1". Also change the page orientation of section 4 to landscape.

o. Change the vertical alignment of section 4 to center. (*Hint:* Use the Vertical Alignment list arrow on the Layout tab in the Page Setup dialog box.)

p. Apply an appropriate table style to the table, such as the style shown in Figure D-27. (*Hint:* Check and uncheck the options in the Table Style Options group on the Table Tools Design tab to customize the style so it enhances the table data.)

q. Save your changes, submit your work, close the document, then exit Word.

FIGURE D-26

Frequently Asked Questions (FAQ)

Parking & Shuttle Service Office

Pacific State College Department of Campus Safety

FIGURE D-27

Sample Parking Permit

Pacific State College
Office of Parking and Shuttle Service

2013-14 Student Parking Permit

License number:	VA 498 359
Make:	Subaru
Model:	Forester
Year:	2004
Color:	Red
Permit Issue Date:	September 8, 2013
Permit Expiration Date:	June 4, 2014

Restrictions:
Parking is permitted in the Pacific State College Greene Street lot 24 hours a day, 7 days a week. Shuttle service is available from the Greene Street lot to campus from 7 a.m. to 7 p.m. Monday through Friday. Parking is also permitted in any on-campus lot from 4:30 p.m. Friday to midnight Sunday.

Independent Challenge 3

A book publisher would like to publish an article you wrote on stormwater pollution in Australia as a chapter in a forthcoming book called *Environmental Issues for the New Millennium*. The publisher has requested that you format your article like a book chapter before submitting it for publication, and has provided you with a style sheet. According to the style sheet, the citations and bibliography should be formatted in Chicago style. You have already created the sources for the chapter, but you need to insert the citations.

FIGURE D-28

a. Start Word, open the file WD D-5.docx from the drive and folder where you store your Data Files, then save it as **WD D-Chapter 7**.

b. Change the font of the entire document to 11-point High Tower Text. If this font is not available to you, select a different font suitable for the pages of a book. Change the alignment to justified.

c. Change the paper size to 6" × 9".

d. Create mirror margins. (*Hint*: Use the Multiple pages list arrow.) Change the top and bottom margins to .8", change the inside margin to .4", change the outside margin to .6", and create a .3" gutter to allow room for the book's binding.

e. Change the Zoom level to Page Width, open the Header and Footer areas, then apply the setting to create different headers and footers for odd- and even-numbered pages.

f. In the odd-page header, type **Chapter 7**, insert a symbol of your choice, then type **The Fairy Creek Catchment and Stormwater Pollution**.

g. Format the header text in 9-point High Tower Text italic, then right-align the text.

h. In the even-page header, type your name.

i. Format the header text in 9-point High Tower Text italic. The even-page header should be left-aligned.

j. Insert a left-aligned page number field in the even-page footer area, format it in 10-point High Tower Text, insert a right-aligned page number field in the odd-page footer area, then format it in 10-point High Tower Text.

k. Format the page numbers so that the first page of your chapter, which is Chapter 7 in the book, begins on page 101. (*Hint*: Select a page number field, click the Page Number button, then click Format Page Numbers.)

l. Go to the beginning of the document, press [Enter] 10 times, type **Chapter 7: The Fairy Creek Catchment and Stormwater Pollution**, press [Enter] twice, type your name, then press [Enter] twice.

m. Format the chapter title in 16-point Calibri bold, format your name in 14-point Calibri, then left-align the title text and your name.

n. Click the References tab, make sure the citations and bibliography style is set to Chicago Fifteenth Edition, place the insertion point at the end of the first body paragraph on page 1 but before the ending period, insert a citation for Alice Burke, et. al., then add the page number 40 to the citation, as shown in Figure D-28.

o. Add the citations listed in Table D-3 to the document using the sources already associated with the document.

TABLE D-3

page	location for citation	source	page number
2	End of the first complete paragraph (after …WCSMP, but before the period)	City of Weston	3
3	End of the first complete paragraph (after …pollution, but before the colon)	Jensen	135
4	End of second paragraph (after …health effects, but before the period)	City of Weston	5
4	End of fourth bulleted list (after 1 month)	Seawatch	None
5	End of third paragraph (after …problem arises, but before the period)	Burke, et. al.	55
6	End of first sentence (after …stormwater system, but before the period)	City of Weston	7
6	End of first paragraph under Conclusion (after …include, but before the colon)	Jensen	142

Independent Challenge 3 (continued)

p. Press [Ctrl][End], insert a Works Cited list, format the Works Cited heading in 11-point High Tower Text, black font color, bold, then format the list of works cited in High Tower Text.

Advanced Challenge Exercise

- Scroll to page 4 in the document, place the insertion point at the end of the paragraph above the Potential health effects... heading, press [Enter] twice, type **Table 1: Total annual pollutant loads per year in the Fairy Creek Catchment**, format the text as bold, then press [Enter] twice.
- Insert a table with four columns and four rows.
- Type the text shown in Figure D-29 in the table. Do not be concerned when the text wraps to the next line in a cell.
- Apply the Light List table style. Make sure the text in the header row is bold, then remove any bold formatting from the text in the remaining rows.
- Use AutoFit to make the table fit the contents, then use AutoFit to make the table fit the window.

FIGURE D-29

Area	Nitrogen	Phosphorus	Suspended solids
Fairy Creek	9.3 tonnes	1.2 tonnes	756.4 tonnes
Durras Arm	6.2 tonnes	.9 tonnes	348.2 tonnes
Cabbage Tree Creek	9.8 tonnes	2.3 tonnes	485.7 tonnes

q. Save your changes, submit your work, then close the document and exit Word.

Real Life Independent Challenge

One of the most common opportunities to use the page layout features of Word is when formatting a research paper. The format recommended by the *MLA Handbook for Writers of Research Papers*, a style guide that includes information on preparing, writing, and formatting research papers, is the standard format used by many schools, colleges, and universities. In this independent challenge, you will research the MLA guidelines for formatting a research paper and use the guidelines you find to format the pages of a sample research report.

a. Use your favorite search engine to search the Web for information on the MLA guidelines for formatting a research report. Use the keywords **MLA Style** and **research paper format** to conduct your search.

b. Look for information on the proper formatting for the following aspects of a research paper: paper size, margins, title page or first page of the report, line spacing, paragraph indentation, and page numbers. Also find information on proper formatting for citations and a works cited page. Print the information you find.

c. Start Word, open the file WD D-6.docx from the drive and folder where you store your Data Files, then save it as **WD D-Research Paper**. Using the information you learned, format this document as a research report.

d. Adjust the margins, set the line spacing, and add page numbers to the document in the format recommended by the MLA. Use **The Maori History of New Zealand** as the title for your sample report, use your name as the author name, and use the name of the course you are enrolled in currently as well as the instructor's name for that course. Make sure to format the title page exactly as the MLA style dictates.

e. Format the remaining text as the body of the research report. Indent the first line of each paragraph rather than use quadruple spacing between paragraphs.

f. Create three sources, insert three citations in the document—a book, a journal article, and a Web site—and create a works cited page, following MLA style. If necessary, edit the format of the citations and works cited page to conform to MLA format. (*Note*: For this practice document, you are allowed to make up sources. Never make up sources for real research papers.)

g. Save the document, submit a copy to your instructor, close the document, then exit Word.

Open the file WD D-7.docx from the drive and folder where you store your Data Files, then modify it to create the article shown in Figure D-30. (*Hint*: Change all four margins to .6". Add the footnotes as shown in the figure. To locate the flower clip art image, search using the keyword **wildflowers**, and be sure only the Photographs check box in the Results should be in list box in the Clip Art task pane has a check mark. Select a different clip if the clip shown in the figure is not available to you.) Save the document with the filename **WD D-Gardener's Corner**, then print a copy.

FIGURE D-30

GARDENER'S CORNER

Putting a Perennial Garden to Bed

By Your Name

A certain sense of peace descends when a perennial garden is put to bed for the season. The plants are safely tucked in against the elements, and the garden is ready to welcome the first signs of life. When the work is done, you can sit back and anticipate the bright blooms of spring. Many gardeners are uncertain about how to close a perennial garden. This week's column demystifies the process.

Clean up

Garden clean up can be a gradual process—plants will deteriorate at different rates, allowing you to do a little bit each week.

- Edge beds and borders and remove stakes, trellises, and other plant supports.
- Dig and divide irises, daylilies, and other early bloomers.
- Cut back plants when foliage starts to deteriorate, then rake all debris out of the garden and pull any weeds that remain.

Plant perennials

Fall is the perfect time to plant perennials.[1] The warm, sunny days and cool nights provide optimal conditions for new root growth, without the stress of summer heat.

- Dig deeply and enhance soil with organic matter.
- Use a good starter fertilizer to speed up new root growth and establish a healthy base.
- Untangle the roots of new plants before planting.
- Water deeply after planting as the weather dictates, and keep plants moist for several days after planting.

Add compost

Organic matter is the key ingredient to healthy garden soil. Composting adds nutrients to the soil, helps the soil retain water and nutrients, and keeps the soil well aerated. If you take care of the soil, your plants will become strong and disease resistant.[2]

Before adding compost, use an iron rake to loosen the top few inches of soil. Spread a one to two inch layer of compost over the entire garden—the best compost is made up of yard waste and kitchen scraps—and then refrain from stepping on the area and compacting the soil.

Winter mulch

Winter protection for perennial beds can only help plants survive the winter. Winter mulch prevents the freezing and thawing cycles, which cause plants to heave and eventually die. Here's what works and what doesn't:

- Always apply mulch after the ground is frozen.
- Never apply generic hay because it contains billions of weed seeds. Also, whole leaves and bark mulch hold too much moisture.[3]
- Use a loose material to allow air filtration. Straw and salt marsh hay are excellent choices for mulch.
- Remove the winter mulch in the spring as soon as new growth begins.

---

[1] Fall is also an excellent time to plant shrubs and trees.

[2] You can buy good compost, but it is easy and useful to make it at home. Composting kitchen scraps reduces household garbage by about one-third.

[3] If using leaves, use only stiff leaves such as Oak or Beech. Soft leaves, such as Maple, make it difficult for air and water to filtrate.

Creating and Formatting Tables

Files You Will Need:

WD E-1.docx
WD E-2.docx

Tables are commonly used to display information for quick reference and analysis. In this unit, you learn how to create and modify a table in Word, how to sort table data and perform calculations, and how to format a table with borders and shading. You also learn how to use a table to structure the layout of a page.  You are preparing a summary budget for an advertising campaign aimed at the San Francisco market. The goal of the ad campaign is to promote winter tours to tropical destinations. You decide to format the budget information as a table so that it is easy to read and analyze.

OBJECTIVES

Insert a table

Insert and delete rows and columns

Modify rows and columns

Sort table data

Split and merge cells

Perform calculations in tables

Apply a table style

Create a custom format for a table

Inserting a Table

A **table** is a grid made up of rows and columns of cells that you can fill with text and graphics. A **cell** is the box formed by the intersection of a column and a row. The lines that divide the columns and rows and help you see the grid-like structure of a table are called **borders**. You can create a table in a document by using the Table command in the Tables group on the Insert tab. Once you have created a table, you can add text and graphics to it. 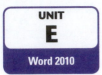 You begin by inserting a blank table and adding text to it.

STEPS

1. **Start Word, click the View tab, then click the Page Width button in the Zoom group**

QUICK TIP
Click the View Ruler button at the top of the vertical scroll bar to display the rulers if they are not already displayed.

2. **Click the Insert tab, then click the Table button in the Tables group**

   The Table menu opens. It includes a grid for selecting the number of columns and rows you want the table to contain, as well as several commands for inserting a table. Table E-1 describes these commands. As you move the pointer across the grid, a preview of the table with the specified number of columns and rows appears in the document at the location of the insertion point.

3. **Point to the second box in the fourth row to select 2×4 Table, then click**

   A table with two columns and four rows is inserted in the document, as shown in Figure E-1. Black borders surround the table cells. The insertion point is in the first cell in the first row.

TROUBLE
Don't be concerned if the paragraph spacing under the text in your table is different from that shown in the figures.

4. **Type Location, then press [Tab]**

   Pressing [Tab] moves the insertion point to the next cell in the row.

5. **Type Cost, press [Tab], then type San Francisco Chronicle**

   Pressing [Tab] at the end of a row moves the insertion point to the first cell in the next row.

6. **Press [Tab], type 27,600, press [Tab], then type the following text in the table, pressing [Tab] to move from cell to cell**

   | SFGate.com | 25,000 |
   | Taxi tops | 18,000 |

7. **Press [Tab]**

   Pressing [Tab] at the end of the last cell of a table creates a new row at the bottom of the table, as shown in Figure E-2. The insertion point is located in the first cell in the new row.

TROUBLE
If you pressed [Tab] after the last row, click the Undo button on the Quick Access toolbar to remove the new blank row.

8. **Type the following, pressing [Tab] to move from cell to cell and to create new rows**

The Independent	18,760
Examiner.com	3,250
Muni bus stops	12,000
San Francisco Magazine	12,400

9. **Click the Save button on the Quick Access toolbar, then save the document as WD E-San Francisco Ad Budget to the drive and folder where you store your Data Files**

   The table is shown in Figure E-3.

TABLE E-1: Table menu commands

command	use to
Insert Table	Create a table with any number of columns and rows and select an AutoFit behavior
Draw Table	Create a complex table by drawing the table columns and rows
Convert Text to Table	Convert text that is separated by tabs, commas, or another separator character into a table
Excel Spreadsheet	Insert a blank Excel worksheet into the document as an embedded object
Quick Tables	Insert a preformatted table template and replace the placeholder data with your own data

FIGURE E-1: Blank table

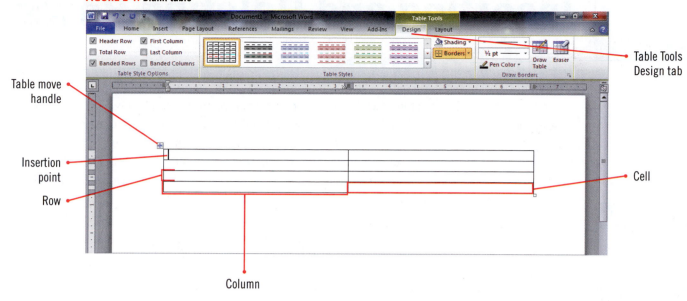

FIGURE E-2: New row in table

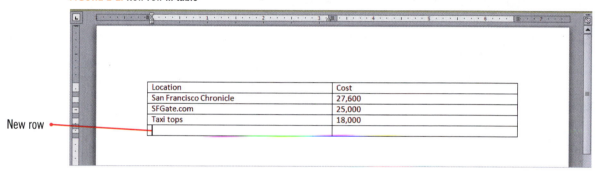

FIGURE E-3: Text in the table

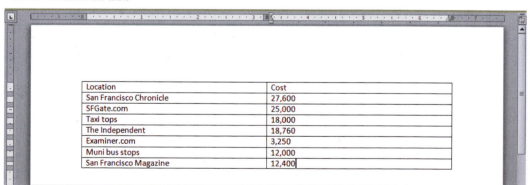

Converting text to a table and a table to text

Another way to create a table is to convert text that is separated by a tab, a comma, or another separator character into a table. For example, to create a two-column table of last and first names, you could type the names as a list with a comma separating the last and first name in each line, and then convert the text to a table. The separator character—a comma in this example—indicates where you want to divide the table into columns, and a paragraph mark indicates where you want to begin a new row. To convert text to a table, select the text, click the Table button in the Tables group on the Insert tab, and then click Convert Text to Table. In the Convert Text to Table dialog box, select from the options for structuring and formatting the table, and then click OK to create the table.

Conversely, you can convert a table to text that is separated by tabs, commas, or some other character by selecting the table, clicking the Table Tools Layout tab, and then clicking the Convert to Text button in the Data group.

Inserting and Deleting Rows and Columns

You can easily modify the structure of a table by adding and removing rows and columns. First, you must click or select an existing row or column in the table to indicate where you want to insert or delete a row or a column. You can select any element of a table using the Select command in the Table group on the Table Tools Layout tab, but it is often easier to select rows and columns using the mouse. To insert or delete rows and columns, you use the commands in the Rows & Columns group on the Table Tools Layout tab. 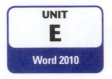 You add new rows and columns to the table, and delete unnecessary rows.

STEPS

1. **Click the Home tab, then click the Show/Hide ¶ button ¶ in the Paragraph group to display formatting marks**

   An end of cell mark appears at the end of each cell and an end of row mark appears at the end of each row.

QUICK TIP
You can also insert a row by right-clicking a row, pointing to Insert, then clicking Insert Rows Above or Insert Rows Below.

2. **Click the Table Tools Layout tab, click the first cell of the Examiner.com row, then click the Insert Above button in the Rows & Columns group**

   A new row is inserted directly above the Examiner.com row, as shown in Figure E-4. To insert a single row, you simply place the insertion point in the row above or below where you want the new row to be inserted, and then insert the row.

3. **Click the first cell of the new row, type San Francisco Examiner, press [Tab], then type 15,300**

QUICK TIP
If the end of row mark is not selected, you have selected only the text in the row, not the row itself.

4. **Place the pointer in the margin to the left of the SFGate.com row until the pointer changes to ⇗, click to select the row, press and hold the mouse button, drag down to select the Taxi tops row, then release the mouse button**

   The two rows are selected, including the end of row marks.

5. **Click the Insert Below button in the Rows & Columns group**

   Two new rows are added below the selected rows. To insert multiple rows, you select the number of rows you want to insert before inserting the rows.

6. **Click the The Independent row, click the Delete button in the Rows & Columns group, click Delete Rows, select the two blank rows, right-click the selected rows, then click Delete Rows on the menu that opens**

   The Independent row and the two blank rows are deleted. If you select a row and press [Delete], you delete only the contents of the row, not the row itself.

7. **Place the pointer over the top border of the Location column until the pointer changes to ↓, then click**

   The entire column is selected.

QUICK TIP
To select a cell, place the ➤ pointer near the left border of the cell, then click.

8. **Click the Insert Left button in the Rows & Columns group, then type Type**

   A new column is inserted to the left of the Location column, as shown in Figure E-5.

9. **Click in the Location column, click the Insert Right button in the Rows & Columns group, then type Details in the first cell of the new column**

   A new column is added to the right of the Location column.

10. **Press [↓] to move the insertion point to the next cell in the Details column, click the Home tab, click ¶ to turn off the display of formatting marks, enter the text shown in Figure E-6 in each cell in the Details and Type columns, then save your changes**

   You can use the arrow keys to move the insertion point from cell to cell. Notice that text wraps to the next line in the cell as you type. Compare your table to Figure E-6.

Creating and Formatting Tables

FIGURE E-4: Inserted row

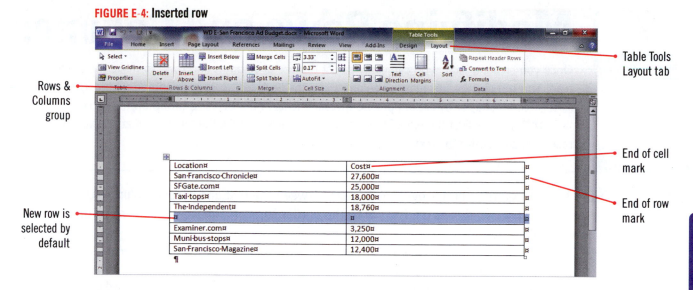

Table Tools Layout tab

Rows & Columns group

End of cell mark

End of row mark

New row is selected by default

FIGURE E-5: Inserted column

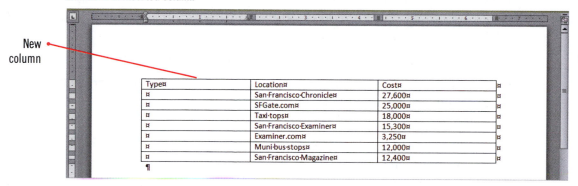

New column

FIGURE E-6: Text in Type and Details columns

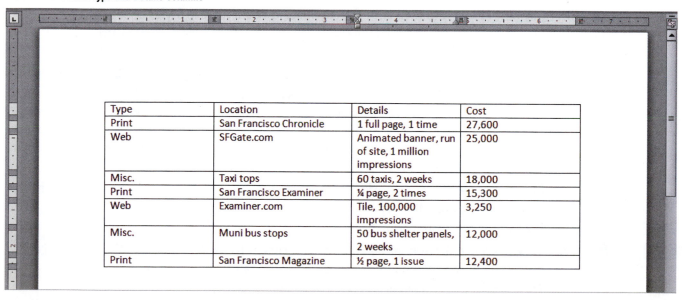

Type	Location	Details	Cost
Print	San Francisco Chronicle	1 full page, 1 time	27,600
Web	SFGate.com	Animated banner, run of site, 1 million impressions	25,000
Misc.	Taxi tops	60 taxis, 2 weeks	18,000
Print	San Francisco Examiner	¼ page, 2 times	15,300
Web	Examiner.com	Tile, 100,000 impressions	3,250
Misc.	Muni bus stops	50 bus shelter panels, 2 weeks	12,000
Print	San Francisco Magazine	½ page, 1 issue	12,400

Copying and moving rows and columns

You can copy and move rows and columns within a table in the same manner you copy and move text. Select the row or column you want to move, then use the Copy or Cut button to place the selection on the Clipboard. Place the insertion point in the location where you want to insert the row or column, then click the Paste button to paste the selection. Rows are inserted above the row containing the insertion point; columns are inserted to the left of the column containing the insertion point. You can also copy or move columns and rows by selecting them and using the pointer to drag them to a new location in the table.

Modifying Rows and Columns

Once you create a table, you can easily adjust the size of columns and rows to make the table easier to read. You can change the width of columns and the height of rows by dragging a border, by using the AutoFit command, or by setting precise measurements in the Cell Size group on the Table Tools Layout tab. 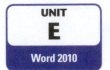 You adjust the size of the columns and rows to make the table more attractive and easier to read. You also center the text vertically in each table cell.

QUICK TIP
Press [Alt] as you drag a border to display the column width or row height measurements on the ruler.

1. **Position the pointer over the border between the first and second columns until the pointer changes to ╬, then drag the border to approximately the ½" mark on the horizontal ruler**

   The dotted line that appears as you drag represents the border. Dragging the column border changes the width of the first and second columns: the first column is narrower and the second column is wider. When dragging a border to change the width of an entire column, make sure no cells are selected in the column. You can also drag a row border to change the height of the row above it.

2. **Position the pointer over the right border of the Location column until the pointer changes to ╬, then double-click**

   Double-clicking a column border automatically resizes the column to fit the text.

3. **Double-click the right border of the Details column with the ╬ pointer, then double-click the right border of the Cost column with the ╬ pointer**

   The widths of the Details and Cost columns are adjusted.

4. **Move the pointer over the table, then click the table move handle ⊞ that appears outside the upper-left corner of the table**

   Clicking the table move handle selects the entire table. You can also use the Select button in the Table group on the Table Tools Layout tab to select an entire table.

5. **Click the Home tab, then click the No Spacing button in the Styles group**

   Changing the style to No Spacing removes the paragraph spacing below the text in each table cell, if your table included extra paragraph spacing.

QUICK TIP
Quickly resize a table by dragging the table resize handle to a new location.

6. **With the table still selected, click the Table Tools Layout tab, click the Distribute Rows button ⊞ in the Cell Size group, then click in the table to deselect it**

   All the rows in the table become the same height, as shown in Figure E-7. You can also use the Distribute Columns button to make all the columns the same width, or you can use the AutoFit button to make the width of the columns fit the text, to adjust the width of the columns so the table is justified between the margins, or to set fixed column widths.

7. **Click in the Details column, click the Table Column Width text box in the Cell Size group, type 3.5, then press [Enter]**

   The width of the Details column changes to 3.5".

QUICK TIP
Quickly center a table on a page by selecting the table and clicking the Center button in the Paragraph group on the Home tab.

8. **Click the Select button in the Table group, click Select Table, click the Align Center Left button ▤ in the Alignment group, deselect the table, then save your changes**

   The text is centered vertically in each table cell, as shown in Figure E-8. You can use the alignment buttons in the Alignment group to change the vertical and horizontal alignment of the text in selected cells or in the entire table.

FIGURE E-7: Resized columns and rows

Table move handle: click to select the table; drag to move the table

Rows are all the same height

Table resize handle; drag to change the size of all the rows and columns

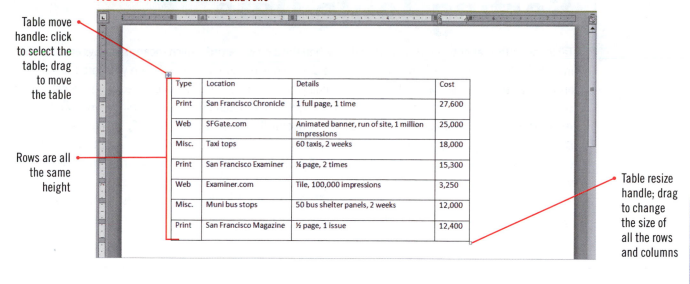

Type	Location	Details	Cost
Print	San Francisco Chronicle	1 full page, 1 time	27,600
Web	SFGate.com	Animated banner, run of site, 1 million impressions	25,000
Misc.	Taxi tops	60 taxis, 2 weeks	18,000
Print	San Francisco Examiner	¼ page, 2 times	15,300
Web	Examiner.com	Tile, 100,000 impressions	3,250
Misc.	Muni bus stops	50 bus shelter panels, 2 weeks	12,000
Print	San Francisco Magazine	½ page, 1 issue	12,400

FIGURE E-8: Text centered vertically in cells

Column is widened

Text is centered vertically in the cell

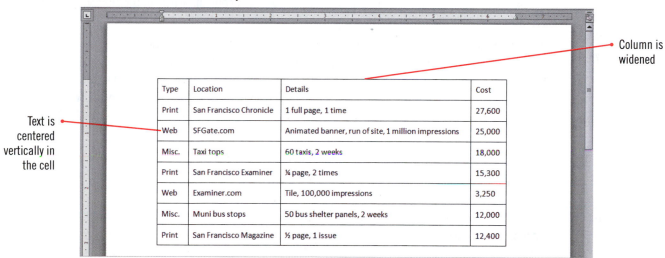

Type	Location	Details	Cost
Print	San Francisco Chronicle	1 full page, 1 time	27,600
Web	SFGate.com	Animated banner, run of site, 1 million impressions	25,000
Misc.	Taxi tops	60 taxis, 2 weeks	18,000
Print	San Francisco Examiner	¼ page, 2 times	15,300
Web	Examiner.com	Tile, 100,000 impressions	3,250
Misc.	Muni bus stops	50 bus shelter panels, 2 weeks	12,000
Print	San Francisco Magazine	½ page, 1 issue	12,400

Setting advanced table properties

When you want to wrap text around a table, indent a table, or set other advanced table properties, you click the Properties command in the Table group on the Table Tools Layout tab to open the Table Properties dialog box, shown in Figure E-9. Using the Table tab in this dialog box, you can set a precise width for the table, change the horizontal alignment of the table between the margins, indent the table, and set text wrapping options for the table. You can also click Options on the Table tab to open the Table Options dialog box, which you use to customize the table's default cell margins and the spacing between table cells. Alternatively, click Borders and Shading on the Table tab to open the Borders and Shading dialog box, which you can use to create a custom format for the table.

The Column, Row, and Cell tabs in the Table Properties dialog box allow you to set an exact width for columns, to specify an exact height for rows, and to indicate an exact size for individual cells. The Alt Text tab is used to add alternative text for a table that will appear on a Web page.

FIGURE E-9: Table Properties dialog box

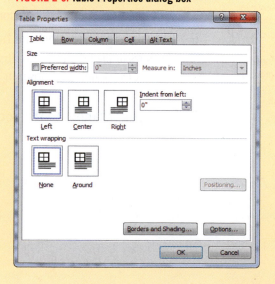

Sorting Table Data

Tables are often easier to interpret and analyze when the data is **sorted**, which means the rows are organized in alphabetical or sequential order based on the data in one or more columns. When you sort a table, Word arranges all the table data according to the criteria you set. You set sort criteria by specifying the column (or columns) you want to sort by and indicating the sort order—ascending or descending—you want to use. **Ascending order** lists data alphabetically or sequentially (from A to Z, 0 to 9, or earliest to latest). **Descending order** lists data in reverse alphabetical or sequential order (from Z to A, 9 to 0, or latest to earliest). You can sort using the data in one column or multiple columns. When you sort by multiple columns you must select primary, secondary, and tertiary sort criteria. You use the Sort command in the Data group on the Table Tools Layout tab to sort a table.  You sort the table so that all ads of the same type are listed together. You also add secondary sort criteria so that the ads within each type are listed in descending order by cost.

STEPS

1. **Place the insertion point anywhere in the table**

   To sort an entire table, you simply need to place the insertion point anywhere in the table. If you want to sort specific rows only, then you must select the rows you want to sort.

2. **Click the Sort button in the Data group on the Table Tools Layout tab**

   The Sort dialog box opens, as shown in Figure E-10. You use this dialog box to specify the column or columns you want to sort by, the type of information you are sorting (text, numbers, or dates), and the sort order (ascending or descending). Column 1 is selected by default in the Sort by list box. Since you want to sort your table first by the information in the first column—the type of ad (Print, Web, or Misc.)—you don't change the Sort by criteria.

3. **Click the Descending option button in the Sort by section**

   The ad type information will be sorted in descending—or reverse alphabetical—order, so that the "Web" ads will be listed first, followed by the "Print" ads, and then the "Misc." ads.

4. **Click the Then by list arrow in the first Then by section, click Column 4, click the Type list arrow, click Number if it is not already selected, then click the Descending option button**

   Within the Web, Print, and Misc. groups, the rows will be sorted by the cost of the ad, which is the information contained in the fourth column. The rows will appear in descending order within each group, with the most expensive ad listed first.

5. **Click the Header row option button in the My list has section to select it**

   The table includes a **header row**, which is the first row of a table that contains the column headings. You select the Header row option button when you do not want the header row included in the sort.

6. **Click OK, then deselect the table**

   The rows in the table are sorted first by the information in the Type column and second by the information in the Cost column, as shown in Figure E-11. The first row of the table, which is the header row, is not included in the sort.

7. **Save your changes to the document**

QUICK TIP
To repeat the header row on every page of a table that spans multiple pages, click the Repeat Header Rows button in the Data group on the Table Tools Layout tab.

FIGURE E-10: Sort dialog box

Select the primary sort column

Choose the sort order

Select the type of data in the sort column

Include or exclude the header row in the sort

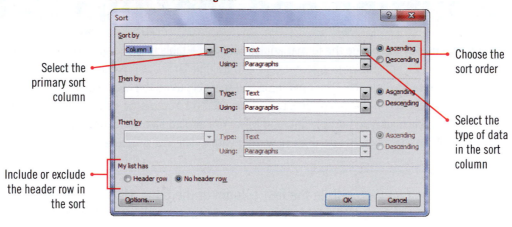

FIGURE E-11: Sorted table

Header row is not included in the sort

First, rows are sorted by type in descending order

Second, within each type, rows are sorted by cost in descending order

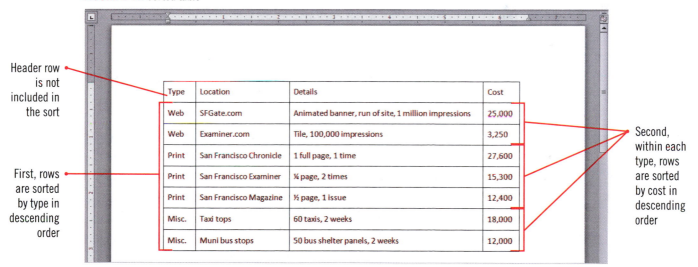

Type	Location	Details	Cost
Web	SFGate.com	Animated banner, run of site, 1 million impressions	25,000
Web	Examiner.com	Tile, 100,000 impressions	3,250
Print	San Francisco Chronicle	1 full page, 1 time	27,600
Print	San Francisco Examiner	¼ page, 2 times	15,300
Print	San Francisco Magazine	½ page, 1 issue	12,400
Misc.	Taxi tops	60 taxis, 2 weeks	18,000
Misc.	Muni bus stops	50 bus shelter panels, 2 weeks	12,000

Sorting lists and paragraphs

In addition to sorting table data, you can use the Sort command to alphabetize text or sort numerical data. When you want to sort data that is not formatted as a table, such as lists and paragraphs, you use the Sort command in the Paragraph group on the Home tab. To sort lists and paragraphs, select the items you want included in the sort, then click the Sort button. In the Sort Text dialog box, use the Sort by list arrow to select the sort by criteria (paragraphs or fields), use the Type list arrow to select the type of data (text, numbers, or dates), and then click the Ascending or Descending option button to choose a sort order.

When sorting text information in a document, the term "fields" refers to text or numbers that are separated by a character, such as a tab or a comma. For example, you might want to sort a list of names alphabetically. If the names you want to sort are listed in "Last name, First name" order, then last name and first name are each considered a field. You can choose to sort the list in alphabetical order by last name or by first name. Use the Options button in the Sort Text dialog box to specify the character that separates the fields in your lists or paragraphs, along with other sort options.

Splitting and Merging Cells

A convenient way to change the format and structure of a table is to merge and split the table cells. When you **merge** cells, you combine adjacent cells into a single larger cell. When you **split** a cell, you divide an existing cell into multiple cells. You can merge and split cells using the Merge Cells and Split Cells commands in the Merge group on the Table Tools Layout tab.  You merge cells in the first column to create a single cell for each ad type—Web, Print, and Misc. You also add a new row to the bottom of the table, and split the cells in the row to create three new rows with a different structure.

STEPS

TROUBLE

If you click below the table to deselect it, the active tab changes to the Home tab. If necessary, click in the table, then click the Table Tools Layout tab to continue with the steps in this lesson.

1. **Select the two Web cells in the first column of the table, click the Merge Cells button in the Merge group on the Table Tools Layout tab, then deselect the text**

   The two Web cells merge to become a single cell. When you merge cells, Word converts the text in each cell into a separate paragraph in the merged cell.

2. **Select the first Web in the cell, then press [Delete]**

3. **Select the three Print cells in the first column, click the Merge Cells button, type Print, select the two Misc. cells, click the Merge Cells button, then type Misc.**

   The three Print cells merge to become one cell and the two Misc. cells merge to become one cell.

4. **Click the Muni bus stops cell, then click the Insert Below button in the Rows & Columns group**

   A row is added to the bottom of the table.

5. **Select the first three cells in the new last row of the table, click the Merge Cells button, then deselect the cell**

   The three cells in the row merge to become a single cell.

QUICK TIP

To split a table in two, click the row you want to be the first row in the second table, then click the Split Table button in the Merge group.

6. **Click the first cell in the last row, then click the Split Cells button in the Merge group**

   The Split Cells dialog box opens, as shown in Figure E-12. You use this dialog box to split the selected cell or cells into a specific number of columns and rows.

7. **Type 1 in the Number of columns text box, press [Tab], type 3 in the Number of rows text box, click OK, then deselect the cells**

   The single cell is divided into three rows of equal height. When you split a cell into multiple rows, the width of the original column does not change. When you split a cell into multiple columns, the height of the original row does not change. If the cell you split contains text, all the text appears in the upper-left cell.

8. **Click the last cell in the Cost column, click the Split Cells button, repeat Step 7, then save your changes**

   The cell is split into three rows, as shown in Figure E-13. The last three rows of the table now have only two columns.

Creating and Formatting Tables

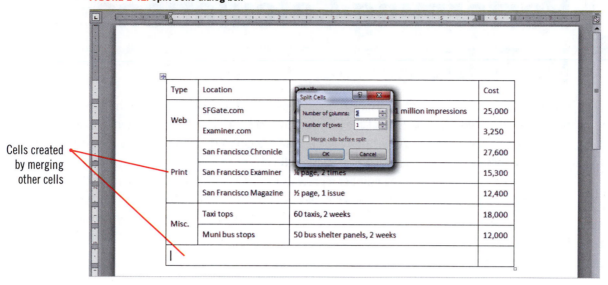

Cells created by merging other cells

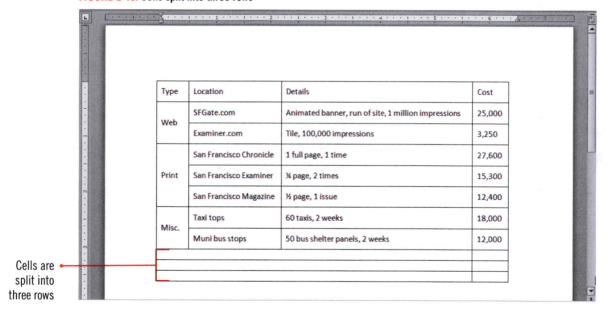

Cells are split into three rows

Changing cell margins

By default, table cells have .08" left and right cell margins with no spacing between the cells, but you can adjust these settings for a table using the Cell Margins button in the Alignment group on the Table Tools Layout tab. First, place the insertion point in the table, and then click the Cell Margins button to open the Table Options dialog box. Enter new settings for the top, bottom, left, and right cell margins in the text boxes in the Default cell margins section of the dialog box, or select the Allow spacing between cells check box and then enter a setting in the Cell spacing section to increase the spacing between table cells. You can also deselect the Automatically resize to fit contents check box in the Options section of the dialog box to turn off the setting that causes table cells to widen to fit the text as you type. Any settings you change in the Table Options dialog box are applied to the entire table.

Performing Calculations in Tables

If your table includes numerical information, you can perform simple calculations in the table. The Formula command allows you to quickly total the numbers in a column or row, and to perform other standard calculations, such as averages. When you calculate data in a table using formulas, you use cell references to refer to the cells in the table. Each cell has a unique **cell reference** composed of a letter and a number; the letter represents its column and the number represents its row. For example, the cell in the third row of the fourth column is cell D3. Figure E-14 shows the cell references in a simple table. 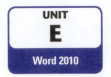 You use the Formula command to calculate the total cost of the San Francisco ad campaign. You also add information about the budgeted cost, and create a formula to calculate the difference between the total and budgeted costs.

STEPS

QUICK TIP
If a column or row contains blank cells, you must type a zero in any blank cell before using the SUM function.

1. **Click the first blank cell in column 1, type Total Cost, press [Tab], then click the Formula button in the Data group on the Table Tools Layout tab**

   The Formula dialog box opens, as shown in Figure E-15. The SUM function appears in the Formula text box followed by the reference for the cells to include in the calculation, (ABOVE). The formula =SUM(ABOVE) indicates that Word will sum the numbers in the cells above the active cell.

2. **Click OK**

   Word totals the numbers in the cells above the active cell and inserts the sum as a field. You can use the SUM function to quickly total the numbers in a column or a row. If the cell you select is at the bottom of a column of numbers, Word totals the column. If the cell is at the right end of a row of numbers, Word totals the row.

3. **Select 12,000 in the cell above the total, then type 13,500**

   If you change a number that is part of a calculation, you must recalculate the field result.

QUICK TIP
To change a field result to regular text, click the field to select it, then press [Ctrl][Shift][F9].

4. **Press [↓], right-click the cell, then click Update Field**

   The information in the cell is updated. When the insertion point is in a cell that contains a formula, you can also press [F9] to update the field result.

5. **Press [Tab], type Budgeted, press [Tab], type 113,780, press [Tab], type Difference, then press [Tab]**

   The insertion point is in the last cell of the table.

6. **Click the Formula button**

   The Formula dialog box opens. Word proposes to sum the numbers above the active cell, but you want to insert a formula that calculates the difference between the total and budgeted costs. You can type simple custom formulas using a plus sign (+) for addition, a minus sign (–) for subtraction, an asterisk (*) for multiplication, and a slash (/) for division.

QUICK TIP
Cell references are determined by the number of columns in each row, not by the number of columns in the table. Therefore, rows 9 and 10 have only two columns.

7. **Select =SUM(ABOVE) in the Formula text box, then type =B9–B10**

   You must type an equal sign (=) to indicate that the text following it is a formula. You want to subtract the budgeted cost in the second column of row 10 from the total cost in the second column of row 9; therefore, you type a formula to subtract the value in cell B10 from the value in cell B9.

8. **Click OK, then save your changes**

   The difference appears in the cell, as shown in Figure E-16.

FIGURE E-14: Cell references in a table

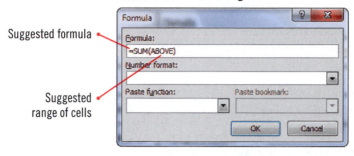

Column D (fourth column)

	A	B	C	D
1	A1	B1	C1	D1
2	A2	B2	C2	D2
3	A3	B3	C3	D3

Row 3

Cell reference indicates the cell's column and row

FIGURE E-15: Formula dialog box

Suggested formula

Suggested range of cells

FIGURE E-16: Difference calculated

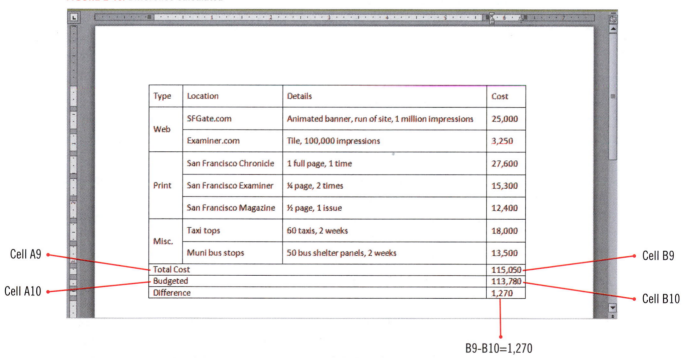

Cell A9

Cell A10

Cell B9

Cell B10

Type	Location	Details	Cost
Web	SFGate.com	Animated banner, run of site, 1 million impressions	25,000
	Examiner.com	Tile, 100,000 impressions	3,250
Print	San Francisco Chronicle	1 full page, 1 time	27,600
	San Francisco Examiner	¼ page, 2 times	15,300
	San Francisco Magazine	½ page, 1 issue	12,400
Misc.	Taxi tops	60 taxis, 2 weeks	18,000
	Muni bus stops	50 bus shelter panels, 2 weeks	13,500
Total Cost			115,050
Budgeted			113,780
Difference			1,270

B9-B10=1,270

Working with formulas

In addition to the SUM function, Word includes formulas for averaging, counting, and rounding data, to name a few. To use a Word formula, delete any text in the Formula text box, type =, click the Paste function list arrow in the Formula dialog box, select a function, and then insert the cell references of the cells you want to include in the calculation in parentheses after the name of the function. When entering formulas, you must separate cell references by a comma. For example, if you want to average the values in cells A1, B3, and C4, enter the formula =AVERAGE(A1,B3,C4). You must separate cell ranges by a colon. For example, to total the values in cells A1 through A9, enter the formula =SUM(A1:A9). To display the result of a calculation in a particular number format, such as a decimal percentage (0.00%), click the Number format list arrow in the Formula dialog box and select a number format. Word inserts the result of a calculation as a field in the selected cell.

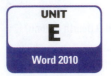
Applying a Table Style

Adding shading and other design elements to a table can help give it a polished appearance and make the data easier to read. Word includes predefined, built-in table styles that you can apply to a table to format it quickly. Table styles include borders, shading, fonts, alignment, colors, and other formatting effects. You can apply a table style to a table using the buttons in the Table Styles group on the Table Tools Design tab. ██ You want to enhance the appearance of the table with shading, borders, and other formats, so you apply a table style to the table. After applying a style, you change the theme colors to a more pleasing palette.

1. **Click the Table Tools Design tab**

   The Table Tools Design tab includes buttons for applying table styles and for adding, removing, and customizing borders and shading in a table.

2. **Click the More button ▾ in the Table Styles group**

   The gallery of table styles opens, as shown in Figure E-17. You point to a table style in the gallery to preview the style applied to the table.

3. **Move the pointer over several styles in the gallery, then click the Light Grid – Accent 4 style**

   The Light Grid – Accent 4 style is applied to the table, as shown in Figure E-18. Because of the structure of the table, this style neither enhances the table nor helps make the data more readable.

4. **Click the More button ▾ in the Table Styles group, then click the Light List – Accent 4 style**

   This style works better with the structure of the table, and makes the table data easier to read. Notice that the alignment of the text in the table changed back to top left when you applied a table style.

5. **In the Table Style Options group, click the First Column check box to clear it, then click the Banded Columns check box to select it**

   The bold formatting is removed from the first column, and column borders are added to the table. When the banded columns or banded rows setting is active, the odd columns or rows are formatted differently from the even columns or rows to make the table data easier to read.

6. **Click the Page Layout tab, click the Theme Colors list arrow ██ in the Themes group, then click Paper in the gallery that opens**

   The color palette for the document changes to the colors used in the Paper theme, and the table color changes to lavender.

7. **Click the Table Tools Design tab, click the More button ▾ in the Table Styles group, then click the Light List – Accent 6 style**

   The table color changes to blue-gray.

8. **Click the Table Tools Layout tab, click the table move handle ██ to select the table, click the Align Center Left button ██ in the Alignment group, select the Type column, click the Align Center button ██ in the Alignment group, select the Cost column, then click the Align Center Right button ██ in the Alignment group**

   First, the data in the table is left-aligned and centered vertically, then the data in the Type column is centered, and finally the data in the Cost column is right-aligned.

9. **Select the last three rows of the table, click the Bold button B on the Mini toolbar, then click the Align Center Right button ██ in the Alignment group on the Table Tools Layout tab**

   The text in the last three rows is right-aligned and bold is applied.

10. **Select the first row of the table, click the Center button ██ on the Mini toolbar, click the Font Size list arrow on the Mini toolbar, click 14, deselect the row, then save your changes**

    The text in the header row is centered and enlarged, as shown in Figure E-19. You can also use the alignment buttons in the Paragraph group on the Home tab to change the alignment of text in a table.

FIGURE E-17: Gallery of table styles

Options for customizing table style settings

Gallery of table styles (your display may differ)

Light List, Accent 4 style

Modify an existing table style

Remove a table style from a table

Create a new table style

Light Grid, Accent 4 style

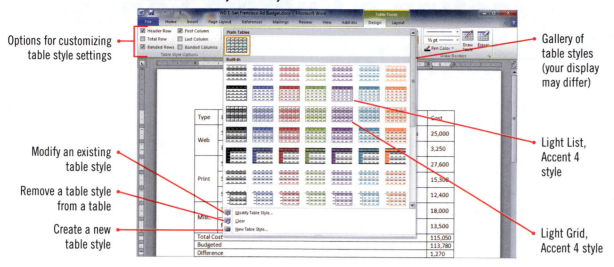

FIGURE E-18: Light Grid, Accent 4 style applied to table

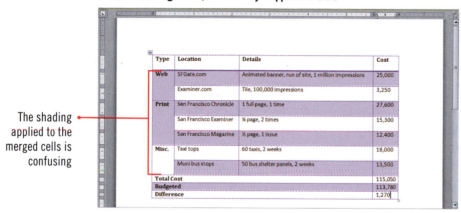

The shading applied to the merged cells is confusing

FIGURE E-19: Light List, Accent 6 style (Paper theme) applied to table

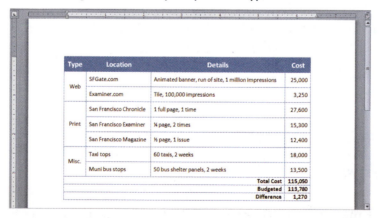

Using tables to lay out a page

Tables are often used to display information for quick reference and analysis, but you can also use tables to structure the layout of a page. You can insert any kind of information in the cell of a table—including graphics, bulleted lists, charts, and other tables (called **nested tables**). For example, you might use a table to lay out a résumé, a newsletter, or a Web page. When you use a table to lay out a page, you generally remove the table borders to hide the table structure from the reader. After you remove borders, it can be helpful to display the table gridlines onscreen while you work. **Gridlines** are blue dotted lines that show the boundaries of cells, but do not print. If your document will be viewed online—for example, if you are planning to e-mail your résumé to potential employers—you should turn off the display of gridlines before you distribute the document so that it looks the same online as it looks when printed. To turn gridlines off or on, click the View Gridlines button in the Table group on the Table Tools Layout tab.

Creating a Custom Format for a Table

You can also use the formatting tools available in Word to create your own table designs. For example, you can add or remove borders and shading; vary the line style, thickness, and color of borders; and change the orientation of text from horizontal to vertical.  You adjust the text direction, shading, and borders in the table to make it easier to understand at a glance.

STEPS

1. **Select the Type and Location cells in the first row, click the Merge Cells button in the Merge group on the Table Tools Layout tab, then type Ad Location**

   The two cells are combined into a single cell containing the text "Ad Location."

2. **Select the Web, Print, and Misc. cells in the first column, click the Bold button B on the Mini toolbar, click the Text Direction button in the Alignment group twice, then deselect the cells**

   The text is rotated 270 degrees.

3. **Position the pointer over the right border of the Web cell until the pointer changes to ◂‖▸, then drag the border to approximately the ¼" mark on the horizontal ruler**

   The width of the column containing the vertical text narrows.

QUICK TIP

In cells with vertical text, the I-beam pointer is rotated 90 degrees, and the buttons in the Alignment group change to vertical alignment.

4. **Place the insertion point in the Web cell, click the Table Tools Design tab, then click the Shading list arrow in the Table Styles group**

   The gallery of shading colors for the Paper theme opens.

5. **Click Gold, Accent 3 in the gallery as shown in Figure E-20, click the Print cell, click the Shading list arrow, click Lavender, Accent 4, click the Misc. cell, click the Shading list arrow, then click Blue-Gray, Accent 6**

   Shading is applied to each cell.

6. **Drag to select the six white cells in the Web rows (rows 2 and 3), click the Shading list arrow, then click Gold, Accent 3, Lighter 60%**

7. **Repeat Step 6 to apply Lavender, Accent 4, Lighter 60% shading to the Print rows and Blue-Gray, Accent 6, Lighter 60% shading to the Misc. rows**

   Shading is applied to all the cells in rows 1–8.

TROUBLE

If gridlines appear, click the Borders list arrow, then click View Gridlines to turn off the display.

8. **Select the last three rows of the table, click the Borders list arrow in the Table Styles group, click No Border on the menu that opens, then click in the table to deselect the rows**

   The top, bottom, left, and right borders are removed from each cell in the selected rows.

QUICK TIP

On the Borders menu, click the button that corresponds to the border you want to add or remove.

9. **Click the Pen Color list arrow in the Draw Borders group, click Blue-Gray, Accent 6, select the Total Cost row, click the Borders list arrow, click Top Border, click the 113,780 cell, click the Borders list arrow, then click the Bottom Border**

   The active pen color for borders is Blue-Gray, Accent 6. You use the buttons in the Draw Borders group to change the active pen color, line weight, and line style settings before adding a border to a table. A top border is added to each cell in the Total Cost row, and a bottom border is added below 113,780. The completed table is shown in Figure E-21.

10. **Press [Ctrl][Home], press [Enter], type your name, save your changes, submit the document to your instructor, close the document, then exit Word**

    Press [Enter] at the beginning of a table to move the table down one line in a document.

FIGURE E-20: Gallery of shading colors from the Origin theme

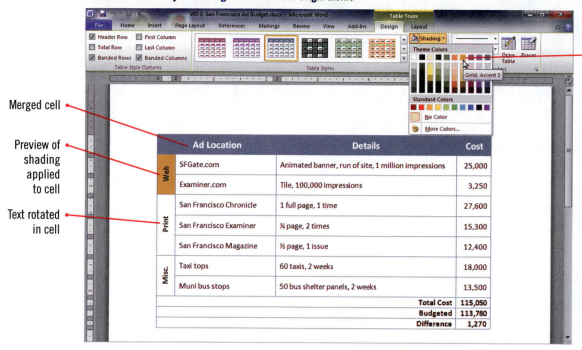

Merged cell

Preview of shading applied to cell

Text rotated in cell

Gold, Accent 3; use ScreenTips as needed to identify colors

FIGURE E-21: Completed table

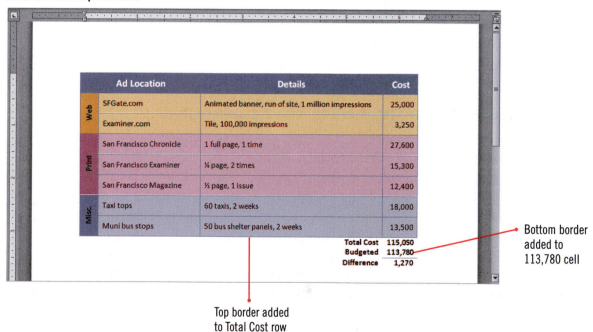

Bottom border added to 113,780 cell

Top border added to Total Cost row

Drawing a table

The Word Draw Table feature allows you to draw table cells exactly where you want them. To draw a table, click the Table button on the Insert tab, and then click Draw Table. If a table is already started, you can click the Draw Table button in the Draw Borders group on the Table Tools Design tab to turn on the Draw pointer, and then click and drag to draw a cell. Using the same method, you can draw borders within the cell to create columns and rows, or draw additional cells attached to the first cell. Click the Draw Table button to turn off the draw feature. The borders you draw are added using the active line style, line weight, and pen color settings.

If you want to remove a border from a table, click the Eraser button in the Draw Borders group to activate the Eraser pointer, and then click the border you want to remove. Click the Eraser button to turn off the erase feature. You can use the Draw pointer and the Eraser pointer to change the structure of any table, not just the tables you draw from scratch.

Word 2010

Practice

Concepts Review

For current SAM information, including versions and content details, visit SAM Central (http://www.cengage.com/samcentral). If you have a SAM user profile, you may have access to hands-on instruction, practice, and assessment of the skills covered in this unit. Since various versions of SAM are supported throughout the life of this text, check with your instructor for the correct instructions and URL/Web site for accessing assignments.

Label each element shown in Figure E-22.

FIGURE E-22

Type	Location	Details	Cost
Print	San Francisco Chronicle	1 full page, 1 time	27,600
Web	SFGate.com	Animated banner, run of site, 1 million impressions	25,000
Misc.	Taxi tops	60 taxis, 2 weeks	18,000
Print	San Francisco Examiner	¼ page, 2 times	15,300
Web	Examiner.com	Tile, 100,000 impressions	3,250
Misc.	Muni bus stops	50 bus shelter panels, 2 weeks	12,000
Print	San Francisco Magazine	½ page, 1 issue	12,400

Match each term with the statement that best describes it.

6. Split

7. Borders

8. Ascending order

9. Merge

10. Nested table

11. Descending order

12. Cell

13. Header row

14. Cell reference

15. Gridlines

a. Sort order that organizes text from A to Z

b. The box formed by the intersection of a column and a row

c. An object inserted in a table cell

d. The first row of a table that contains the column headings

e. To combine two or more adjacent cells into one larger cell

f. Lines that separate columns and rows in a table and that print

g. To divide an existing cell into multiple cells

h. Lines that show columns and rows in a table but that do not print

i. A cell address composed of a column letter and a row number

j. Sort order that organizes text from Z to A

Select the best answer from the list of choices.

16. **Which button do you use to change the alignment of text in a cell?**

   a.
   b.
   c.
   d.

17. **Which of the following is the cell reference for the third cell in the second column?**

   a. 3B
   b. B3
   c. C2
   d. 2C

18. **What happens when you double-click a column border?**

   a. The column width is adjusted to fit the text.
   b. The columns in the table are distributed evenly.
   c. A new column is added to the left.
   d. A new column is added to the right.

Creating and Formatting Tables

19. Which of the following is *not* a valid way to add a new row to the bottom of a table?

   a. Click in the bottom row, open the Properties dialog box, then insert a row using the options on the Row tab.

   b. Place the insertion point in the last cell of the last row, then press [Tab].

   c. Right-click the bottom row, point to Insert, then click Insert Rows Below.

   d. Click in the bottom row, then click the Insert Below button in the Rows & Columns group on the Table Tools Layout tab.

20. Which of the following is *not* a correct formula for adding the values in cells A1, A2, and A3?

   a. =A1+A2+A3

   b. =SUM(A1~A3)

   c. =SUM(A1,A2,A3)

   d. =SUM(A1:A3)

Skills Review

1. Insert a table.

   a. Start Word, then save the new blank document as **WD E-Mutual Funds** to the drive and folder where you store your Data Files.

   b. Type your name, press [Enter] twice, type **Mutual Funds Performance**, then press [Enter].

   c. Insert a table that contains four columns and four rows.

   d. Type the text shown in Figure E-23, pressing [Tab] to add rows as necessary. (*Note*: Do not format text or the table at this time.)

   e. Save your changes.

2. Insert and delete rows and columns.

   a. Insert a row above the Health Care row, then type the following text in the new row:

      Canada   **8.24**   **8.12**   **8.56**

   b. Delete the Europe row.

   c. Insert a column to the right of the 10 Year column, type **Date Purchased** in the header row, then enter a date in each cell in the column using the format MM/DD/YY (for example, 11/27/02).

   d. Move the Date Purchased column to the right of the Fund Name column, then save your changes.

FIGURE E-23

Fund Name	1 Year	5 Year	10 Year
Computers	16.47	25.56	27.09
Europe	-6.15	13.89	10.61
Natural Resources	19.47	12.30	15.38
Health Care	32.45	24.26	22.25
Financial Services	22.18	22.79	24.44
500 Index	10.34	15.34	13.69

3. Modify rows and columns.

   a. Double-click the border between the first and second columns to resize the columns.

   b. Drag the border between the second and third columns to the $2\frac{1}{4}$" mark on the horizontal ruler.

   c. Double-click the right border of the 1 Year, 5 Year, and 10 Year columns.

   d. Select the 1 Year, 5 Year, and 10 Year columns, then distribute the columns evenly.

   e. Select the table, apply the No Spacing style, select rows 2–7, set the row height to exactly .3", then save your changes.

4. Sort table data.

Perform three separate sorts as follows:

   a. Sort the table data, excluding the header row, in descending order by the information in the 1 Year column, then click OK.

   b. Sort the table data, excluding the header row, in ascending order by date purchased, then click OK.

   c. Sort the table data, excluding the header row, by fund name in alphabetical order, click OK, then save your changes.

5. Split and merge cells.

   a. Insert a row above the header row, then merge the first cell in the new row with the Fund Name cell.

   b. Merge the second cell in the new row with the Date Purchased cell.

   c. Merge the three remaining blank cells in the first row into a single cell, then type **Average Annual Returns** in the merged cell.

   d. Add a new row to the bottom of the table.

   e. Merge the first two cells in the new row, then type **Average Return** in the merged cell.

   f. Select the first seven cells in the first column (from Fund Name to Natural Resources), open the Split Cells dialog box, clear the Merge cells before split check box, then split the cells into two columns.

g. Type **Trading Symbol** as the heading for the new column, then enter the following text in the remaining cells in the column: **FINX**, **CAND**, **COMP**, **FINS**, **HCRX**, **NARS**.

h. Double-click the right border of the first column to resize the column, then save your changes.

6. Perform calculations in tables.

a. Place the insertion point in the last cell in the 1 Year column.

b. Open the Formula dialog box, delete the text in the Formula text box, type **=average(above)**, click the Number format list arrow, scroll down, click 0.00%, then click OK.

c. Repeat Step b to insert the average return in the last cell in the 5 Year and 10 Year columns.

d. Change the value of the 1-year return for the Natural Resources fund to **10.35**.

e. Recalculate the average return for 1 year, then save your changes. (*Hint*: Right-click the cell and select Update Field, or use [F9].)

7. Apply a table style.

a. Click the Table Tools Design tab, preview table styles applied to the table, and then apply an appropriate style. Was the style you chose effective?

b. Apply the Light Shading style to the table, then remove the style from First Column and Banded Rows.

c. Apply bold to the 1 Year, 5 Year, and 10 Year column headings, and to the bottom row of the table.

d. Center the table between the margins, center the table title **Mutual Funds Performance**, increase the font size of the title to 14 points, apply bold, then save your changes.

8. Create a custom format for a table.

a. Select the entire table, then use the Align Center button in the Alignment group on the Table Tools Layout tab to center the text in every cell vertically and horizontally.

b. Center right-align the dates in column 3 and the numbers in columns 4–6.

c. Center left-align the fund names and trading symbols in columns 1 and 2, but not the column headings.

d. Center right-align the text in the bottom row. Make sure the text in the header row is still centered.

e. Change the theme colors to Executive.

f. Select all the cells in the header row, including the 1 Year, 5 Year, and 10 Year column headings, change the shading color to Dark Green, Accent 5, then change the font color to white.

g. Apply Dark Green, Accent 5, Lighter 60% shading to the cells containing the fund names and trading symbols, and Dark Green Accent 5, Lighter 80% shading to the cells containing the purchase dates.

h. To the cells containing the 1 Year, 5 Year, and 10 Year data (excluding the Average Return data), apply Indigo, Accent 1, Lighter 60% shading; Orange, Accent 3, Lighter 60% shading; and Red, Accent 2, Lighter 60% shading, respectively.

i. Apply Dark Green Accent 5, Lighter 80% shading to the last row of the table.

j. Add a ½-point white bottom border to the Average Annual Returns cell in the header row.

k. Add a 1½-point black border around the outside of the table.

l. Add a ½-point black top border to the 500 Index row and to the last row of the table. (*Hint*: Do not remove any borders.)

m. Compare your table to Figure E-24, make any necessary adjustments, save your changes, submit a copy to your instructor, close the file, then exit Word.

FIGURE E-24

Mutual Funds Performance

Fund Name	Trading Symbol	Date Purchased	Average Annual Returns		
			1 Year	5 Year	10 Year
500 Index	FINX	5/9/96	10.34	15.34	13.69
Canada	CAND	11/13/03	8.24	8.12	8.56
Computers	COMP	9/23/01	16.47	25.56	27.09
Financial Services	FINS	2/12/01	22.18	22.79	24.44
Health Care	HCRX	3/24/96	32.45	24.26	22.25
Natural Resources	NARS	6/2/98	10.35	12.30	15.38
Average Return			16.67%	18.06%	18.57%

Independent Challenge 1

You are the director of sales for a publishing company with branch offices in six cities around the globe. In preparation for the upcoming sales meeting, you create a table showing your sales projections for the fiscal year 2013.

a. Start Word, then save the new blank document as **WD E-2013 Sales** to the drive and folder where you store your Data Files.

b. Type the table heading **Projected Sales in Millions, Fiscal Year 2013** at the top of the document, then press [Enter] twice.

c. Insert a table with five columns and four rows, then enter the data shown in Figure E-25 into the table, adding rows as necessary. (*Note*: Do not format text or the table at this time.)

d. Resize the columns to fit the text.

e. Sort the table rows in alphabetical order by Office.

f. Add a new row to the bottom of the table, type **Total** in the first cell, then enter a formula in each remaining cell in the new row to calculate the sum of the cells above it.

FIGURE E-25

Office	Q1	Q2	Q3	Q4
London	9500	5800	3900	9800
Tokyo	6700	8900	4500	4900
Frankfurt	8800	8500	6800	7400
Shanghai	5800	7200	4700	8200
New York	8500	7800	9800	9400
Sydney	7900	6800	3800	6200

g. Add a new column to the right side of the table, type **Total** in the first cell, then enter a formula in each remaining cell in the new column to calculate the sum of the cells to the left of it. (*Hint*: Make sure the formula you insert in each cell sums the cells to the left, not the cells above. In the last cell in the last column, you can sum the cells to the left or the cells above; either way the total should be the same.)

h. Apply a table style to the table. Select a style that enhances the information contained in the table, and adjust the Table Style Options to suit the content.

i. Center the text in the header row, left-align the remaining text in the first column, then right-align the numerical data in the table.

j. Enhance the table with fonts, font colors, shading, and borders to make the table attractive and easy to read at a glance.

k. Increase the font size of the table heading to 18 points, then center the table heading and the table on the page.

l. Press [Ctrl][End], press [Enter], type your name, save your changes, submit the file to your instructor, close the file, then exit Word.

Independent Challenge 2

You have been invited to speak to your local board of realtors about the economic benefits of living in your city. To illustrate some of your points, you want to distribute a handout comparing the cost of living and other economic indicators in the U.S. cities that offer features similar to your city. You decide to format the data as a table.

a. Start Word, open the file WD E-1.docx, then save it as **WD E-City Data** to the drive and folder where you store your Data Files.

b. Center the table heading, then increase the font size to 18 points.

c. Turn on formatting marks, select the tabbed text in the document, then convert the text to a table.

d. Add a row above the first row in the table, then enter the following column headings in the new header row: **City**, **Cost of Living**, **Median Income**, **Average House Cost**, **Bachelor Degree Rate**.

e. Apply an appropriate table style to the table. Add or remove the style from various elements of the table using the options in the Table Style Options group, as necessary.

f. Adjust the column widths so that the table is attractive and readable. (*Hint*: Allow the column headings to wrap to two lines.)

g. Make the height of each row at least .25".

h. Center left-align the text in each cell in the first column, including the column head.

i. Center right-align the text in each cell in the remaining columns, including the column heads.

j. Center the entire table on the page.

k. Sort the table by cost of living in descending order.

Independent Challenge 2 (continued)

Advanced Challenge Exercise

- Add a new row to the bottom of the table, then type **Average** in the first cell in the new row.
- In each subsequent cell in the Average row, insert a formula that calculates the averages of the cells above it. (*Hint*: For each cell, replace SUM with **AVERAGE** in the Formula text box, but do not make other changes.)
- Format the Average row with borders, shading, fonts, and other formats, as necessary to enhance the data, then adjust the formatting of the table so it fits on one page.

l. On the blank line below the table, type **Note: The average cost of living in the United States is 100.**, italicize the text, then use a tab stop and indents to align the text with the left side of the table if it is not aligned.

m. Enhance the table with borders, shading, fonts, and other formats, if necessary, to make it attractive and readable.

n. Type your name at the bottom of the document or in the footer, save your changes, submit a copy of the table to your instructor, close the document, then exit Word.

Independent Challenge 3

You work in the advertising department at a magazine. Your boss has asked you to create a fact sheet on the ad dimensions for the magazine. The fact sheet should include the dimensions for each type of ad. As a bonus, you could also add a visual representation of the different ad shapes and sizes, shown in Figure E-26. You'll use tables to lay out the fact sheet, present the dimension information, and, if you are performing the ACE steps, illustrate the ad shapes and sizes.

a. Start Word, open the file WD E-2.docx from the drive and folder where you store your Data Files, then save it as **WD E-Ad Fact Sheet**. Turn on the display of gridlines, then read the document to get a feel for its contents.

b. Drag the border between the first and second column to approximately the $2\frac{3}{4}$" mark on the horizontal ruler, resize the second and third columns to fit the text, then make each row in the table .5".

c. Change the alignment of the text in the first column to center left, then change the alignment of the text in the second and third columns to center right.

d. Remove all the borders from the table, then apply a $2\frac{1}{4}$-point, orange, dotted line, inside horizontal border to the entire table. This creates an orange dotted line between each row. (*Hint*: Use the Orange, Accent 6 color.)

e. In the second blank paragraph under the table heading, insert a new table with three columns and four rows, then merge the cells in the third column of the new blank table.

f. Drag the border between the first and second columns of the new blank table to the $1\frac{1}{4}$" mark on the horizontal ruler. Drag the border between the second and third columns to the $1\frac{1}{2}$" mark.

g. Select the table that contains text, cut it to the Clipboard, then paste it in the merged cell in the blank table. The table with text is now a nested table in the main table.

h. Split the nested table above the Unit Size (Bleed) row. (*Hint*: Place the insertion point in the Unit Size (Bleed) row, then use the Split Table button.)

i. Scroll up, merge the four cells in the first column of the main table, then merge the four cells in the second column.

j. Split the first column into one column and seven rows.

k. Using the Table Row Height text box in the Cell Size group, change the row height of each cell in the first column so that the rows alternate between exactly 1.8" and .25" in height. Make the height of the first, third, fifth, and seventh rows 1.8". (*Hint*: You can also use the Table Properties dialog box.)

FIGURE E-26

1 Full page

2 2/3 page — 1/3 page vertical

3 1/3 page horizontal — 1/6 page vertical — 1/2 page horizontal

4 1/2 page vertical — 1/12 — 1" — 1/6 page horizontal — 1/6 page

Independent Challenge 3 (continued)

l. Add Orange, Accent 6 shading to the first, third, fifth, and seventh cells in the first column, remove all the borders from the main table, then turn off the display of gridlines. The orange dotted line borders in the nested table remain.

Advanced Challenge Exercise

- In the first orange cell, type **Full Page**, change the font color to white, then center the text horizontally and vertically in the cell.
- In the Draw Borders group on the Table Tools Design tab, change the Line Style to a single line, change the Line Weight to $2\frac{1}{4}$ pt, then change the Pen Color to white.
- Be sure the Draw Table pointer is active, then, referring to Figure E-26, draw a vertical border that divides the second orange cell into 2/3 and 1/3.
- Label the cells and align the text as shown in the figure. (*Hint*: Change the font color, text direction, and alignment before typing text. Take care not to change the size of the cells when you type. If necessary, press [Enter] to start a new line of text in a cell, or reduce the font size of the text.)
- Referring to Figure E-26, divide the third and fourth orange cells, then label the cells as shown in the figure.

m. Examine the document for errors, then make any necessary adjustments.

n. Press [Ctrl][End], type your name, save your changes to the document, preview it, submit the file to your instructor, close the file, then exit Word.

Real Life Independent Challenge

This Independent Challenge requires an Internet connection.

A well-written and well-formatted résumé gives you an advantage when it comes to getting a job interview. In a winning résumé, the content and format support your career objective and effectively present your background and qualifications. One simple way to create a résumé is to lay out the page using a table. In this exercise you research guidelines for writing and formatting résumés. You then create your own résumé using a table for its layout.

a. Use your favorite search engine to search the Web for information on writing and formatting résumés. Use the keywords **resume advice**.

b. Print helpful advice on writing and formatting résumés from at least two Web sites.

c. Think about the information you want to include in your résumé. The header should include your name, address, telephone number, and e-mail address. The body should include your career objective and information on your education, work experience, and skills. You may want to add additional information.

d. Sketch a layout for your résumé using a table as the underlying grid. Include the table rows and columns in your sketch.

e. Start Word, open a new blank document, then save it as **WD E-My Resume** to the drive and folder where you store your Data Files.

f. Set appropriate margins, then insert a table to serve as the underlying grid for your résumé. Split and merge cells, and adjust the size of the table columns as necessary.

g. Type your résumé in the table cells. Take care to use a professional tone and keep your language to the point.

h. Format your résumé with fonts, bullets, and other formatting features. Adjust the spacing between sections by resizing the table columns and rows.

i. When you are satisfied with the content and format of your résumé, remove the borders from the table, then hide the gridlines if they are visible. You may want to add some borders back to the table to help structure the résumé for readers.

j. Check your résumé for spelling and grammar errors.

k. Save your changes, preview your résumé, submit a copy to your instructor, close the file, then exit Word.

Visual Workshop

Create the calendar shown in Figure E-27 using a table to lay out the entire page. (*Hints*: The top and bottom margins are .9", the left and right margins are 1", and the font is Century Gothic. The clip art image is inserted in the table. The clip art image is found using the keyword **chalk**. Use a different clip art image or font if the ones shown in the figure are not available.) Type your name in the last table cell, save the calendar with the file name **WD E-October 2013** to the drive and folder where you store your Data Files, then print a copy.

FIGURE E-27

October 2013

Sunday	Monday	Tuesday	Wednesday	Thursday	Friday	Saturday
		1	2	3	4	5
6	7	8	9	10	11	12
13	14	15	16	17	18	19
20	21	22	23	24	25	26
27	28	29	30	31		Your Name

Creating and Formatting Tables

Working with Windows Live and Office Web Apps

Files You Will Need:

WEB-1.pptx
WEB-2.xlsx

If the computer you are using has an active Internet connection, you can go to the Microsoft Windows Live Web site and access a wide variety of services and Web applications. For example, you can check your e-mail through Windows Live, network with your friends and coworkers, and use SkyDrive to store and share files. From SkyDrive, you can also use Office Web Apps to create and edit Word, PowerPoint, Excel, and OneNote files, even when you are using a computer that does not have Office 2010 installed.  You work in the Vancouver branch of Quest Specialty Travel. Your supervisor, Mary Lou Jacobs, asks you to explore Windows Live and learn how she can use SkyDrive and Office Web Apps to work with her files online.

(*Note*: SkyDrive and Office Web Apps are dynamic Web pages, and might change over time, including the way they are organized and how commands are performed. The steps and figures in this appendix were accurate at the time this book was published.)

OBJECTIVES

Explore how to work online from Windows Live

Obtain a Windows Live ID and sign in to Windows Live

Upload files to Windows Live

Work with the PowerPoint Web App

Create folders and organize files on SkyDrive

Add people to your network and share files

Work with the Excel Web App

Exploring How to Work Online from Windows Live

You can use your Web browser to upload your files to Windows Live from any computer connected to the Internet. You can work on the files right in your Web browser using Office Web Apps and share your files with people in your Windows Live network. You review the concepts and services related to working online from Windows Live.

DETAILS

- ### What is Windows Live?

  Windows Live is a collection of services and Web applications that you can use to help you be more productive both personally and professionally. For example, you can use Windows Live to send and receive e-mail, to chat with friends via instant messaging, to share photos, to create a blog, and to store and edit files using SkyDrive. Table WEB-1 describes the services available on Windows Live. Windows Live is a free service that you sign up for. When you sign up, you receive a Windows Live ID, which you use to sign in to Windows Live. When you work with files on Windows Live, you are cloud computing.

- ### What is Cloud Computing?

  The term **cloud computing** refers to the process of working with files online in a Web browser. When you save files to SkyDrive on Windows Live, you are saving your files to an online location. SkyDrive is like having a personal hard drive in the cloud.

- ### What is SkyDrive?

  SkyDrive is an online storage and file sharing service. With a Windows Live account, you receive access to your own SkyDrive, which is your personal storage area on the Internet. On your SkyDrive, you are given space to store up to 25 GB of data online. Each file can be a maximum size of 50 MB. You can also use SkyDrive to access Office Web Apps, which you use to create and edit files created in Word, OneNote, PowerPoint, and Excel online in your Web browser.

- ### Why use Windows Live and SkyDrive?

  On Windows Live, you use SkyDrive to access additional storage for your files. You don't have to worry about backing up your files to a memory stick or other storage device that could be lost or damaged. Another advantage of storing your files on SkyDrive is that you can access your files from any computer that has an active Internet connection. Figure WEB-1 shows the SkyDrive Web page that appears when accessed from a Windows Live account. From SkyDrive, you can also access Office Web Apps.

- ### What are Office Web Apps?

  Office Web Apps are versions of Microsoft Word, Excel, PowerPoint, and OneNote that you can access online from your SkyDrive. An Office Web App does not include all of the features and functions included with the full Office version of its associated application. However, you can use the Office Web App from any computer that is connected to the Internet, even if Microsoft Office 2010 is not installed on that computer.

- ### How do SkyDrive and Office Web Apps work together?

  You can create a file in Office 2010 using Word, Excel, PowerPoint, or OneNote and then upload the file to your SkyDrive. You can then open the Office file saved to SkyDrive and edit it using your Web browser and the corresponding Office Web App. Figure WEB-2 shows a PowerPoint presentation open in the PowerPoint Web App. You can also use an Office Web App to create a new file, which is saved automatically to SkyDrive while you work. In addition, you can download a file created with an Office Web App and continue to work with the file in the full version of the corresponding Office application: Word, Excel, PowerPoint, or OneNote. Finally, you can create a SkyDrive network that consists of the people you want to be able to view your folders and files on your SkyDrive. You can give people permission to view and edit your files using any computer with an active Internet connection and a Web browser.

FIGURE WEB-1: SkyDrive on Windows Live

Browser window

SkyDrive - Windows Live tab

By default, one folder is available on SkyDrive; you can create additional folders

The name of the person who signed into Windows Live and SkyDrive appears here

Monitors the amount of space still available on your SkyDrive

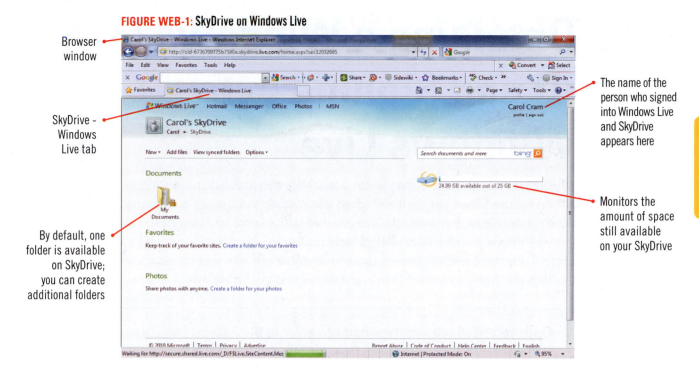

FIGURE WEB-2: PowerPoint presentation open in the PowerPoint Web App

Browser window

Ribbon available in PowerPoint Web App

The presentation in PowerPoint Web App maintains the same look and feel as the same presentation in the desktop version of PowerPoint

Name of PowerPoint presentation open in PowerPoint Web App

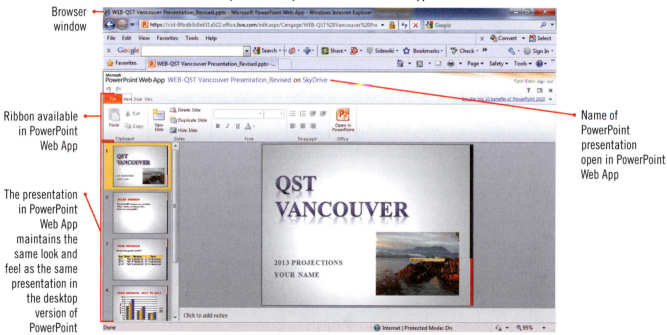

TABLE WEB-1: Services available via Windows Live

service	description
E-mail	Send and receive e-mail using a Hotmail account
Instant Messaging	Use Messenger to chat with friends, share photos, and play games
SkyDrive	Store files, work on files using Office Web Apps, and share files with people in your network
Photos	Upload and share photos with friends
People	Develop a network of friends and coworkers, then use the network to distribute information and stay in touch
Downloads	Access a variety of free programs available for download to a PC
Mobile Device	Access applications for a mobile device: text messaging, using Hotmail, networking, and sharing photos

Obtaining a Windows Live ID and Signing In to Windows Live

To work with your files online using SkyDrive and Office Web Apps, you need a Windows Live ID. You obtain a Windows Live ID by going to the Windows Live Web site and creating a new account. Once you have a Windows Live ID, you can access SkyDrive and then use it to store your files, create new files, and share your files with friends and coworkers. Mary Lou Jacobs, your supervisor at QST Vancouver, asks you to obtain a Windows Live ID so that you can work on documents with your coworkers. You go to the Windows Live Web site, create a Windows Live ID, and then sign in to your SkyDrive.

STEPS

QUICK TIP
If you already have a Windows Live ID, go to the next lesson and sign in as directed using your account.

1. **Open your Web browser, type home.live.com in the Address bar, then press [Enter]**

   The Windows Live home page opens. From this page, you can create a Windows Live account and receive your Windows Live ID.

2. **Click the Sign up button** (*Note: You may see a Sign up link instead of a button*)

   The Create your Windows Live ID page opens.

3. **Click the Or use your own e-mail address link under the Check availability button or if you are already using Hotmail, Messenger, or Xbox LIVE, click the Sign in now link in the Information statement near the top of the page**

4. **Enter the information required, as shown in Figure WEB-3**

   If you wish, you can sign up for a Windows Live e-mail address such as yourname@live.com so that you can also access the Windows Live e-mail services.

TROUBLE
The code can be difficult to read. If you receive an error message, enter the new code that appears.

5. **Enter the code shown at the bottom of your screen, then click the I accept button**

   The Windows Live home page opens. The name you entered when you signed up for your Windows Live ID appears in the top right corner of the window to indicate that you are signed in to Windows Live. From the Windows Live home page, you can access all the services and applications offered by Windows Live. See the Verifying your Windows Live ID box for information on finalizing your account set up.

6. **Point to Windows Live, as shown in Figure WEB-4**

   A list of options appears. SkyDrive is one of the options you can access directly from Windows Live.

TROUBLE
Click I accept if you are asked to review and accept the Windows Live Service Agreement and Privacy Statement.

7. **Click SkyDrive**

   The SkyDrive page opens. Your name appears in the top right corner, and the amount of space available is shown on the right side of the SkyDrive page. The amount of space available is monitored, as indicated by the gauge that fills with color as space is used. Using SkyDrive, you can add files to the existing folder and you can create new folders.

8. **Click sign out in the top right corner under your name, then exit the Web browser**

   You are signed out of your Windows Live account. You can sign in again directly from the Windows Live page in your browser or from within a file created with PowerPoint, Excel, Word, or OneNote.

FIGURE WEB-3: Creating a Windows Live ID

Click to sign in using a Hotmail, Messenger, or Xbox Live account

Once your registration is complete, you will be asked to verify your ID

A different code will appear on your screen

Type your e-mail address

You can choose to get a Windows Live e-mail address

Enter the information required

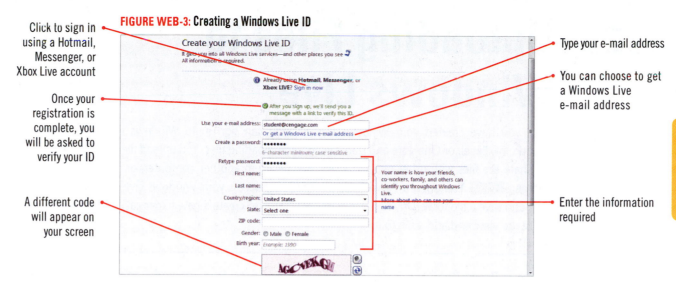

FIGURE WEB-4: Selecting SkyDrive

SkyDrive in the list of Windows Live options

Information about your Windows Live network

Your name appears here

Click to quickly add people to your network

An advertisement appropriate for your location appears here

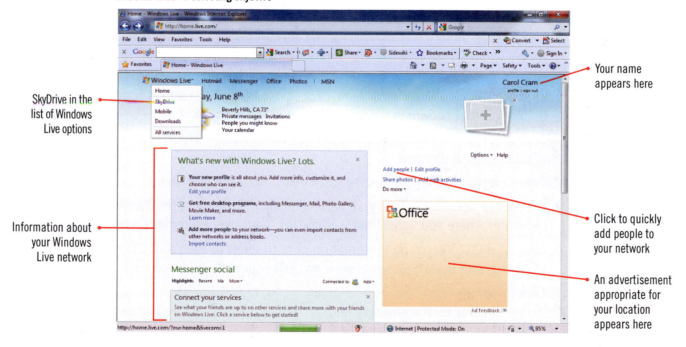

Verifying your Windows Live ID

As soon as you accept the Windows Live terms, an e-mail is sent to the e-mail address you supplied when you created your Windows Live ID. Open your e-mail program, and then open the e-mail from Microsoft with the Subject line: Confirm your e-mail address for Windows Live. Follow the simple, step-by-step instructions in the e-mail to confirm your Windows Live ID. When the confirmation is complete, you will be asked to sign in to Windows Live, using your e-mail address and password. Once signed in, you will see your Windows Live Account page.

Uploading Files to Windows Live

Once you have created your Windows Live ID, you can sign in to Windows Live directly from Word, PowerPoint, Excel, or OneNote and start saving and uploading files. You upload files to your SkyDrive so you can share the files with other people, access the files from another computer, or use SkyDrive's additional storage.  You open a PowerPoint presentation, access your Windows Live account from Backstage view, and save a file to SkyDrive on Windows Live. You also create a new folder called Cengage directly from Backstage view and add a file to it.

STEPS

1. Start PowerPoint, open the file WEB-1.pptx from the drive and folder where you store your Data Files, then save the file as WEB-QST Vancouver Presentation

2. Click the File tab, then click Save & Send
   The Save & Send options available in PowerPoint are listed in Backstage view, as shown in Figure WEB-5.

3. Click Save to Web

> **QUICK TIP**
> Skip this step if the computer you are using signs you in automatically.

4. Click Sign In, type your e-mail address, press [Tab], type your password, then click OK
   The My Documents folder on your SkyDrive appears in the Save to Windows Live SkyDrive information area.

5. Click Save As, wait a few seconds for the Save As dialog box to appear, then click Save
   The file is saved to the My Documents folder on the SkyDrive that is associated with your Windows Live account. You can also create a new folder and upload files directly to SkyDrive from your hard drive.

6. Click the File tab, click Save & Send, click Save to Web, then sign in if the My Documents folder does not automatically appear in Backstage view

7. Click the New Folder button in the Save to Windows Live SkyDrive pane, then sign in to Windows Live if directed

8. Type Cengage as the folder name, click Next, then click Add files

9. Click select documents from your computer, then navigate to the location on your computer where you saved the file WEB-QST Vancouver Presentation in Step 1

10. Click WEB-QST Vancouver Presentation.pptx to select it, then click Open
    You can continue to add more files; however, you have no more files to upload at this time.

11. Click Continue
    In a few moments, the PowerPoint presentation is uploaded to your SkyDrive, as shown in Figure WEB-6. You can simply store the file on SkyDrive or you can choose to work on the presentation using the PowerPoint Web App.

12. Click the PowerPoint icon 🔲 on your taskbar to return to PowerPoint, then close the presentation and exit PowerPoint

FIGURE WEB-5: Save & Send options in Backstage view

PowerPoint file

Save & Send area in Backstage view

Save to Web option

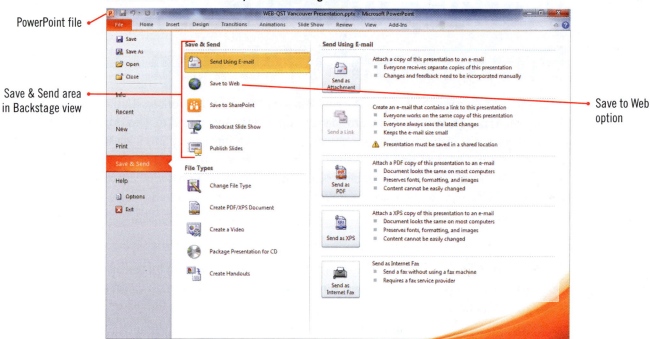

FIGURE WEB-6: File uploaded to the Cengage folder on Windows Live

Browser window

Path to file

Current folder menu bar

Uploaded file

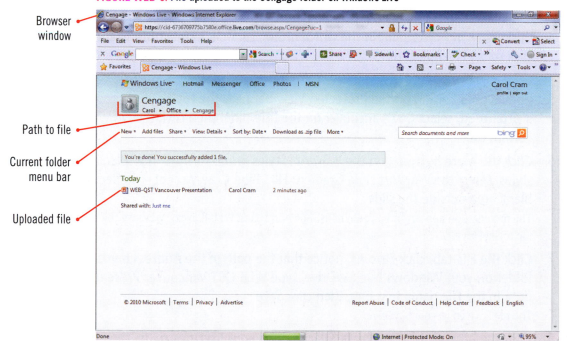

Working with the PowerPoint Web App

Once you have uploaded a file to SkyDrive on Windows Live, you can work on it using its corresponding Office Web App. **Office Web Apps** provide you with the tools you need to view documents online and to edit them right in your browser. You do not need to have Office programs installed on the computer you use to access SkyDrive and Office Web Apps. From SkyDrive, you can also open the document directly in the full Office application (for example, PowerPoint) if the application is installed on the computer you are using.  You use the PowerPoint Web App to make some edits to the PowerPoint presentation. You then open the presentation in PowerPoint and use the full version to make additional edits.

STEPS

TROUBLE
Click the browser button on the task-bar, then click the Windows Live SkyDrive window to make it the active window.

1. **Click the WEB-QST Vancouver Presentation file in the Cengage folder on SkyDrive**

   The presentation opens in your browser window. A menu is available, which includes the options you have for working with the file.

2. **Click Edit in Browser, then if a message appears related to installing the Sign-in Assistant, click the Close button ☒ to the far right of the message**

   In a few moments, the PowerPoint presentation opens in the PowerPoint Web App, as shown in Figure WEB-7. Table WEB-2 lists the commands you can perform using the PowerPoint Web App.

QUICK TIP
The changes you make to the presentation are saved automatically on SkyDrive.

3. **Enter your name where indicated on Slide 1, click Slide 3 (New Tours) in the Slides pane, then click Delete Slide in the Slides group**

   The slide is removed from the presentation. You decide to open the file in the full version of PowerPoint on your computer so you can apply WordArt to the slide title. You work with the file in the full version of PowerPoint when you want to use functions, such as WordArt, that are not available on the PowerPoint Web App.

4. **Click Open in PowerPoint in the Office group, click OK in response to the message, then click Allow if requested**

   In a few moments, the revised version of the PowerPoint slide opens in PowerPoint on your computer.

5. **Click Enable Editing on the Protected View bar near the top of your presentation window if prompted, select QST Vancouver on the title slide, then click the Drawing Tools Format tab**

QUICK TIP
Use the ScreenTips to help you find the required WordArt style.

6. **Click the More button ▼ in the WordArt Styles group to show the selection of WordArt styles, select the WordArt style Gradient Fill - Blue-Gray, Accent 4, Reflection, then click a blank area outside the slide**

   The presentation appears in PowerPoint as shown in Figure WEB-8. Next, you save the revised version of the file to SkyDrive.

7. **Click the File tab, click Save As, notice that the path in the Address bar is to the Cengage folder on your Windows Live SkyDrive, type WEB-QST Vancouver Presentation_Revised. pptx in the File name text box, then click Save**

   The file is saved to your SkyDrive.

TROUBLE
The browser opens to the Cengage folder but the file is not visible. Follow Step 8 to open the Cengage folder and refresh the list of files in the folder.

8. **Click the browser icon on the taskbar to open your SkyDrive page, then click Office next to your name in the SkyDrive path, view a list of recent documents, then click Cengage in the list to the left of the recent documents list to open the Cengage folder**

   Two PowerPoint files now appear in the Cengage folder.

9. **Exit the Web browser and close all tabs if prompted, then exit PowerPoint**

FIGURE WEB-7: Presentation opened in the PowerPoint Web App from Windows Live

Browser window

Name of Web App

PowerPoint Web App Ribbon

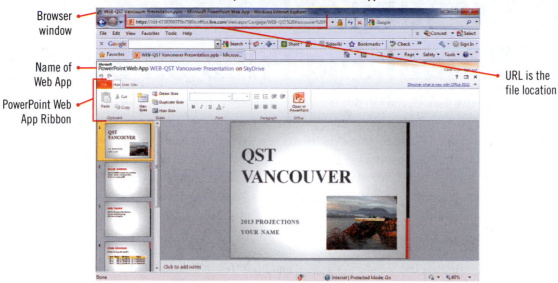

URL is the file location

FIGURE WEB-8: Revised PowerPoint presentation

PowerPoint title bar

PowerPoint Ribbon

Presentation title enhanced using full version of PowerPoint

Name added using PowerPoint Web App

TABLE WEB-2: Commands on the PowerPoint Web App

tab	commands available
File	• Open in PowerPoint: select to open the file in PowerPoint on your computer • Where's the Save Button?: when you click this option, a message appears telling you that you do not need to save your presentation when you are working on it with PowerPoint Web App. The presentation is saved automatically as you work. • Print • Share • Properties • Give Feedback • Privacy • Terms of Use • Close
Home	• Clipboard group: Cut, Copy, Paste • Slides group: Add a New Slide, Delete a Slide, Duplicate a Slide, and Hide a Slide • Font group: Work with text: change the font, style, color, and size of selected text • Paragraph group: Work with paragraphs: add bullets and numbers, indent text, align text • Office group: Open the file in PowerPoint on your computer
Insert	• Insert a Picture • Insert a SmartArt diagram • Insert a link such as a link to another file on SkyDrive or to a Web page
View	• Editing view (the default) • Reading view • Slide Show view • Notes view

Creating Folders and Organizing Files on SkyDrive

As you have learned, you can sign in to SkyDrive directly from the Office applications PowerPoint, Excel, Word, and OneNote, or you can access SkyDrive directly through your Web browser. This option is useful when you are away from the computer on which you normally work or when you are using a computer that does not have Office applications installed. You can go to SkyDrive, create and organize folders, and then create or open files to work on with Office Web Apps.  You access SkyDrive from your Web browser, create a new folder called Illustrated, and delete one of the PowerPoint files from the My Documents folder.

STEPS

> **TROUBLE**
> Go to Step 3 if you are already signed in.

1. **Open your Web browser, type home.live.com in the Address bar, then press [Enter]**
   The Windows Live home page opens. From here, you can sign in to your Windows Live account and then access SkyDrive.

> **TROUBLE**
> Type your Windows Live ID (your e-mail) and password, then click Sign in if prompted to do so.

2. **Sign into Windows Live as directed**
   You are signed in to your Windows Live page. From this page, you can take advantage of the many applications available on Windows Live, including SkyDrive.

3. **Point to Windows Live, then click SkyDrive**
   SkyDrive opens.

4. **Click Cengage, then point to WEB-QST Vancouver Presentation.pptx**
   A menu of options for working with the file, including a Delete button to the far right, appears to the right of the filename.

5. **Click the Delete button ⊠, then click OK**
   The file is removed from the Cengage folder on your SkyDrive. You still have a copy of the file on your computer.

6. **Point to Windows Live, then click SkyDrive**
   Your SkyDrive screen with the current selection of folders available on your SkyDrive opens, as shown in Figure WEB-9.

7. **Click New, click Folder, type Illustrated, click Next, click Office in the path under Add documents to Illustrated at the top of the window, then click View all in the list under Personal**
   You are returned to your list of folders, where you see the new Illustrated folder.

8. **Click Cengage, point to WEB-QST Vancouver Presentation_Revised.pptx, click More, click Move, then click the Illustrated folder**

9. **Click Move this file into Illustrated, as shown in Figure WEB-10**
   The file is moved to the Illustrated folder.

FIGURE WEB-9: Folders on your SkyDrive

Current location

Folders currently available

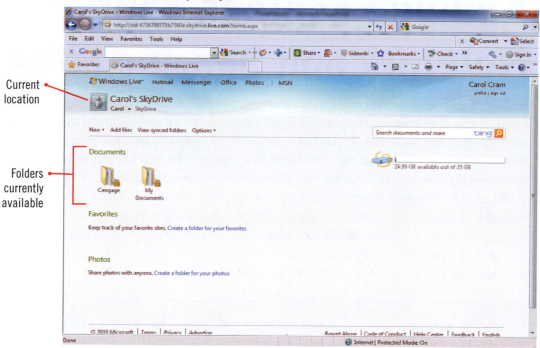

FIGURE WEB-10: Moving a file to the Illustrated folder

Click to move file to this location

Be sure to rename a file before moving it if you are moving it to a location where another copy of the same file exists

Name of file to be moved

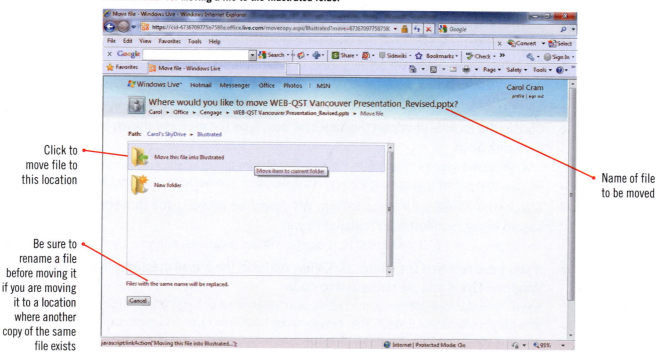

Adding People to Your Network and Sharing Files

One of the great advantages of working with SkyDrive on Windows Live is that you can share your files with others. Suppose, for example, that you want a colleague to review a presentation you created in PowerPoint and then add a new slide. You can, of course, e-mail the presentation directly to your colleague, who can then make changes and e-mail the presentation back. Alternatively, you can save time by uploading the PowerPoint file directly to SkyDrive and then giving your colleague access to the file. Your colleague can edit the file using the PowerPoint Web App, and then you can check the updated file on SkyDrive, also using the PowerPoint Web App. In this way, you and your colleague are working with just one version of the presentation that you both can update.  You have decided to share files in the Illustrated folder that you created in the previous lesson with another individual. You start by working with a partner so that you can share files with your partner and your partner can share files with you.

STEPS

TROUBLE
If you cannot find a partner, read the steps so you understand how the process works.

1. **Identify a partner with whom you can work, and obtain his or her e-mail address; you can choose someone in your class or someone on your e-mail list, but it should be someone who will be completing these steps when you are**

2. **From the Illustrated folder, click Share**

3. **Click Edit permissions**

   The Edit permissions page opens. On this page, you can select the individual with whom you would like to share the contents of the Illustrated folder.

4. **Click in the Enter a name or an e-mail address text box, type the e-mail address of your partner, then press [Tab]**

   You can define the level of access that you want to give your partner.

5. **Click the Can view files list arrow shown in Figure WEB-11, click Can add, edit details, and delete files, then click Save**

   You can choose to send a notification to each individual when you grant permission to access your files.

6. **Click in the Include your own message text box, type the message shown in Figure WEB-12, then click Send**

   Your partner will receive a message from Windows Live advising him or her that you have shared your Illustrated folder. If your partner is completing the steps at the same time, you will receive an e-mail from your partner.

TROUBLE
If you do not receive a message from Windows Live, your partner has not yet completed the steps to share the Illustrated folder.

7. **Check your e-mail for a message from Windows Live advising you that your partner has shared his or her Illustrated folder with you**

   The subject of the e-mail message will be "[Name] has shared documents with you."

QUICK TIP
You will know you are on your partner's SkyDrive because you will see your partner's first name at the beginning of the SkyDrive path.

8. **If you have received the e-mail, click View folder in the e-mail message, then sign in to Windows Live if you are requested to do so**

   You are now able to access your partner's Illustrated folder on his or her SkyDrive. You can download files in your partner's Illustrated folder to your own computer where you can work on them and then upload them again to your partner's Illustrated shared folder.

9. **Exit the browser**

FIGURE WEB-11: Editing folder permissions

Folder permissions will be changed for the Illustrated folder

Click to select network permission options

Type email address to continue to add people

Person whose permission status will change

Click to select person from list of contacts

Click to select permission option

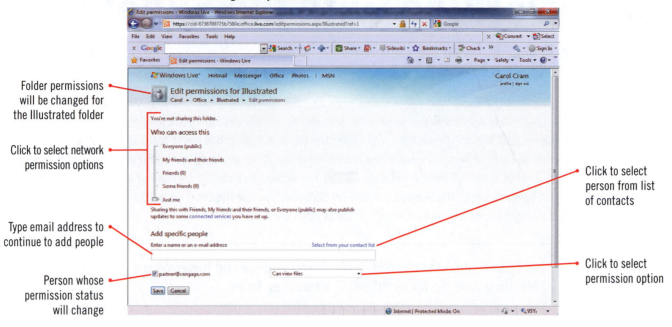

FIGURE WEB-12: Entering a message to notify a person that file sharing permission has been granted

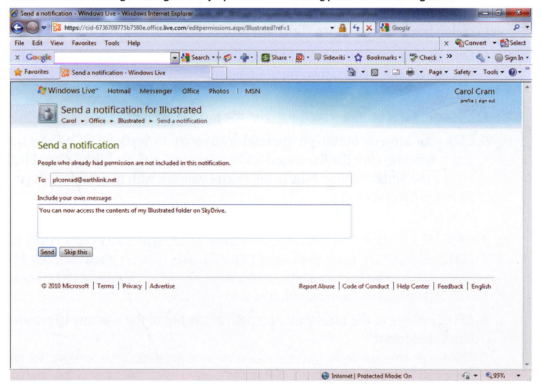

Sharing files on SkyDrive

When you share a folder with other people, the people with whom you share a folder can download the file to their computers and then make changes using the full version of the corresponding Office application.

Once these changes are made, each individual can then upload the file to SkyDrive and into a folder shared with you and others. In this way, you can create a network of people with whom you share your files.

Working with the Excel Web App

You can use the Excel Web App to work with an Excel spreadsheet on SkyDrive. Workbooks opened using the Excel Web App have the same look and feel as workbooks opened using the full version of Excel. However, just like the PowerPoint Web App, the Excel Web App has fewer features available than the full version of Excel. When you want to use a command that is not available on the Excel Web App, you need to open the file in the full version of Excel.  You upload an Excel file containing a list of the tours offered by QST Vancouver to the Illustrated folder on SkyDrive. You use the Excel Web App to make some changes, and then you open the revised version in Excel 2010 on your computer.

STEPS

1. **Start Excel, open the file WEB-2.xlsx from the drive and folder where you store your Data Files, then save the file as WEB-QST Vancouver Tours**

   The data in the Excel file is formatted using the Excel table function.

TROUBLE

If prompted, sign in to your Windows Live account as directed.

2. **Click the File tab, click Save & Send, then click Save to Web**

   In a few moments, you should see three folders to which you can save spreadsheets. My Documents and Cengage are personal folder that contains files that only you can access. Illustrated is a shared folder that contains files you can share with others in your network. The Illustrated folder is shared with your partner.

3. **Click the Illustrated folder, click the Save As button, wait a few seconds for the Save As dialog box to appear, then click Save**

QUICK TIP

Alternately, you can open your Web browser and go to Windows Live to sign in to SkyDrive.

4. **Click the File tab, click Save & Send, click Save to Web, click the Windows Live SkyDrive link above your folders, then sign in if prompted**

   Windows Live opens to your SkyDrive.

5. **Click the Excel program button 🗷 on the taskbar, then exit Excel**

6. **Click your browser button on the taskbar to return to SkyDrive if SkyDrive is not the active window, click the Illustrated folder, click the Excel file, click Edit in Browser, then review the Ribbon and its tabs to familiarize yourself with the commands you can access from the Excel Web App**

   Table WEB-3 summarizes the commands that are available.

7. **Click cell A12, type Gulf Islands Sailing, press [TAB], type 3000, press [TAB], type 10, press [TAB], click cell D3, enter the formula =B3*C3, press [Enter], then click cell A1**

   The formula is copied automatically to the remaining rows as shown in Figure WEB-13 because the data in the original Excel file was created and formatted as an Excel table.

8. **Click SkyDrive in the Excel Web App path at the top of the window to return to the Illustrated folder**

   The changes you made to the Excel spreadsheet are saved automatically on SkyDrive. You can download the file directly to your computer from SkyDrive.

9. **Point to the Excel file, click More, click Download, click Save, navigate to the location where you save the files for this book, name the file WEB-QST Vancouver Tours_Updated, click Save, then click Close in the Download complete dialog box**

   The updated version of the spreadsheet is saved on your computer and on SkyDrive.

10. **Exit the Web browser**

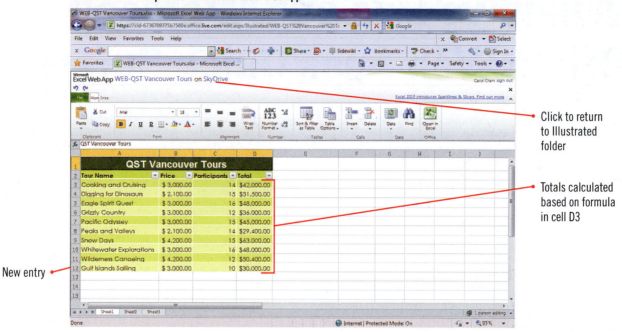

FIGURE WEB-13: Updated table In the Excel Web App

Click to return to Illustrated folder

Totals calculated based on formula in cell D3

New entry

TABLE WEB-3: Commands on the Excel Web App

tab	commands available
File	• Open in Excel: select to open the file in Excel on your computer • Where's the Save Button?: when you click this option, a message appears telling you that you do not need to save your spreadsheet when you are working in it with Excel Web App; the spreadsheet is saved automatically as you work • Save As • Share • Download a Snapshot: a snapshot contains only the values and the formatting; you cannot modify a snapshot • Download a Copy: the file can be opened and edited in the full version of Excel • Give Feedback • Privacy Statement • Terms of Use • Close
Home	• Clipboard group: Cut, Copy, Paste • Font group: change the font, style, color, and size of selected labels and values, as well as border styles and fill colors • Alignment group: change vertical and horizontal alignment and turn on the Wrap Text feature • Number group: change the number format and increase or decrease decimal places • Tables: sort and filter data in a table and modify Table Options • Cells: insert and delete cells • Data: refresh data and find labels or values • Office: open the file in Excel on your computer
Insert	• Insert a Table • Insert a Hyperlink to a Web page

Exploring other Office Web Apps

Two other Office Web Apps are Word and OneNote. You can share files on SkyDrive directly from Word or from OneNote using the same method you used to share files from PowerPoint and Excel. After you upload a Word or OneNote file to SkyDrive, you can work with it in its corresponding Office Web App. To familiarize yourself with the commands available in an Office Web App, open the file and then review the commands on each tab on the Ribbon. If you want to perform a task that is not available in the Office Web App, open the file in the full version of the application.

In addition to working with uploaded files, you can create files from new on SkyDrive. Simply sign in to SkyDrive and open a folder. With a folder open, click New and then select the Web App you want to use to create the new file.

Windows Live and Microsoft Office Web Apps Quick Reference

To Do This	Go Here
Access Windows Live	From the Web browser, type **home.live.com**, then click Sign In
Access SkyDrive on Windows Live	From the Windows Live home page, point to Windows Live, then click SkyDrive
Save to Windows Live from Word, PowerPoint, or Excel	File tab | Save & Send | Save to Web | Select a folder | Save As
Create a New Folder from Backstage view	File tab | Save & Send | Save to Web | New Folder button
Edit a File with a Web App	From SkyDrive, click the file, then click Edit in Browser
Open a File in a desktop version of the application from a Web App: Word, Excel, PowerPoint	Click Open in [Application] in the Office group in each Office Web App
Share files on Windows Live	From SkyDrive, click the folder containing the files to share, click Share on the menu bar, click Edit permissions, enter the e-mail address of the person to share files with, click the Can view files list arrow, click Can add, edit details, and delete files, then click Save

Glossary

Active The currently available document, program, or object; on the taskbar, the button of the active document appears in a darker shade while the buttons of other open documents are dimmed.

Alignment The position of text in a document relative to the margins.

Ascending order Lists data alphabetically or sequentially (from A to Z, 0 to 9, or earliest to latest).

AutoComplete A feature that automatically suggests text to insert.

AutoCorrect A feature that automatically detects and corrects typing errors, minor spelling errors, and capitalization, and inserts certain typographical symbols as you type.

Automatic page break A page break that is inserted automatically at the bottom of a page.

Backstage view The set of commands related to managing files and the information about them, including opening, printing, and saving a document, creating a new document, and protecting a document before sharing it with others.

Backward-compatible Software feature that enables documents saved in an older version of a program to be opened in a newer version of the program.

Bibliography A list of sources that you consulted or cited while creating a document.

Blog An informal journal that is created by an individual or a group and available to the public on the Internet; short for weblog.

Blogger The person who creates and maintains a blog.

Bold Formatting applied to text to make it thicker and darker.

Border A line that can be added above, below, or to the sides of a paragraph, text, or table cell; a line that divides the columns and rows of a table.

Building block A reusable piece of formatted content or document part that is stored in a gallery.

Bullet A small graphic symbol used to identify an item in a list.

Cell The box formed by the intersection of a table row and a table column.

Cell reference A code that identifies a cell's position in a table. Each cell reference contains a letter (A, B, C, and so on) to identify its column and a number (1, 2, 3, and so on) to identify its row.

Center Alignment in which an item is centered between the margins.

Character spacing Formatting that changes the width or scale of characters, expands or condenses the amount of space between characters, raises or lowers characters relative to the line of text, and adjusts kerning (the space between standard combinations of letters).

Citation A parenthetical reference in the document text that gives credit to the source for a quotation or other information used in a document.

Click and Type A feature that allows you to automatically apply the necessary paragraph formatting to a table, graphic, or text when you insert the item in a blank area of a document in Print Layout or Web Layout view.

Click and Type pointer A pointer used to move the insertion point and automatically apply the paragraph formatting necessary to insert text at that location in the document.

Clip A media file, such as a graphic, photograph, sound, movie, or animation, that can be inserted into a document.

Clip art A collection of graphic images that can be inserted into documents, presentations, Web pages, spreadsheets, and other Office files.

Clip Organizer A library of the clips that come with Word.

Clipboard A temporary storage area for items that are cut or copied from any Office file and are available for pasting. *See* Office Clipboard and System Clipboard.

Cloud computing When data, applications, and resources are stored on servers accessed over the Internet or a company's internal network rather than on users' computers.

Compatible The capability of different programs to work together and exchange data.

Content control An interactive object that is embedded in a document you create from a template and that expedites your ability to customize the document with your own information.

Contextual tab Tab on the Ribbon that appears when needed to complete a specific task; for example, if you select a graphic, the Picture Tools Format tab appears.

Copy To place a copy of an item on the Clipboard without removing it from a document.

Copy and paste To move text or graphics using the Copy and Paste commands.

Cut To remove an item from a document and place it on the Clipboard.

Cut and paste To move text or graphics using the Cut and Paste commands.

Delete To permanently remove an item from a document.

Descending order Lists data in reverse alphabetical or sequential order (from Z to A, 9 to 0, or latest to earliest).

Dialog box launcher An icon available in many groups on the Ribbon that you can click to open a dialog box or task pane, offering an alternative way to choose commands. *Also called* launcher.

Document The electronic file you create using Word.

Document properties Details about a file, such as author name or the date the file was created, that are used to describe, organize, and search for files.

Document window The workspace in the program window that displays the current document.

Draft view A view that shows a document without margins, headers and footers, or graphics.

Drag and drop To move text or a graphic by dragging it to a new location using the mouse.

Drop cap A large dropped initial capital letter that is often used to set off the first paragraph of an article.

Endnote Text that provides additional information or acknowledges sources for text in a document and that appears at the end of a document.

Field A code that serves as a placeholder for data that changes in a document, such as a page number.

File An electronic collection of stored data that has a unique name, distinguishing it from other files.

File tab Provides access to Backstage view and the Word Options dialog box.

Filename The name given to a document when it is saved.

First line indent A type of indent in which the first line of a paragraph is indented more than the subsequent lines.

Floating graphic A graphic to which text wrapping has been applied, making the graphic independent of text and able to be moved anywhere on a page.

Font The typeface or design of a set of characters (letters, numbers, symbols, and punctuation marks).

Font effect Font formatting that applies a special effect to text, such as small caps or superscript.

Font size The size of characters, measured in points (pts).

Footer Information, such as text, a page number, or a graphic, that appears at the bottom of every page in a document or a section.

Footnote Text that provides additional information or acknowledges sources for text in a document and that appears at the bottom of the page on which the note reference mark appears.

Format Painter A feature used to copy the format settings applied to the selected text to other text you want to format the same way.

Formatting marks Nonprinting characters that appear on screen to indicate the ends of paragraphs, tabs, and other formatting elements.

Full Screen Reading view A view that shows only the document text on screen, making it easier to read and annotate.

Gallery A visual collection of choices you can browse through to make a selection. Often available with Live Preview.

Gridlines Nonprinting lines that appear on screen to show the boundaries of table cells or to help you size, align, and position graphics. *See also* table gridlines.

Group A collection of related commands on a tab on the Ribbon.

Gutter Extra space left for a binding at the top, left, or inside margin of a document.

Hanging indent A type of indent in which the second and subsequent lines of a paragraph are indented more than the first.

Hard page break *See* Manual page break.

Header Information, such as text, a page number, or a graphic, that appears at the top of every page in a document or a section.

Header row The first row of a table that usually contains the column headings.

Highlighting Transparent color that can be applied to text to call attention to it.

Horizontal ruler A ruler that appears at the top of the document window in Print Layout, Draft, and Web Layout view.

Horizontal scroll bar *See* Scroll bar.

Hyperlink Text or a graphic that opens a file, Web page, or other item when clicked. *Also called* link.

I-beam pointer The pointer used to move the insertion point and select text.

Indent The space between the edge of a line of text or a paragraph and the margin.

Indent marker A marker on the horizontal ruler that shows the indent settings for the active paragraph.

Inline graphic A graphic that is part of a line of text.

Insertion point The blinking vertical line that shows where text will appear when you type in a document.

Integrate To incorporate a document and parts of a document created in one program into another program; for example, to incorporate an Excel chart into a PowerPoint slide, or an Access table into a Word document.

Interface The look and feel of a program; for example, the appearance of commands and the way they are organized in the program window.

Italic Formatting applied to text to make the characters slant to the right.

Justify Alignment in which an item is flush with both the left and right margins.

Keyboard shortcut A combination of keys or a function key that can be pressed to perform a command.

Landscape orientation Page orientation in which the page is wider than it is tall.

Launch To open or start a program on your computer.

Launcher *See* Dialog box launcher.

Left-align Alignment in which the item is flush with the left margin.

Left indent A type of indent in which the left edge of a paragraph is moved in from the left margin.

Line spacing The amount of space between lines of text.

Live Preview A feature that lets you point to a choice in a gallery or palette and see the results in the document without actually clicking the choice.

Manual page break A page break inserted to force the text following the break to begin at the top of the next page.

Margin The blank area between the edge of the text and the edge of a page.

Merge To combine adjacent cells into a single larger cell.

Microsoft Word Help button A button used to access the Word Help system.

Mini toolbar A toolbar that appears faintly above text when you first select it and includes the most commonly used text and paragraph formatting commands.

Mirror margins Margins used in documents with facing pages, where the inside and outside margins are mirror images of each other.

Multilevel list A list with a hierarchical structure; an outline.

Negative indent A type of indent in which the left edge of a paragraph is moved to the left of the left margin.

Nested table A table inserted in a cell of another table.

Note reference mark A mark (such as a letter or a number) that appears next to text to indicate that additional information is offered in a footnote or endnote.

Office Clipboard A temporary storage area shared by all Office programs that can be used to cut, copy, and paste multiple items within and between Office programs. The Office Clipboard can hold up to 24 items collected from any Office program. *See also* System Clipboard.

Office Web App Versions of the Microsoft Office applications with limited functionality that are available online from Windows Live SkyDrive. Users can view documents online and then edit them in the browser using a selection of functions. Office Web Apps are available for Word, PowerPoint, Excel, and One Note.

Online collaboration The ability to incorporate feedback or share information across the Internet or a company network or intranet.

Open To use one of the methods for opening a document to retrieve it and display it in the document window.

Orphan The first line of a paragraph when it appears alone at the bottom of a page.

Outdent *See* Negative indent.

Outline view A view that shows the headings of a document organized as an outline.

Paragraph spacing The amount of space between paragraphs.

Paste To insert items stored on the Clipboard into a document.

Point The unit of measurement for text characters and the space between paragraphs and characters; 1/72 of an inch.

Portrait orientation Page orientation in which the page is taller than it is wide.

Previewing Viewing a document on screen to see exactly how it will look when printed.

Print Layout view A view that shows a document as it will look on a printed page.

Print Preview A view of a file as it will appear when printed.

Quick Access toolbar A customizable toolbar that contains buttons you can click to perform frequently used commands.

Quick Part A reusable piece of content that can be inserted into a document, including a field, document property, or a preformatted building block.

Quick Style A set of format settings that can be applied to text or an object to format it quickly and easily; Quick Styles appear in galleries. *See also* Style.

Ribbon An area that displays Word commands, organized into tabs and groups.

Right-align Alignment in which an item is flush with the right margin.

Right indent A type of indent in which the right edge of a paragraph is moved in from the right margin.

Sans serif font A font (such as Calibri) whose characters do not include serifs, which are small strokes at the ends of letters.

Save To store a file permanently on a disk or to overwrite the copy of a file that is stored on a disk with the changes made to the file.

Save As Command used to save a file for the first time or to create a new file with a different filename, leaving the original file intact.

Screen capture A snapshot of your screen, as if you took a picture of it with a camera, which you can paste into a document.

ScreenTip A label that identifies the name of a button or feature, briefly describes its function, conveys any keyboard shortcut for the command, and includes a link to associated help topics, if any.

Scroll To use the scroll bars or the arrow keys to display different parts of a document in the document window.

Scroll arrow The arrow at the end of a scroll bar that is clicked to scroll a document one line at a time, or to scroll a document left and right in the document window.

Scroll bar The bar on the right edge (vertical scroll bar) or bottom edge (horizontal scroll bar) of the document window that is used to display different parts of the document in the document window.

Scroll box The box in a scroll bar that can be dragged to scroll a document.

Section A portion of a document that is separated from the rest of the document by section breaks.

Section break A formatting mark inserted to divide a document into sections.

Select To click or highlight an item in order to perform some action on it.

Serif font A font (such as Times New Roman) whose characters include serifs, which are small strokes at the ends of letters.

Shading A background color or pattern that can be applied to text, tables, or graphics.

Shortcut key *See* Keyboard shortcut.

Sizing handles The white circles that appear around a graphic when it is selected; used to change the size or shape of a graphic.

SkyDrive An online storage and file sharing service. Access to SkyDrive is through a Windows Live account. Up to 25 GB of data can be stored in a personal SkyDrive, with each file a maximum size of 50 MB.

Soft page break *See* Automatic page break.

Sort To organize data, such as table rows, items in a list, or records in a mail merge, in ascending or descending order.

Split To divide a cell into two or more cells, or to divide a table into two tables.

Status bar The bar at the bottom of the Word program window that shows information about the document, including the current page number, the total number of pages in a document, the document word count, and the on/off status of spelling and grammar checking, and contains the view buttons, the Zoom level button, and the Zoom slider.

Style A named collection of character and paragraph formats that are stored together and can be applied to text to format it quickly. *See also* Quick Style.

Subscript A font effect in which text is formatted in a smaller font size and placed below the line of text.

Suite A group of programs that are bundled together and share a similar interface, making it easy to transfer skills and program content among them.

Superscript A font effect in which text is formatted in a smaller font size and placed above the line of text.

Symbol A special character that can be inserted into a document using the Symbol command.

System Clipboard A clipboard that stores only the last item cut or copied from a document. *See also* Clipboard and Office Clipboard.

Tab A part of the Ribbon that includes groups of buttons for related commands. *See also* Tab stop.

Tab leader A line that appears in front of tabbed text.

Tab stop A location on the horizontal ruler that indicates where to align text.

Table A grid made up of rows and columns of cells that can contain text and graphics.

Table gridlines Nonprinting blue dotted lines that show the boundaries of table cells. *See also* Gridlines.

Table style A named set of table format settings that can be applied to a table to format it all at once.

Template A formatted document that contains placeholder text you can replace with your own text.

Text effect Formatting that applies a visual effect to text, such as a shadow, glow, outline, or reflection.

Theme A set of unified design elements, including theme colors, theme fonts for body text and headings, and theme effects for graphics that can be applied to a document all at once.

Title bar The bar at the top of the program window that indicates the program name and the name of the current file.

Toggle button A button that turns a feature on and off.

User interface A collective term for all the ways you interact with a software program.

Vertical alignment The position of text in a document relative to the top and bottom margins.

Vertical ruler A ruler that appears on the left side of the document window in Print Layout view.

Vertical scroll bar *See* Scroll bar.

View A way of displaying a document in the document window; each view provides features useful for editing and formatting different types of documents.

View buttons Buttons on the status bar that are used to change document views.

Web Layout view A view that shows a document as it will look when viewed with a Web browser.

Widow The last line of a paragraph when it is carried over to the top of the following page, separate from the rest of the paragraph.

Windows Live A collection of services and Web applications that people can access through a login. Windows Live services include access to e-mail and instant messaging, storage of files on SkyDrive, sharing and storage of photos, networking with people, downloading software, and interfacing with a mobile device.

Word processing program A software program that includes tools for entering, editing, and formatting text and graphics.

Word program window The window that contains the Word program elements, including the document window, Quick Access toolbar, Ribbon, and status bar.

Word-wrap A feature that automatically moves the insertion point to the next line as you type.

Works cited A list of sources that you cited while creating a document.

XML Acronym that stands for eXtensible Markup Language, which is a language used to structure, store, and send information.

XML format New file format for Word documents beginning with Word 2007.

Zoom level button A button on the status bar that is used to change the zoom level of the document in the document window.

Zoom slider An adjustment on the status bar that is used to enlarge or decrease the display size of the document in the document window.

Zooming in A feature that makes a document appear bigger but shows less of it on screen at once; does not affect actual document size.

Zooming out A feature that shows more of a document on screen at once but at a reduced size; does not affect actual document size.

Index

Note: The following abbreviations have been used before page numbers: WD=Word; OFF=Office A; WEB=Web Apps.